Between Two Gileads

Between Two Gileads

Christian Nationalism, Fundamentalism, Romans 13:1–7, and the Future of Political Theology

HENRY WALTER SPAULDING III

Foreword by Rodney Clapp

CASCADE *Books* • Eugene, Oregon

BETWEEN TWO GILEADS

Christian Nationalism, Fundamentalism, Romans 13:1–7, and the Future of Political Theology

Copyright © 2026 Henry Walter Spaulding III. All rights reserved. Except for brief quotations in critical publications or reviews, no part of this book may be reproduced in any manner without prior written permission from the publisher. Write: Permissions, Wipf and Stock Publishers, 199 W. 8th Ave., Suite 3, Eugene, OR 97401.

Cascade Books
An Imprint of Wipf and Stock Publishers
199 W. 8th Ave., Suite 3
Eugene, OR 97401

www.wipfandstock.com

PAPERBACK ISBN: 979-8-3852-1835-6
HARDCOVER ISBN: 979-8-3852-1836-3
EBOOK ISBN: 979-8-3852-1837-0

Cataloguing-in-Publication data:

Names: Spaulding, Henry Walter, III, author. | Clapp, Rodney, foreword.

Title: Between two Gileads : Christian nationalism, fundamentalism, Romans 13:1–7, and the future of political theology / Henry Walter Spaulding III; foreword by Rodney Clapp.

Description: Eugene, OR: Cascade Books, 2026 | Includes bibliographical references and index.

Identifiers: ISBN 979-8-3852-1835-6 (paperback) | ISBN 979-8-3852-1836-3 (hardcover) | ISBN 979-8-3852-1837-0 (ebook)

Subjects: LCSH: Bible—Use—History. | White supremacy movements—Religious aspects—Christianity. | Atwood, Margaret—Criticism and intepretation. | Robinson, Marilynne—Criticism and interpretation.

Classification: BT82.2 S695 2026 (paperback) | BT82.2 (ebook)

04/01/26

To the Love of My Life:

Michaela Renā Spaulding

You are my courage and heart

Contents

Foreword

The American church suffers sickness and desperately stands in need of an intervention. We need not rehearse the current polarization, division, and ugly actions and states of mind. They weigh heavily and clearly enough on everyone. It is enough, and germane to the book you are preparing to read, to remember 1985. That was the year Margaret Atwood published *The Handmaid's Tale,* about a dystopian United States refashioned as the draconian, patriarchal Republic of Gilead, lorded over by grim Christian white males. At the time Atwood's novel was published, many dismissed it as overwrought and fantastical. Nothing of the sort could ever happen here! But around just forty years later, look where we are.

Hank Spaulding in these pages offers exactly the sort of intervention so desperately needed. He immerses himself and his readers in Atwood's dark and frightening Gilead. But he sees and hopes in another fictional Gilead—the small Iowa town of Marilynne Robinson's novelistic quadrilogy. In Robinson's vision, the Christian faith encompasses complicated, patient and impatient, sometimes broken people. They attempt not to lord it over one another, but to live together amid their imperfections.

To great effect, Spaulding juxtaposes these two fictional Gileads, both of which have much to suggest about our real world today. But before he enters richly into these fictional universes, he begins where any effective intervention must: by taking account of where things have run amiss. Make no mistake. The American church's present illness did not spring to life suddenly or develop overnight. Such gross misappropriations of the gospel as the Christian nationalism on our soil and in our habits of thought have a history. In his early chapters, Spaulding explores how a defective biblical hermeneutics is at the heart of our problems. This fundamentalist hermeneutic, widely shared in popular evangelicalism, envisions the Bible as an inerrant, encyclopedic answer book. Assuming clear, indisputable answers to discrete problems, this account of the Bible belies its riches, both literarily and spiritually. It forgets, or at least radically plays down, the reality that the Bible is a collection of books, in various literary genres, written and edited by scores of authors over several centuries. And with its easy presumption of clear, indisputable answers, it lends itself to the weaponization of Scripture.

Extended, the arguments of the early chapters could easily have constituted an entire book. But Hank Spaulding is after healing, not simply dissection, and his account really hits its stride in chapter 3. There he begins to recover and portray a literary theology, one that opens us to the breadth and depth of the biblical testimony, to the story of the God met in Israel and Jesus Christ, to something that is so much more challenging and promising than a giant answer book.

Subsequent chapters remind and open us to the counsel of luminaries of the tradition, not least Karl Barth and Jacques Ellul. And they unpack Augustine's great hermeneutic of love: to wit, that solely those interpretations that deepen us in love of God and neighbor are truly faithful and commendable. Only then does Spaulding turn to our two Gileads. We are helped to see how Atwood's Gilead paints a profound picture of how wrong anti-Augustinian interpretation can go, and how we are seeing that Gilead tenuously and partially instantiated in the current US. And we turn to Robinson's Gilead for a picture of a very different sort of Christian community and hope. Even here, though, the better Gilead does not reflect the wounds of the nation's racist past and present, so Spaulding vitally complements his account with the indispensable counsel and imagination of thinkers and artists such as James Cone and Toni Morrison.

It is the likes of Cone and Morrison, whose people have been maimed and oppressed for centuries, who most strikingly remind us that seven verses in Romans 13 have again and again been interpreted to the advantage of oppression and not liberation. Spaulding's literary theology shows the way to a more faithful and true reading of those dangerous verses. *Between Two Gileads*, difficult and challenging as it is, ends, somehow, with a conclusion that positively soars.

These are dark times. Can a deathly ill church ever soar again? Under God's mercy, and following the profound leads such as Hank Spaulding offers in these pages, it might.

Rodney Clapp

Preface

This book was born from a collision of stories—some imagined, some tragically real—that stirred something deep in my theological imagination. One of the earliest sparks came while watching *The Handmaid's Tale*, the harrowing television adaptation of Margaret Atwood's novel. One scene in particular lodged in my heart: Offred and Ofglen, two handmaids in the theocratic Republic of Gilead, come across a Catholic priest hanging from a wall marked "traitor." As they walk, Offred points out while watching the demolition of St. Paul's Cathedral in New York that it was her father's parish and the location of her daughter's baptism. Ofglen quietly adds that she was there when Gilead blew up St. Patrick's Cathedral and dumped its stones in the Hudson River. The memory of those destroyed churches, the literal erasure of sacred space, and the violent purging of Christian difference revealed a terrifying reality: in the world of Gilead, even Christ becomes a threat to Christians. When faith becomes wholly absorbed into the power machinery, the church turns against itself. Christians hang other Christians. Altars are razed. Worship becomes idolatry masquerading as orthodoxy.

That fictional vision became devastatingly real on January 6, 2021. I watched, heartbroken and theologically shaken, as Christian symbols flooded the steps of the US Capitol—not in repentance or peace, but in violence. Crosses were held high above a crowd that beat officers with flagpoles. Rioters read Scripture while storming the halls of democracy. They invoked the name of Jesus as justification for chaos, hatred, and death. It was a moment when something long-simmering boiled over: the fusion of white fundamentalism, nationalist fervor, and the thirst for control erupting in the name of God, and I could not look away.

What haunted me most was how it mirrored the world about which Atwood warned us. *The Handmaid's Tale* is dystopian fiction, but watching January 6 unfold, I wondered whether that label still held. In both Atwood's Gilead and our American moment, politicians and Christians weaponized Scripture and used religious language to justify domination. Those who claimed to follow Christ were crucifying their neighbors—not metaphorically but with literal violence. The story was not speculative anymore. It was a documentary.

However, amid these dark parallels, I also found myself returning to another "Gilead"—the one imagined by Marilynne Robinson. Her small Iowa town, bearing the same name as Atwood's regime, offered a striking contrast. In Robinson's Gilead, difference is not feared but embraced. John Ames, a quiet, aging pastor, falls in love with Lila, a woman with a painful past, and together they imagine a life shaped by grace rather than fear. Robinson's Gilead is slow, thoughtful, and open to mystery. It is a place where theology is inseparable from love. Reading Robinson while watching Atwood brought the tension into sharp relief: we live between two Gileads. One where power erases the church and one where the church embraces the powerless. One where Scripture is used to dominate and one where it invites us to love. One where God is an idol of the ruling class, and one where God remains wholly Other—disruptive, gracious, uncontainable.

The book in your hands is in an in-between space. It is a sequel—spiritually and intellectually—to my earlier work, *The Just and Loving Gaze of God with Us: Paul's Apocalyptic Political Theology*. That book was my first attempt to wrestle with the dangerous co-opting of Christianity, and in particular the apostle Paul, by political ideologies. January 6 broke something open in me. I could no longer ignore how easily faith can twist into something cruel. I could no longer write or preach as if Scripture speaks only in our lives' quiet, private corners. I needed to say clearly: when Christians wield the Bible as a weapon, they betray the very heart of the gospel.

The present book is my attempt to reclaim the Bible, and Paul, not as an instrument of domination but as a wellspring of grace. It is also a celebration of literature, of the novelists whose imagined worlds have helped me *see* reality more clearly. Writers like Atwood and Robinson have taught me to read human beings with empathy, recognize holiness in hidden places, and sit with complexity and resist easy answers. If this book helps anyone read Scripture more honestly or deeply, it owes a debt to those literary voices who shaped my imagination.

I am profoundly grateful to my parents, Henry and Sharon Spaulding, who raised me in love and truth. Their example taught me what it means to hold faith and compassion together. To my wife, Michaela Spaulding—your fierce love and unwavering hope are the soul of this book. You embody the kind of radical hospitality I write about, and I dedicate this work to you with gratitude and awe. Luke Harbaugh and Patrick Taylor, your friendship and insight have strengthened me more than you know. And to Michael Thomson, Rodney Clapp, and Charlie Collier at Cascade, thank you for believing in this project. Rodney, your editorial eye and gracious spirit have made this book possible. I also want to thank Rodney especially for his kind foreword. I hope the book proves to be as fruitful as he suggests.

We are living in a time when Scripture is being twisted to serve an ideology, when the gospel is shouted as a slogan rather than whispered as good news. However, the kingdom of God still comes—quietly, unexpectedly, and always in resistance to the powers of this world. I hope that this book helps us hear that kingdom's call and that it nurtures communities shaped by vulnerability, hospitality, and love. It bears witness to the God who refuses to be used and is always found among the crucified, not the conquerors.

May we choose the better Gilead. And may the Word who became flesh continue to speak, even through the ruins.

Henry Walter Spaulding III
Eastertide 2025

"There is a balm in Gilead that makes her people whole."

Harry Thacker Burleigh

Introduction

American Christianity in the Twenty-First Century

A PAULINE LITERARY IMAGINATION AGAINST NATIONALISM

Paul's theology and writings stand at the center of Christian thought and, as such, undergo a myriad of interpretations by Christians and non-Christians, interpretations that align his vision with interests unfamiliar to his context. A clear example of this alignment arises from the nationalistic interpretation of Romans 13:1–7 by former Attorney General Jeff Sessions' in his defense of President Trump's infamous immigration policy. The policy was an extension of an earlier policy instituted by President Obama to separate children from their parents at the US/Mexico border. In response to the critics of the policy, Sessions states a clear Christian nationalistic agenda: "I would cite to you the apostle Paul and his clear and wise command in Romans 13:1–7, to obey the laws of the government because God has ordained the government for his purposes."[1] On the surface, Sessions merely recites a literal reading of Scripture. However, the simplicity of his statement betrays a complex array of moral teachings, assumptions about the policy itself, and about the correct interpretation of Scripture. All aspects of this array require privileging certain forms of American policy. By hermeneutically reading an American policy into his interpretation of Romans 13:1–7, Sessions

1. Sessions, "Speech to Law Enforcement Officials."

extends a theological rationale to US interests and "America first" policies to garner support for the policy from Christians.

Sessions and his theological interpretation of immigration appealed to citizens such as Shelia, who was interviewed a month after Sessions's speech. A Sunday school teacher, she reflects on the speech and the rebuttal made by Christians in their call to love their neighbor despite the call from Sessions to obey the governmental authorities.

> Love thy neighbor, she said, meant "love thy American neighbor." Welcome the stranger, she said, meant the "legal immigrant stranger." "The Bible says, 'If you do this to the least of these, you do it to me,'" Sheila said, quoting Jesus. "But the least of these are Americans, not the ones crossing the border."[2]

For Sessions and Shelia, Romans 13:1–7 preserves a well-ordered, America-first society above all else, one that uses the Bible and Christian themes to create and maintain a power that privileges certain people over others. The qualifications they placed on the text are logical and necessary even though the text itself does not make such stipulations. Furthermore, one must adopt such a hermeneutic to read Scripture properly in this way. Thus, a certain perspective exists for a sector of Christianity that cannot read the Bible outside of this cultural lens.

Sessions and Shelia are neither the first nor the most recent politicians to engage in Christian nationalist logic. For example, on August 5, 2022, Representative Marjorie Taylor Greene of Georgia stated clearly that *Christian nationalism* is not a term Americans should be ashamed of and that members of her (Republican) party should focus more heavily on restoring "biblical principles" to the heart of America.[3] Representative Greene defines these terms as an extremist form of conservative ideology and sees no issue with them as such. Nevertheless, Christian nationalism presents a troubling history to which Christians and Americans must pay attention. As Paul Miller, professor of political science at Georgetown and a committed Southern Baptist, comments, Christian nationalism should not be adopted as a mark of patriotism and Christian faith. Miller defines Christian nationalism as "the belief that the American Nation is defined by Christianity, and that the government should take active steps to keep it that way."[4] Miller's definition highlights that a certain sector of Christi-

2. Quoted in Bruenig, "Judgment Days."
3. Greene quoted in Jenkins, "Republicans Mostly Mum."
4. Miller, "What Is Christian Nationalism?"

anity prizes the creation of Christian codes and principles to guide and control a vision for American success. Christianity, in Christian nationalism, concerns itself entirely with the domination of what philosopher Charles Taylor terms the "immanent frame," namely a constructed space of instrumental rationality devoid of transcendence.[5] The concern for the immanent frame exposes that the Christian story, for Christian nationalists, is less about an encounter with a transcendent God than power over an immanent space closed off from the transcendent. Humans, in this perspective, must secure this space *for* God. Such a perspective illustrates the modern shift in Christian political theology wherein God does not secure meaning, but rather, this is the responsibility of humans. As such, Christian nationalists must require absolute adherence to the instrumental reason of their position, such as a radical conservative agenda, which must be upheld and policed. The power of such a belief is obvious in political life. Politicians such as Greene see a clear need to preserve only a certain structure of government that favors certain privileged Christian symbols and narratives to keep a select group of politicians in power.

Such political strategies, which emphasize the preservation of a certain structure of government, have proven effective, as the appeal of this language can be traced to several politicians both in the past and present. For example, former President Ronald Reagan appealed in several speeches to America as a shining city on a hill, which is a scriptural allusion to Jesus's teaching in the Sermon on the Mount (Matt 5:14) and first said in reference to the church by Puritan minister John Winthrop.[6] In addition, even progressive politicians such as President Joe Biden performed similar gestures when he equated the military's willingness to enter the battlefield with the call to Isaiah.[7] Most recently, House Speaker Mike Johnson claimed that the Bible clearly states that God "raised up . . . to this specific moment in time" each conservative leader in the Republican-controlled House to lead America to the promised land.[8]

The frequent invocation of biblical imagery by political leaders, whether conservative or progressive, reflects a long-standing tradition of using Scripture to frame national identity and moral authority. However, when such language is repeatedly employed to justify political agendas,

5. Taylor, *Secular Age*, 542–54.

6. For the history of appropriation of the phrase, and its confusion with the nation rather than the church, see Van Engen, *City on a Hill*.

7. Biden, "Remarks on the Terror Attack."

8. Johnson, "Remarks upon Election."

it fosters an environment where theological concepts become entangled with nationalist ideologies. This entanglement has contributed to the rise of Christian nationalism in many Western nations, particularly the United States, where religious rhetoric increasingly asserted political dominance. At the core of Christian nationalism is a fundamentalist approach to Scripture—one that imposes a rigid, divinely sanctioned vision of governance. While Christian nationalism and fundamentalism have distinct historical roots, they often reinforce one another, emerging as reactionary movements to perceived threats against religious, ideological, and cultural norms.

The word *fundamentalism* became a key term for a certain kind of theological thinking in the late nineteenth and early twentieth centuries. Defining the term in light of those who bear it, George Marsden writes that "an American fundamentalist is an evangelical who is militant in opposition to liberal theology in the churches or to changes in cultural values or mores, such as those associated with 'secular humanism.'"[9] The term *fundamentalist* fell out of prominence in the 1930s but experienced a resurgence in response to the sexual revolution. It first emerged as a label for those who followed and, in some cases, produced a set of tracts, *The Fundamentals: A Testimony to the Truth.* The authors of this work, pastors and theologians in the late nineteenth century, desired a definitive affirmation of their perceived core tenets of the faith, such as the inerrancy of Scripture, penal substitutionary atonement, and an almost universal rejection of science, to name a few. However, this document is not without its history. *The Fundamentals* emerged in response to the political progressivism present in the West and sought to preserve a more conservative form of the faith and subsequent political life. Fundamentalism, as such, is as much a political movement seeking to guarantee its identity.

Fundamentalism presupposes foundational principles, such as inerrancy, that one must adopt to be faithful. A fundamentalist assumes that these "foundational principles" equate with faith itself. These eternal truths exist in the text, and if the Bible contradicts itself, then it must be ignored due to these presuppositions. For example, suppose a passage presents a different understanding of the atonement than penal substitution theory, which is one of the fundamentals. In that case, fundamentalists argue that the supposed error is not in the original manuscripts. Inerrancy cultivates a fideism that one cannot escape. Even though the principles are not eternal,

9. Marsden, *Understanding Fundamentalism*, 1.

they are immutable because, as the fundamentalists confess, they arise from Scripture. As Mark Noll famously presented, this inserted an "anti-intellectualism" into Christianity from which it has not recovered.[10] The result is the simplification of Christianity into a set of immutable propositions or codes that replace God as the one in which one puts their faith.

This "exegetical" position does not require serious engagement with the biblical texts but rather the adoption of a set of fundamentals. To be "biblical" is an adherence to a preset worldview arising from the cultural moment of *The Fundamentals*. The language of a biblical worldview, biblical morality, or any word modified adjectivally by "biblical," is a cultural identity more than one rooted in serious engagement with the biblical texts. One can see that those who identify with these "biblical" positions largely do not read the Bible. As the Pew Research Center illustrates, only 35 percent of Christian adults admit to reading the Bible frequently.[11] This frequency is down among all sectors of Christianity and illustrates that the use of the word *biblical* does not require engagement with the biblical texts. This posture leads to the desire to simplify nuanced ideas, biblical passages, and even policies down to a tagline, an ontological anxiety about a progressing world, and a particular kind of eschatological vision. With something as vast as Scripture, a set of fundamentals invariably distorts its complexity. As such, "biblical" is a "dog whistle" in many of its deployments within *evangelical* social norms.

The simplicity of fundamentalism and Christian nationalism lead us to texts such as Romans 13:1–7. More than others, this text funds a theological foundation of power that maintains a certain cultural order. In short, the history of this text finds perfection in a Puritan context in the fledgling United States, where God enters a covenant with the colonial inhabitants of the new world and must obey certain rules to avoid divine judgment and enact God's justice in the world. One must see how this interpretation naturally assumes a culture (*Kultur*) of belief rather than exegetical work. The fundamentalist position is a Trojan horse that makes possible the disguising of a cultural norm as a biblical one.

Now, to be clear, Christian nationalism and fundamentalism interpenetrate each other, but fundamentalism manufactures much of the consent sought by Christian nationalists. Though nationalism and fundamentalism do necessitate one another, the connection is unmistakable in

10. Noll, *Scandal of the Evangelical Mind*, 114.

11. Pew Research Center, "5 Facts."

the history of biblical interpretation. Through a strict view of inerrancy, fundamentalists contend that the Bible, from start to finish, is without error and aligns perfectly with empirical fact. Furthermore, as such an authority it also confirms their prejudices about the just order of society. This view is an epistemological prerequisite that divinizes the culture and misappropriates the Bible. Fundamentalism has undeniable power, and through the political mobilization of fundamentalists, nationalism has succeeded.

Therefore, I argue that fundamentalism creates conditions for Christian nationalism and vice versa. It is only in this light that Shelia's comments about immigration makes sense. In fundamentalism, the Bible is merely a collection of timeless rules that stretch across time and context. These rules must be obeyed and should structure society according to divinely ordained hierarchies that code certain forms of life at the top. Thus, in the hands of Christian nationalism, a fundamentalist handling of Scripture serves as nothing more than a zero-sum guide for a code fetishism that rewards those who fit its description and punishes those who do not. The quest for national power and reading of the Bible dovetail around this modern concern for the domination of an imminent world frame with no concern for the God beyond it.

Many in the United States and all over the world find the fundamentalist approach to Scripture attractive. However, it is not faithful or the only way to engage the biblical texts. Instead, this book will present a literary, ultimately figurative, allegorical approach to Scripture. Such an approach will focus on the narrative of the biblical text and locating isolated texts, like Romans 13:1–7, within the broader unfolding of the story of the triune Lord. Instead of reducing Scripture to a set of propositions (moral rules, empirical claims, doctrinal presuppositions), a literary approach will cultivate a taste for beauty that apocalyptically disrupts fundamentalist Christian nationalist readings of Scripture in general and Romans 13:1–7 in particular. A literary theology frees Scripture and subordinates it to the transcendent, triune God and encourages love of that God and of neighbor.[12] As such, this book provides a hermeneutic for reading Scripture and a spiritual engagement that illustrates how the biblical texts aid moral discernment. The literary theology developed here does not explicitly utilize a literary critical method but instead borrows a rhythm for reading from literature. The literary approach flips the fundamentalist approach on its

12. I borrow the phrase "literary theology" from theologian Brian Bantum. See Bantum, "Clothed in Flesh."

head, not misappropriating literal readings that merely confirm certain principles exterior to the text that support a specific culture.

Beyond providing a better way to read Scripture, a literary theology develops a particular taste as its mode of ethical discernment. Rather than privileging the epistemological precondition of code and empiricism (fundamentalism), a literary approach to Scripture examines the literary themes, artistic qualities, and aesthetics present to develop a certain *taste* for transcendence and virtue that reads Scripture accordingly. A greater emphasis on taste loosens the biblical text from fundamentalist captivity and opens Christians to a different, more beautiful way of living. The theological and moral development of taste translates into a scriptural, practical reason that transcends mere repetitions of certain codes but searches for the deeper reality of the true, good, and beautiful presented in and by the text. Theologian David Bentley Hart describes this taste well in a recent debate on the death penalty. Hart describes his astonishment at those who read the Gospels and think it permits the death penalty. He believes the imagination in such readings represents bad taste. He writes,

> I have to admit that what struck me most forcibly was . . . appalling bad taste. Those who think it possible to be faithful to the figure of Christ as he appears in the gospels and also to argue in favor of the death penalty are, before all else, philistines. Their sensibilities are manifestly too barbarous and obtuse to see and appreciate the style of Christ at all because it is simply too refined, subtle, and elegant for them and certainly too negligent of common sensible, ethical expectations and the regrettable necessities those sometimes entail; it is a style rather, that expresses a form of life thoroughly absorbed in a far more essential and otherworldly loveliness.[13]

Hart describes the goal of literary theology, which privileges the embodied graciousness of Jesus of Nazareth as a larger trope that organizes readings of biblical texts around the center of graciousness and love of God for the world. One can gather a collection of verses and prove whatever one would like through the pages of Scripture, but as Hart states, this can betray the bad taste one brings *to* the text. A literary theology that develops good taste seeks instead the elegance of the beauty embodied in the life of Christ as the hermeneutic by which to understand the whole of Scripture. As Connor Cunningham succinctly summarizes, "Christ is . . . truth, goodness, and beauty. For this reason, the truth our

13. Hart, "Sense of Style," 249.

reading explicates is *a good way and a beautiful life.*"[14] Christ's life forms the moral imagination around it so that moral positions such as the death penalty are no longer palatable. To be clear, a literary theology does not wholesale reject literal readings of the text but moves literal readings into the orbit of the beauty of God in Christ so that one might locate literal readings within that larger frame of reference.

The literary theologian loves the biblical text, but does not turn it into an idol; furthermore, such reading develops a reflex to move from the transcendent God present in Jesus Christ to the text, which must inevitably move into the world. Thus, literary theology does not lose a passion for the immanent world and the biblical text but locates it within an artistic, transcendent frame where each dance is in mutual recognition. Only such an impulse can face the immanent world and realities with the strength to confront Christian nationalism and fundamentalism.

The Two Gileads: Life and Death

Before moving to the roadmap, I want to clarify the central imagery of the book, namely the two Gileads, which emerge from two separate novels (*The Handmaid's Tale* by Margaret Atwood and *Gilead* by Marilynne Robinson). The difference between the two Gileads illustrates the difference between the fundamentalist Christian nationalism of the West and the possibility of a literary theology beyond it. The Republic of Gilead and the small town of Gilead, Iowa, both exist in fictional spaces but inform their readers respectively of the threat and promise of Christian Scripture. The former is a nation structured around power and submission, while the latter is a town haunted by transcendence amid the messiness of people's lives. Though they share a name, the compelling feature of both fictional places arises from their different imaginative embodiment of various biblical texts. Discerning the different ways that Scripture operates at the heart of these two communities leads to a richer understanding of the literary theology of this book.

Margaret Atwood's *The Handmaid's Tale* presents a dystopian vision of a theocratic society, the Republic of Gilead, where fundamentalist interpretations of Scripture sustain systemic oppression, particularly against women. Unlike other post-apocalyptic literature, Atwood's world draws on real historical events, making its horrors all the more plausible. The narrative

14. Cunningham, *Genealogy of Nihilism*, 205. Emphasis original.

follows Offred, a handmaid forced into ritualized sexual servitude to high-ranking officials under the pretense of biblical justification. The governing authorities manipulate Scripture to serve their political aims, selectively reading passages such as Genesis 30:1–3 to legitimize their control while suppressing any counter-narrative. In this rigid society, biblical interpretation is wielded as a tool of power, privileging a patriarchal hierarchy that demands submission and enforces order through coercion and violence.

In contrast, Marilynne Robinson's Gilead series presents a different vision of faith and biblical engagement, embodied in the small town of Gilead, Iowa. Unlike the Republic of Gilead, which enforces a narrow, exclusionary religious order, Robinson's Gilead offers a model of faith marked by openness, imperfection, and a longing for something beyond rigid legalism. The town's inhabitants, particularly John Ames, Jack Boughton, and Lila, grapple with their struggles and uncertainties, yet they remain bound together by an underlying grace. Rather than enforcing Scripture as a system of control, the people of Gilead, Iowa, encounter it as a living text that invites wonder, inclusion, and transformation rather than fear and submission.

Lila's journey exemplifies this alternative approach to faith and biblical interpretation. Having lived on the margins of society, she arrives in Gilead as an outsider, wary of the kindness extended to her by Pastor Ames and his church. However, as she immerses herself in Scripture, she does not read it as a rigid code but as a story interwoven with her experiences of grace and survival. Her acts of kindness—offering shelter to a runaway boy and lovingly reflecting on the people who shaped her—become an extension of the love she unexpectedly finds in Gilead. For Lila, Scripture does not impose a system of exclusion but points beyond itself to a God who embraces even those deemed unworthy by the world. In this way, Robinson's Gilead provides a counter-narrative to the Republic of Gilead, demonstrating that true faith does not demand rigid conformity but fosters a community of grace shaped by a vision of love that transcends the limits of human judgment.

Robinson and Atwood employ literary theology to critique communities that manipulate Scripture in pursuit of societal perfection, offering instead a vision of faith that transcends fundamentalist Christian nationalism. Their works guide readers toward a posture that looks beyond rigid textualism to the God who calls for inclusive and compassionate communities. Rather than restricting life through coded cultural norms, Scripture aims to reveal the transcendent God who fosters love for the neighbor. This book argues that literary theology prioritizes divine beauty and communal embrace. It is the most effective response to fundamentalist nationalism, challenging its grip on Scripture and reorienting biblical interpretation toward justice, inclusion, and love.

ROADMAP: AN OVERVIEW OF THE CHAPTERS AND ARGUMENT

The central theme of the two Gileads will be woven through the entire book but will require a robust presentation of a literary theology. This section overviews the chapters, briefly connecting them to the book's larger argument and how each chapter's themes advance the argument. The thesis is that a literary approach to Scripture apocalyptically disrupts fundamentalist Christian nationalism (henceforth termed FCN) through the unfolding history of God with humanity that yields love of neighbor. The aim of this book is not only the ability to read texts like Romans 13:1–7 outside an FCN grasp but also to name the conditions by which one arrives at such interpretations. In chapter 1, the thesis will be advanced by analyzing the history and theories of fundamentalism and Christian nationalism in the United States separately, but against which a literary theology will emerge. The chapter argues that a fundamentalist reading of Scripture enables Christian nationalist politics. The latter requires the former, and their methods are identical, namely a preference for an efficient technique that achieves optimal ends of creating a desired culture with an optimal hierarchy.

In chapter 2, I advance the thesis by locating the phenomena of FCN as the perfection of secularity and a technological society rather than in opposition to it. Scripture is a focal point for political theology, and historically, Christians use it to determine how they should relate to government. For example, St. Augustine developed the image of the *Civitas Dei* and Martin Luther the two kingdoms. In both perspectives, one sees two distinct spaces: sacred and something else. One might assume that the sacred, for FCN, is an appeal to God against a secular world. However, the FCN, through their interpretation of Scripture, collapses all meaning into the immanent frame, which *they win* for God. This shift to the immanent as a contested space up for grabs departs significantly from the perspective that dominated much of history, namely that the gods/God secured that space *for* humanity. Thus, Christian nationalism and fundamentalism represent the perfection of the logic of secularity because they use faith to win society and public space for God. I explore the modern emergence of secularity in the work of philosopher Charles Taylor, who notes that the secular shifts what possesses authority and believability in modernity. One can find meaning exclusively inside the immanent frame in FCN. What makes non-faith-driven organizations and FCN secular is their expression of faithfulness in numbers, authority, and power over finite, immanent institutions.

Chapter 3 advances my thesis by proposing a literary imagination that subverts the fundamentalist Christian nationalist (FCN) approach to Scripture, which assumes a singular, inerrant interpretation. Instead, this approach seeks a primal narrative expressed through Scripture's literary tropes, opening the reader to a disruptive, transcendent reality that is new, embodied, and transformative. While engaging Christian nationalism, the chapter primarily critiques fundamentalism. It begins with Karl Barth's theology, which affirms Scripture as the word of God while rejecting its heretical conflation with the Second Person of the Trinity. This confusion leads to Bible worship and ideological control. I further nuance Barth's approach by reclaiming the transcendent distance between Scripture and the Word of God, fostering wonder in reading to encounter the triune Lord.

This chapter then explores Scripture's dramatic coherence, engaging Hans Frei's narrative theology while drawing on Kathryn Tanner and Pauline apocalyptic theology to challenge fundamentalist reductionism. Walter Brueggemann's concept of a primal narrative—a recurring motif throughout Scripture—demonstrates how biblical texts resist static readings, pointing instead to the openness of God's future, a vision enriched by Robert Jenson's trinitarian theology. If Scripture participates in divine revelation, it must be approached as a work of art, requiring interpretive tools that direct readers beyond the text to a transcendent reality.

To develop these tools, I turn to Toni Morrison's literary imagination, which, like James Cone's theology of the cross, emerges from a community's struggle and fosters liberation through aesthetic encounters. Cone, engaging W. E. B. Du Bois's *Jesus Christ in Texas*, highlights how Black artistic expressions reveal God's solidarity with the crucified and oppressed, situating beauty at the heart of exegesis and ethics.

Chapter 4 expands on the literary theology of resistance developed in the previous chapter by using hermeneutical tools to challenge fundamentalism and Christian nationalism. Drawing from Augustine and modern hermeneutical voices, I argue that resisting these ideologies requires a dynamic reading of Scripture, seeing it as an unfolding story rather than a static code. Using *The Handmaid's Tale* and *Gilead*, I explore how fundamentalist readings support power structures, revealing their immorality. Atwood critiques Gilead by portraying it as a subversive dystopia that embodies the dangers of Christian nationalism. A Girardian analysis further exposes how Gilead's order mirrors a scapegoating system. In contrast, Marilynne Robinson's Gilead quadrilogy presents a faith that embraces openness, failure, and wonder, critiquing both authoritarianism and secularism. Robinson's characters, particularly Lila, challenge traditional interpretations of Scripture, illustrating a more inclusive and redemptive biblical community.

Chapter 5 serves as the book's culminating argument by bringing the literary theology of the two Gileads into direct conversation with one of the most contested biblical texts in political theology. The chapter begins with a historical survey of Romans 13:1–7, tracing its use from early Christian thought through its varied deployments in Reformation, abolitionist, and nationalist contexts. This historical backdrop reveals how fundamentalist and Christian nationalist interpretations of the passage distort its theological meaning, using it as a justification for authoritarianism and the sanctification of power.

The chapter then advances an alternative, literary-theological reading of Romans 13:1–7 that resists its reduction to an instrument of control. Drawing on the insights of Jacques Ellul, this book challenges the technical and coercive logic that undergirds fundamentalist interpretations. Instead, the text is placed within a figural and apocalyptic framework with several focal images that emphasize the cruciform nature of Christ's reign. This approach reorients Romans 13 as a call not to passive submission but to discerning faithfulness—one that stands in solidarity with the marginalized and resists authoritarian misuse of power.

To illustrate this theological vision, I juxtapose the Republic of Gilead's rigid, ideological use of Scripture with Lila's Gilead, which embodies an open, grace-filled hermeneutic of presence and liberation. By integrating literary theology with a preferential option for the oppressed, the chapter argues that Romans 13 cannot function as a blank check for authoritarian governance but must invite humanity to participate in God's redemptive justice. This book's final section underscores that reclaiming Scripture from fundamentalist control requires a different hermeneutical approach and willingness to stand at the margins, where the true revelation of divine authority is in the crucified and risen Christ.

1

The Birth of a Nation

Fundamentalism and Christian Nationalism

"For we shall be as a city upon a hill, the eyes of all people are upon us"

John Winthrop, a Puritan Minister

INTRODUCTION: A DEEP STORY

The stories of fundamentalism and Christian nationalism share a singular thread in US history. The thread runs through a particular practice of Scripture and certain cultural moments, which presents a particular story about Christianity, the Bible, and the United States. In short, the story is that the Bible is the word of God as the full, complete, inerrant revelation of God without factual error, and that text gives the United States a clear and concise blueprint for God's politics. As such, the interpreters who hold this position argue that the Scriptures privilege conservative politics and evangelical Protestant Christian confessions over all others. Such a story runs deep in the United States, and this "deep story," as Samuel Perry and Philip Gorski term it, captures the imagination of many in the United States.[1]

This chapter examines the deep historical and theological roots of Christian nationalism and fundamentalism, arguing that the fundamentalist

1. Gorski and Perry, *Flag and the Cross*, 3–4.

reading of Scripture fosters a natural theology that ultimately fuels secularity at the heart of Christian nationalism. Rather than directly interpreting Romans 13:1–7, the chapter explores the conditions that make its nationalist and fundamentalist interpretation possible, particularly in response to higher criticism and the pluralization of the United States. In reaction, these movements seek control over social space to preserve a specific cultural order, collapsing meaning into the immanent frame and leading to the worship of the Bible and select individuals through a secular, technological use of Scripture. The chapter begins with an analysis of the shared origins of Christian nationalism and fundamentalism in the Puritan movement, which instilled a biblical literalism and divinely structured politics privileging certain forms of life. From there, it traces the historical development of both movements into the twentieth century and examines their internal logic through key academic and public figures. Ultimately, this chapter uncovers the ideological scaffolding that unites these movements—a natural theology of place, reality, and peoplehood—before concluding with signposts that will shape the remainder of the book.

PART I: ONE RIVER, TWO TRIBUTARIES: FUNDAMENTALISM AND CHRISTIAN NATIONALISM

As this chapter proposes, one cannot understand fundamentalism without Christian nationalism or Christian nationalism without fundamentalism. At the heart of fundamentalism and Christian nationalism is a particular view of Scripture that motivates a sociality of place, reality, and peoplehood. The social movement encourages a Christian responsibility to control and manipulate the public realm through a narrow lens of extremist, conservative politics oriented toward mastery. As will be shown, not only must one master the text, but one must also master a form of life that permits some to live and others to die. I begin by analyzing early Puritan theology as it grew after the English and Scottish Reformations. Puritanical regimes provide the theology, politics, and social constriction from which fundamentalism and Christian nationalism have grown. Even though it would be too large of a claim to lay the existence of both movements at the feet of Puritans, they drink deeply from the wells of Puritan theology.

Puritans

Fundamentalism's origin weaves through many historical moments. However, this study begins with the seventeenth-century Puritan movement, which shaped the emerging American colonies' religious and socio-political identity. Rooted in the Protestant Reformation and England's rising global influence, the Puritans embraced a literal reading of Scripture and a supersessionist theology that framed their theo-political aspirations. Viewing themselves as the new Israel, they saw their migration to the New World as a divine mandate to establish God's holy nation. However, to understand Puritanism's theological and political vision, one must first examine the English Reformation, which set the stage for its emergence.

King Henry VIII's break from the Catholic Church (driven by personal and political motives) consolidated religious and state power under the monarchy, a structure that would define England's religious struggles for decades. The ensuing power struggles between Catholics and Protestants intensified under Mary Tudor's violent restoration of Catholicism and forced many reformers, including John Knox, into exile. Upon returning, these Marian exiles and Knox's influence fueled a more radical Protestant reform. Queen Elizabeth I attempted a middle-way settlement, preserving some Catholic traditions while advancing Protestant reforms, but Puritan factions rejected this compromise as idolatrous. Their insistence on a fully reformed Church of England contributed to the English Civil War. It ultimately led to the Westminster Confession of Faith, a foundational Puritan document to secure a definitive Protestant identity. This legacy of biblical literalism, divine nationalism, and socio-political control carried into the American colonies, laying the groundwork for the fundamentalist impulse that would later shape Christian nationalism.

At the heart of this legacy were two defining characteristics that would continue to shape Puritan identity, as well as the emerging American identity, as they transitioned to the New World—first, the Reformed emphasis on the Bible's complete reliability.[2] Puritans held a Reformed perspective that the Bible was infallible in its plain, literal reading.[3] Their reading of the Bible coupled well with their coordinated belief in the absolute truth of Puritanism.[4] Any innovation or turn to tradition creates an innovation that corrupts the simple reading of the text.

2. Hall, *Puritans,* 21.

3. Hall, *Puritans,* 21.

4. Hall, *Puritans,* 2.

Second, we must consider a federal theology that claimed a history of redemption realized in a sequence of covenants from the Old Testament to the present.[5] As David Hall writes,

> This framework had several benefits. It supported an understanding of the Christian life as grounded in obedience to Old Testament law and buttressed the argument, itself classically Reformed, that law and grace were always intermingled, the law serving as a means of preparing for grace and a framework for the righteousness that the elect were obliged to practice.[6]

Federal theology and upholding covenants will continue to be an emphasis in the movement and American Christianity in general. To be clear, Puritans believed in a theology of replacement, as did many Protestant and Catholic movements in the sixteenth and seventeenth centuries. The covenant once made with Israel is made anew with new nations. Therefore, as the Puritans sought the New World, in a desire to fulfill their covenant, they also sought to live in a new nation blessed by God.

Puritan federal theology led to another consequence, namely a strict understanding of social order and a strong social activism to reform the church and the world.[7] In modern caricatures, Puritans are depicted as prudish, emphasizing punishment for sin. Puritans were very disciplined and borrowed that perspective from their Reformed heritage developed from theologian John Calvin. Hall states, "Calvin took for granted that the progress of reform depended on . . . penalties and, especially, excommunication, which he regarded as the church's most effective means of preserving a semblance of purity."[8] Therefore, the Puritans took for granted the idea that correct behavior was God's desire and led to blessing.

The Puritans found a new life and an enduring legacy in the New World. Puritans believed they practiced the true religion, and the New World offered a chance to enact it. Their religion practiced a strictly literal reading of the Bible, disciplined personal piety, and desired a reformed society. A new opportunity occurred in the Americas to practice their religion and convert the indigenous inhabitants to their way. The New World drew out an important element of Puritan theology: logic and natural theology. Puritans favored literal readings of Scripture, but

5. Hall, *Puritans*, 115.

6. Hall, *Puritans*, 115.

7. Hall, *Puritans*, 24.

8. Hall, *Puritans*, 23.

they sought and found a natural foundation for revelation. This impulse will appear in later movements, such as the fundamentalists' implicit embrace of modernism even as they ostensibly reject it. The Puritan movement believed that the Enlightenment was an opportunity. As Wallace Marshall argues, Puritans "assimilated" the Enlightenment to prove its true religion through logic and adherence to revelation.[9] As Marshall continues, the "overwhelming majority of Puritan theologians were firm believers in the legitimacy of natural theology and evidentialism . . . [and] employed them in a surprising variety of pastoral, evangelical, and polemical contexts."[10] Thus, the literal reading of Scripture that Puritans practiced should be examined in light of their appeal to Enlightenment logic.

The posture in natural theology appears succinctly in the seminal Puritan document, *The Westminster Confession of Faith*. It states,

> The light of nature sheweth that there is a God, who hath lordship and sovereignty over all; it is good, and doeth good unto all; and is therefore to be feared, loved, praised, and called upon, trusted in, and served, with all the heart, and with all the soul, and with all the might.[11]

Not only did Puritans believe that one could extract knowledge of God's existence, but one could also know God's attributes. Thus, the Puritans allowed a greater place for reason than generations before. This emphasis breaks with traditional Thomist descriptions of natural knowledge of God limited only to knowledge of God's existence or the dialectical account of Protestant theology.[12] To be clear, Puritans believed that special revelation would clear up issues concerning God's nature and believed it assisted natural reason.[13] However, some Puritans saw the natural comprehension of God in an evangelical light. As Marshall argues, referencing a sermon by Puritan John Howe (1630–1705), "people's receptivity to biblical revelation rose and fell with the strength and character of their natural theology."[14] Howe's claim gestures toward a very important fea-

9. Marshall, *Puritanism and Natural Theology*, 5.
10. Marshall, *Puritanism and Natural Theology*, 6.
11. *The Westminster Confession of Faith*, ch. 21, art. 1.
12. See Aquinas, *ST*, Prima Pars. Q. 12, Art. 12–13.
13. Marshall, *Puritanism and Natural Theology*, 47.
14. Marshall, *Puritanism and Natural Theology*, 39.

ture of biblical interpretation: revelation will find foundation in reason and nature.

Puritans presented three proofs of God's revelation. First, they found external proofs in miracles and fulfilled prophecies. Second, there were internal proofs, such as the simplicity and suitability of the texts. Third, the transformative impact of the text itself remained.[15] The strongest evidence for the Puritans connected the first and second as it yields the third. Puritans believed that people of good reason, even if not born again, would find internal and external evidence convincing them of God's existence. Furthermore, the Holy Spirit will transform the individual's heart with this knowledge. The conversion of the believer was the strongest proof of the Bible. The form of life they proposed through discipline and strict adherence to their religion would inevitably lead to faith. Thus, no greater natural theology existed than the authority of their proposed life.

Understanding fundamentalism and Christian nationalism requires beginning with the Puritans because they established the theological and socio-political framework that later movements would inherit and adapt. The Puritans were not merely a religious sect; they embodied a vision of a society where biblical authority dictated personal piety and public order, laying the groundwork for the fusion of faith and governance that defines fundamentalism and Christian nationalism. Their insistence on biblical literalism, moral discipline, and a covenantal relationship with God created a model in which religious identity was inseparable from national identity—a model that would shape the trajectory of American Christianity. As the Puritans sought to construct a "city on a hill," they embedded within the American consciousness the idea that divine favor was contingent upon societal adherence to their interpretation of Scripture. This theological framework and their conviction that they were establishing a divinely sanctioned nation provided the ideological DNA for later movements seeking to restore or preserve a "Christian" America. Though fundamentalism and Christian nationalism evolved in response to modern challenges, their core commitments—Scriptural absolutism, divine exceptionalism, and the desire to legislate religious and cultural purity—owe much to the Puritan project of covenantal nation-building.

15. Marshall, *Puritanism and Natural Theology*, 45.

PART II: DIVERGING AND MERGING STREAMS

Building on the Puritan legacy, later Christian generations would inherit and adapt this performative drive to fulfill a divine covenant, seeking God's favor through national and religious identity. In the following sections, we see that the histories of both fundamentalism and Christian nationalism converge at the site of Scripture and the control of social space. Fundamentalists and Christian nationalists alike perceive the surrounding culture as being in a state of moral and spiritual decline, prompting them to take decisive action to restore what they see as a divinely ordained order. Their strategy for correcting this perceived erosion centers on an unwavering reverence for the Bible—not simply as a sacred text but as an authoritative instrument that validates their vision for society. This veneration extends beyond Scripture to a specific group whose identity and values are privileged in all biblical interpretations, effectively aligning religious authority with their cultural and political aspirations.

Fundamentalism: A History

The first stream to consider is fundamentalism. The history of fundamentalism, as historian George Marsden writes, reveals a "militantly antimodernist Protestant evangelicalism."[16] Fundamentalism does not have a singular point of origin but develops in response to cultural shifts perceived as deviations from "biblical" norms. The Great Awakenings and the response to deism serve as prime historical examples of this evangelical emphasis, reinforcing a distinct understanding of biblical authority and personal salvation. In England, the term *evangelical* originally referred to Catholics within the Church of England that desired reform. However, in the American context, it came to denote a movement centered on conversion, evangelism, biblical authority, activism, and Christ's atoning death. The First Great Awakening, which took place in the New England Congregationalist churches during 1730s, exemplified the evangelical fervor, particularly in urban centers, laying the groundwork for the fundamentalist impulses that would later arise in American Protestantism. These Congregationalists, as historian Frances Fitzgerald writes, "were the direct heirs to the Puritans of New England."[17] The Congregationalist

16. Marsden, *Fundamentalism and American Culture*, 2.

17. Fitzgerald, *Evangelicals*, 14.

churches were an aspect of the Puritan plan to form the perfect society. Fitzgerald continues, "Puritans had established close-knit communities, bound by covenant, where church and state cooperated in an effort to build a Holy Commonwealth."[18] The Great Awakening occurred as these Congregationalist churches sent circuit-riding preachers to convert people in rural spaces. They wanted to incorporate the commonwealth into a broader community and include it in the covenant. These circuit riders were uneducated, and their message aimed more at the heart than the head. The movement, as Fitzgerald writes, "introduced a new idea of conversion as a sudden, overwhelming experience of God's grace."[19] The believer should expect their affections to change after the new experience of God's grace. Jonathan Edwards, defender of the Second Great Awakening, argued that while conversion is not strictly about emotion, it is about the intensity of the change of the heart to love God more deeply.

The new conversion experience grounded in the affections radically shifted preaching and teaching in the Christian community in two ways. First, the emotional life of revivalism and subsequent evangelicalism forced faith into constant introspection. The believer was in constant danger in their spiritual life of submitting to demonic influences. The metric that measured one's "spiritual health" was emotional fervor. Furthermore, no greater danger faced the evangelical believer than an intellectual exploration of the faith. Christine Heyrman illustrates this point through the story of William Glendinning. After a traditional evangelical conversion and fervor, Glendinning sought to expand his faith through study. However, Glendinning found that many of the inquiries into the faith were more "curious than useful."[20] Glendinning already suffered from several ailments, such as "chronic rheumatism" and "insomnia."[21] The questions over the divinity of Christ, the authority of the biblical canon, and other theological inquiry elements filled Glendinning with excessive doubt. Though he eventually overcame this doubt, he suffered mental anguish over the inquires that he worried "cost him eternal life."[22] Furthermore, Glendinning's spiritual danger extended beyond his emotional turmoil to his family. At one point, Glendinning considered taking his own life to prevent his contagion of doubt from spreading. He feared

18. Fitzgerald, *Evangelicals*, 14–15.
19. Fitzgerald, *Evangelicals*, 13.
20. Heyrman, *Southern Cross*, 29.
21. Heyrman, *Southern Cross*, 29.
22. Heyrman, *Southern Cross*, 29.

the doubt might impact them and, thus, forced himself to be restrained, not to harm himself and others. As Heyrman concludes,

> to seek evangelical rebirth [in revival] was to court daunting emotional risks . . .And while some who observed kin and friends come under conviction were inspired to emulation, many others shrank back, appalled at the toll it exacted . . . one German Quaker who looked on with terror as his wife, a recruit to Methodism, became so preoccupied by the fear of an eternity in hell that she neglected their children.[23]

Thus, even as revivalism spread through the Great Awakenings, a new emotional fervor arose to take center stage in American Christianity.

Second, the revivals of the Great Awakening destabilized traditional church structures and communities. The emotional appeal called every believer to account for their individual salvation and status before God. Such introspection was the logical conclusion of Martin Luther's Reformation project. While Luther did not intend to produce a culture of inward anxiety, the Reformation's emphasis on individual conscience before God helped generate forms of religious introspection that later became culturally pervasive. New Christian denominations arose after the Great Awakenings focused on emotional fervor and sudden conversion. Such work destabilized the authority of the available church structures and pastors. In addition, suspicion for traditional modes of education increased due to the success of uneducated circuit riders, and the spiritual dangers found in education, as in the case of Glendinning, led to the increased use of a plain reading of Scripture alone.

The Great Awakening also triggered a response to the fledgling deism in some of the more influential figures of American life. Thomas Jefferson, for example, was a staunch deist and a Unitarian. Jefferson rejected the religiosity and emotional nature of evangelicalism arising from the Great Awakening. Heyrman summarizes this well.

> Nothing could have been more contrary to his private convictions than evangelical religiosity—its prizing of feeling more than intellect, its veneration of biblical revelation as a truth higher than reason. Jefferson was a deist for much of his life, a Unitarian during his later years, and an arch-rationalist. He always held that the head rather than the heart should dictate an individual's beliefs. He dismissed the Bible as a collection of myths and derided the notion of a trinity as "Abracadabra." Jesus

23. Heyrman, *Southern Cross*, 39.

> was a mere mortal, albeit one Jefferson regarded as a moralist superior to any other of antiquity's sages, pagan or Jewish. As for eternal outcomes, he gave the matter little thought but once speculated that each person's fate would be decided by whether their life had benefited humanity, not whether they believed in a divine Christ.[24]

Jefferson's educated faith ran contrary to everything in the evangelical movement. Furthermore, due to the heritage gained from the Puritans and Jefferson's embrace of the Enlightenment as well as place in the leadership of the United States, the threat of deism, in the evangelical mind, undermined the covenant between the United States and God. Again, one must recall the theology of replacement baked into the American ethos by the Puritans, which was that covenantal adherence led to divine blessing. Jefferson's deism was nothing less than a threat to the whole of America's soul as Glendinning was to his family. Thus, evangelicals, as the descendants of the Puritans, would double down on the revelation of Scripture, revivalist fervor, and the establishment of a pure community before God.

However, this focus on doctrinal purity and revival stands in contrast to the shifts that began to emerge in some academic circles of Christianity, highlighting a growing tension between neo-Puritan evangelicals and evolving theological perspectives. As with Glendinning, there remained a spiritual threat through corrupting what evangelicals saw as the plain reading of the text. Furthermore, as in the Puritan movement, any reading of the Bible that did not adhere to a plain reading only embellished and distorted the message of the Bible. At stake were covenantal faithfulness and true religion. The purity of faithfulness possesses an eschatological character. Puritans believed in a negative apocalypticism wherein the truly faithful resist the forces of evil. This eschatological posture morphed into premillennial dispensationalism under the evangelical movement. According to this eschatological teaching, time is divided into several dispensations or eras. In these dispensations, humans were unfaithful to a divine command. Each era ended in destruction, and in the present dispensation, Christians await the end. History will keep getting worse, but the faithful will not experience destruction. The goal is merely to remain faithful in history to true religion.

24. Heyrman, *Southern Cross*, 7.

The tension between an increased intellectual approach to Christianity continued into the nineteenth century. Not only deists but other rationalists sought a firmer, measured foundation for Scripture. A new approach to Scripture arose in Europe, placing it on firm scientific grounds. Theologian and historian Paul Bassett summarizes this shift in the modern world.

> The rise of modern science . . . with its redefinition of what a fact must be and of reality itself, based upon these re-defined facts, had narrowed the definition of what truth or a truth must be and how it would be determined to be truth or a truth indeed. Nineteenth century theologians, with varying degrees of awareness and complicity, accepted the definitions of facts, or reality and of truth.[25]

Higher criticism developed along the lines of fact/reality synthesis, and modern scientific tools, such as the one used in biblical scholarship (historical critical, sociological, etc.) were used to interpret ancient texts. It emerges largely from Germany in the nineteenth century as the study of the Bible undergoes a more academic turn. In the Enlightenment suspicion of transcendence, the focus on the scientific study of Scripture took center stage. Like Jefferson's deism, higher criticism rejects the more miraculous elements of Scripture and Christianity in favor of historical-scientific analysis and the formation of moral culture.

Higher criticism spread throughout the world to varying degrees of success as the nineteenth century gave way to the twentieth century. Higher criticism became a staple of many seminaries and schools of theology, especially in the University of Chicago Divinity School in the United States. However, higher criticism would find significant pushback from a group of pastors, lay people, and scholars. This group of concerned Christians endeavored to write a defense of the "fundamentals" of the Christian faith in the face of higher criticism. In March of 1910, pastors and theologians, commissioned by wealthy oil barons, wrote *The Fundamentals*. Historian Michael Kazin writes that *The Fundamentals* "gave biblical literalism a new name that stuck."[26] Puritanism emphasized this literalism, which dictated the course of the movement for centuries; however, fundamentalism would dictate the future of biblical literalism. The text defended specific teachings (e.g., a six-day literal creation, the

25. Bassett, "Fundamentalist Leavening," 68.

26. Kazin, *Godly Hero*, 264.

inerrancy of Scripture, and penal substitutionary atonement). The idea of biblical inerrancy resonated with conservative evangelicals, deepening their suspicion of academic theology as it embraced historical criticism. The publication of *The Fundamentals*, a twelve-volume collection of ninety essays written over five years, sought to defend Christianity from the perceived encroachments of modernist thought. Authors ranged from laypeople to influential theologians like Princeton's B. B. Warfield, and their work laid the foundation for what became known as fundamentalism. Central to the movement was the belief that modernist theology, like Thomas Jefferson's approach to Scripture, dismissed key biblical truths by privileging historical science and human consciousness over divine revelation. Fundamentalists sought to combat these perceived threats by establishing their colleges, seminaries, and publishing houses to train students in the "fundamentals" of the faith and disseminate literature to pastors and laypeople. By the early twentieth century, fundamentalists occupied prominent positions in Reformed churches and academic institutions, but their desire extended beyond intellectual influence and control of ecclesial spaces.

A defining moment in this struggle came in 1922 when Presbyterian minister Harry Emerson Fosdick, in his sermon *Shall the Fundamentalists Win?*, defended higher criticism and rejected key fundamentalist doctrines, prompting a fierce rebuttal from Presbyterian pastor Clarence Edward MacCartney in *Shall Unbelief Win?* This debate sharpened divisions between modernists and fundamentalists, culminating in a confrontation at the 1923 Presbyterian Church's (PCUSA) General Assembly. Seeking to solidify their position, fundamentalists enlisted former presidential nominee William Jennings Bryan, who championed their stance against evolution and the literal interpretation of Genesis. Though Bryan's loss in the PCUSA Assembly election and later humiliation in the 1925 Scopes Trial symbolized fundamentalism's public defeat, the movement continued to thrive through its institutional networks, ensuring its persistence in American religious and cultural life.

Bryan's greatest concern about the Presbyterian Church was its educating young people and ministers in a materialistic, evolutionary philosophy.[27] Bryan contended that since less than 10 percent of Presbyterians held to evolution, the Assembly should not force this theory on the denomination. The Assembly adopted his concern, and Bryan continued

27. See Kazin, *Godly Hero*, 277.

his cross-country rejection of evolution. Though we will investigate the claims of inerrancy later in this chapter, the creationist-evolutionist divide dominated much of the arguments along the modernist-fundamentalist divide. Six-day literal creation is a central tenet of many proponents of inerrancy and fundamentalism. The caricature of fundamentalists is their perceived rejection of science and evolution. However, figures like Bryan, known as Mr. Fundamentalist, were not anti-science. Rather, *certain* elements of evolution and Darwinism were of concern to Bryan. As historian Michael Kazin writes,

> Students who learned that humans were nothing but animals and that animals survived only through violence and hatred had little reason to care for "the weak and the helpless" among them . . . A society run by Darwinists could justify a law barring the feebleminded and poor from having babies and could engage in endless wars of conquest.[28]

In Bryan's time, scientists and philosophers utilizing limited aspects of evolution theorized the essential use of survival of the fittest for social structures that allowed for eugenics and war. To be clear, many fundamentalists rejected science as an empirical discipline. However, a fair reading of fundamentalism and individuals like Bryan must also acknowledge the surrounding anxieties.

At the time of the 1923 Assembly of the PCUSA, the University of Chicago was both the epicenter of higher criticism and eugenics, with notable criminal cases such as Leopold and Loeb, where evolutionary science and Nietzschean philosophy directing heinous murders loomed in the background. The eventual use of Darwinism and eugenics in German Nazi rhetoric led to an increased suspicion by certain fundamentalists after Bryan. The six-day literal creation, for Bryan, provided a means to covertly inserted a traditional Christian ethic to the poor and a logic sufficient to counter evolution. For this purpose, Bryan toured the nation speaking against evolution and eventually served as the prosecuting lawyer in the famed Scopes Trial in Dayton, Tennessee.

An accurate depiction of fundamentalism and evolutionary sciences must work past caricatures. The present work does not possess adequate space to develop a thick description of each and their concern with the other. It must be sufficient to state that not every fundamentalist was a knuckle-dragging anti-science Neanderthal nor the evolutionary

28. Kazin, *Godly Hero*, 275.

scientists out of touch, amoral thinkers that desire genocide and mass sterilization. The present work aims to identify the fundamentalist pitfalls and their relationship to Christian nationalism.

As fundamentalists turned their attention to science and higher criticism, the central issue became the nature of empirical fact. The nineteenth century marked a shift in authority toward empirical verification, including within theological studies, where scholars sought to align theology with the scientific method, undermining biblical literalism by questioning miracles, the resurrection, and a six-day creation. *The Fundamentals* emerged as a response, solidifying the fundamentalist commitment to inerrancy and framing the debate as a struggle over competing claims to empirical truth. Rather than emphasizing God's transcendence or challenging the dominance of scientific inquiry, fundamentalists argued that the Bible itself was the most authoritative source of factual truth. The dispute with higher criticism was thus not about faith versus science but about which framework—modernist historical inquiry or scriptural inerrancy—held the power to define reality. This shift detached Scripture from its theological and ecclesial context, transforming it into a defensive mechanism prioritizing factual accuracy over divine mystery. The Scopes Trial in 1925 became the defining moment of this struggle, as fundamentalists, led by William Jennings Bryan, attempted to prohibit the teaching of evolution. Bryan, a populist politician and devout Christian, was not a fundamentalist in the strictest sense but aligned with the movement against a common enemy. The trial, however, became a public spectacle, with defense attorney Clarence Darrow skillfully exposing the logical inconsistencies of biblical inerrancy. Though John Scopes himself was an unenthusiastic defendant, the case became a referendum on fundamentalism, culminating in Bryan's public embarrassment when Darrow called him to testify as a biblical expert. The trial ended before Bryan could deliver his closing arguments, sealing fundamentalism's defeat in the public eye. In the aftermath, fundamentalists retreated from mainstream culture, shifting their focus to private institutions—seminaries, publishing houses, and independent churches—where they could preserve their beliefs free from external scrutiny. Despite their loss in the public square, they continued to see themselves as the true defenders of Christianity in an increasingly secular world, laying the groundwork for future resurgence.

The fallout of the Scopes trial led not to the end of the fundamentalist movement but a reorganization. Largely, fundamentalists, thanks to their premillennial dispositions, retreated from culture. Fundamentalists did not mind because they did not *need* engagement with a larger culture. They ran educational institutions and publishing houses that allowed them to retreat from larger cultures. As historian Randall Balmer describes, this fundamentalist subculture

> was insular and enveloping, and it was possible . . . to grow up in the evangelical subculture and have very little commerce with anyone outside of that world. Parents could send their children to Sunday school and Bible camp and then to Moody Bible Institute, Multnomah School of the Bible, or Westmont College, reasonably confident that they would not be corrupted by the outside world.[29]

Fundamentalists, then, happily went away from the public eye. More than just losing a court case in Tennessee, the Scopes Trial exposed fundamentalism to public scrutiny and mockery. For example, journalist H. L. Mencken wrote of the trial in the *Baltimore Sun*, "It serves notice on the country that Neanderthal man is organizing in these forlorn backwaters of the land, led by a fanatic, rid of sense and devoid of conscience."[30] The goodwill, fundamentalist emphases on resisting eugenics or caring for people experiencing poverty was lost behind the narrative presented by voices like Mencken. But the loss and mockery led fundamentalists to listen to extremist voices and create fundamentalist echo chambers.

As they entered the middle of the twentieth century, the fundamentalists desperately needed a rebranding. Since fundamentalists were not outsiders but evangelicals themselves, rejoining this coalition represented an important act of self-location rather than realignment. The fundamentalists would turn to successes from their evangelical and Puritan past while also keeping the lessons that did work from the previous decades. Furthermore, fundamentalists would distance themselves from the identifier *fundamentalism*. Key leaders of the fundamentalist movement reorganized in 1942 into the National Association of Evangelicals (NAE) and the more militant American Council of Christian Churches (ACCC). As historian Kristin Kobes Du Mez writes,

> Their choice of the word "evangelical" was strategic. Aware of their image problem, fundamentalists knew they needed to rebrand their movement. The fact that some of the more militant

29. Balmer, *Bad Faith*, 18.

30. Mencken quoted in Balmer, *Bad Faith*, 16.

> fundamentalists had started their organization . . . helped with this project, enabling the NAE to distance itself from more reactionary elements, and it was at this time that "evangelical" came to connote a more forward-looking alternative to the militant, separatist fundamentalism that had become an object of ridicule. But evangelicals never entirely abandoned a combative posture, and even as evangelicals worked to bring a new respectability to their "old-time religion," fundamentalists fought to define the contours of that faith. The affinities ran deep, and it was impossible to distinguish one from the other; eventually, fundamentalists would inject their militancy into the broader evangelical movement.[31]

Du Mez clarifies how the fundamentalists rebranded themselves. Instead of calling themselves "fundamentalists," they faded into the background of the growth of evangelical culture. Instead of calling the essentials of the faith "fundamentals," they called their faith "old-time religion."[32] In addition, fundamentalists would use their publishing houses and schools to influence individuals in the wake of such losses by training a new generation that the world did not accept the *true* religion. The new terminology and media would disguise them as they planned their next move. Even though they were premillennial dispensationalists, the Puritan desire for a well-ordered society never left them. However, their next foray would focus on a classic evangelical staple, revival. If the fundamentalists could not form society through traditional legal means, they would focus on individual conversion and revival to transform hearts. Furthermore, fundamentalists believed that a charismatic leader like William Jennings Bryan could be a very enticing aspect of their movement. Thus, the fundamentalists-turned-evangelicals needed a new public face that could advance the cause of their old-time religion (i.e., fundamentalism) and influence the public less directly.

The new leader of the fundamentalist movement and chief star of their rebrand was America's Pastor, Billy Graham. The "handsome young North Carolina minister" upheld fundamentalist values and would drive the greatest evangelical revival of the twentieth century.[33] He believed in the inerrancy of Scripture and preached individual, personal conversion akin to the Great Awakenings of the early eighteenth century. He was

31. Du Mez, *Jesus and John Wayne*, 21–22.

32. Du Mez, *Jesus and John Wayne*, 18–19.

33. Du Mez, *Jesus and John Wayne*, 22.

the vision of the strong American male, like Bryan, which was essential to the fundamentalist rebrand. After World War II, it became a fertile ground for receiving the fundamentalist message through the image of the masculine Christian. The war placed a clear division between good and evil with a clear mandate to defeat the latter. Graham represented the best fundamentalist message and the US nationalist message. "Graham cut his teeth as a revivalist during the Second World War," as Du Mez writes, and "he worked both to evangelize the nation's youth and to craft heroic Christian citizens who could promote Christianity and democracy at home and abroad."[34] The opportunity of the war was that it distracted from the movement's previous losses and allowed a new face to take fundamentalism to a broader, mainstream audience.

Under Graham, the evangelical (i.e., fundamentalist) movement would experience unprecedented growth. Graham utilized the new media and quickly gained national and international acclaim. Thousands of individuals converted in the evangelical style at Graham's crusades. Soon, Graham's fame would gain him an audience with the president of the United States, Harry S. Truman. Graham, like Truman, was a lifelong Democrat. Du Mez writes, "In the middle of the twentieth century it would have been hard to find a Southern Baptist from North Carolina [like Graham] who didn't identify as a Democrat."[35] This comes as a surprise to those who identify Graham and evangelicals with the Republican Party. Furthermore, it is surprising that when the two Democrats met, it did not go well. Graham quickly challenged President Truman's understanding of the faith and publicly disclosed Truman's lack of evangelical faith on the White House lawn. At this moment, Graham, with his legion of evangelical fans, controlled an important moment in the life of the United States. Graham continued his critique of Truman and even encouraged Republican hopeful Dwight D. Eisenhower to enter the race for president. Graham promised evangelicals would vote for the former war hero, thus guiding evangelicals out of the Democratic Party and toward the Republican Party.[36]

Though Billy Graham played a pivotal role in shaping mid-twentieth-century evangelicalism, the political transformation of fundamentalism between the 1950s and 1980s revealed a broader movement. Graham's focus on personal conversion and masculine, militant faith influenced

34. Du Mez, *Jesus and John Wayne*, 25.

35. Du Mez, *Jesus and John Wayne*, 33.

36. Du Mez, *Jesus and John Wayne*, 34.

evangelical social structures, promoting a patriarchal vision that framed Christianity as a battle against evil. This ethos helped reinforce a "family values" agenda rooted in biblical inerrancy and fundamentalist traditions. However, this reinvention also included a racial imaginary that justified segregationist institutions, particularly in the southeastern United States, as biblically ordained safe havens amidst the civil rights movement. J. Russell Hawkins recounts how, in 1963, President John F. Kennedy convened religious leaders to rally support for civil rights legislation, initially receiving positive responses—yet many fundamentalist leaders remained resistant, seeing integration as a threat to their theological and cultural order. It was "a June afternoon in 1963, [and] nearly 250 religious leaders gathered in the East Room of the White House . . . at the invitation of President John F. Kennedy to discuss how American pastors, priests, and rabbis could rally support for Kennedy's recent call for sweeping civil rights legislation."[37] The meeting began well, with many ministers thanking the president for leading such an important conversation. However, Albert Garner would spoil this mood when he raised his hand and said

> many southern white Christians like himself actually held a "strong moral conviction" that "racial integration . . . is against the will of their Creator." After all, Garner reasoned, "segregation is a principle of the Old Testament and . . . prior to this century neither Christianity nor any denomination of it ever accepted the integration philosophy."[38]

The motivation to reject integration was partly the Bible and the defense of its plain reading. One must realize the lure of plain reading and how it can disguise a larger network of hermeneutical and cultural assumptions. Furthermore, transgressing the plain reading threatened not only a moral offense but a larger sinful offense against the Word of God, which was now collapsed exclusively into the Bible. The text then became the site of worship rather than a means of worship, and defense was an act of disciplined fidelity.

The defense of the plain reading of the Bible embedded within the anti-segregationist movement appeared also in the pro-slavery movement. The connection involves race and certain understandings of it. It also includes a cultural hermeneutic that unites the authority of a literal reading of the Bible to a certain form of life. Like the Puritan natural

37. Hawkins, *Bible Told Them So*, 1.

38. Hawkins, *Bible Told Them So*, 2.

theology, such a reading should be evident in a plain reading of Scripture and available to any logical person observing the natural order. Both hermeneutic elements exist in the Puritan mind through its vision of an orderly society and life. The focus on "true religion" that shaped individuals and society formed an interconnected web of meaning that riveted truth to a particular cultural identity.

Historian Mark Noll goes so far as calling their formation of society a form of biblical despotism.[39] Foundational to this approach was a theology of covenant and replacement that made the English-born Puritans the new Israelites and God's chosen people. Following the written word led to blessing, but failure required corporate repentance.[40] This feature of Puritan theology remained an aspect of evangelicalism in the United States. When abolition became an issue of public concern, evangelicals followed the example of Thomas Thompson, Fellow at Christ's College and missionary to New Jersey, who claimed the obvious evidence from Scripture. Thompson would cite Leviticus 25:45–46a:

> Moreover of the children of the strangers that do sojourn among you, of them shall ye buy, and of their families that are with you, which they begat in your land: and they shall be your possession . . . ye shall take them as an inheritance for your children after you, to inherit them for a possession; they shall be your bondmen for ever: but over your brethren the children of Israel, ye shall not rule one over another with rigour. (KJV)

The defense of slavery is direct. As Noll summarizes, Thompson suggested that when it came to the biblical defense of slavery, Christians should "open the Bible, read it, believe it."[41] Thompson would couple the Leviticus text with a brief reading from Philemon and the apostle Paul's admonition for the enslaved person Onesimus to return to his master. Thompson would concede that the Bible puts limits on slavery but permitted keeping foreigners and strangers as enslaved people. The theology of replacement appears here clearly. The passage in Leviticus addresses the Hebrew people but now addresses those in the United States and England. Its prescription was not to enslave one another, but instead, the foreigner had a specific cultural reference. The European and specifically English imagination that formed the biblical defense of slavery places them in the place of the

39. Noll, *Civil War as a Theological Crisis*, 151.

40. See Noll, *Civil War as a Theological Crisis*, 17–18.

41. Noll, *Civil War as a Theological Crisis*, 33.

Hebrews. God's providence permits them, as God's *chosen* people, to hold enslaved people. The United States and Great Britain before them usurped the status of Israel as the chosen people. Thus, the plain reading, which always possesses a rhetorical authority as the "true" reading, privileges a natural theology that presses subjects imaginatively in the text as recipients of divine blessing while others receive only curses.

The move to read a type of natural theology inside of the claim to exclusive Scriptural authority carried into the defense of segregation and Jim Crow by fundamentalists. As J. Russell Hawkins writes,

> Scripture was never the lone rallying cry of those who interpreted Jim Crow as God's will. Instead, before they ever cracked the cover of the Good Book, Christian segregationists saw divine sanction for segregation manifested in the book of nature. As a theological principle, general revelation suggests that humanity can learn about God through observation of the natural world; for many white southerners in the mid-twentieth century, nature revealed God to be a segregationist.[42]

The interweaving of natural theology (i.e., general revelation in nature) with Scripture created a starting point for segregationists. They argued that not only did heaven and earth reveal God's glory (Psalm 19:1), but they revealed a segregated order. It is a natural order that serves the ends of the reader rather than others. Dr. Mack Stewart, a Louisiana Baptist minister and segregationist, presented this logic one Sunday morning to his congregation: "I am a segregationist because God ordained it. It is true with plants and animal life . . . If you leave plants and animals alone, they will stay separated. Animals will not mix. Birds will not mix . . . God intended it that way."[43] However, Stewart was not alone. Alabama Sunday school teacher and author Fetus Windham appealed to this divinely ordained natural order in the "racial" segregation of ants: "We find much voluntary segregation even in nature . . . Hordes of black ants several times larger than the little red ants do not integrate with any other ants, though they may live not too far apart in their ground tunnels."[44] However, again, one should detect a theology of replacement in this natural theology. It grants not only a status of superiority to Caucasians but implies that those

42. Hawkins, *Bible Told Them So*, 46.

43. Stewart, "Why I am a Segregationist," quoted in Hawkins, *Bible Told Them So*, 47.

44. Windham, *Bible Treatise on Segregation*, 15, quoted in Hawkins, *Bible Told Them So*, 47.

of different races are different species. Furthermore, this natural theology grounds the purported authority of Scripture in an external, observable reality. The racial lines mapped onto creation and Scripture, which led to a reading that favored those of Caucasian, European descent.

The most influential individuals in fundamentalism struggled to mediate between public concern around segregation and their fundamentalist base. Kristin Du Mez reminds readers that fundamentalists were staunch opponents of the civil rights movement.[45] Fundamentalists claimed that desegregation, a key cornerstone of civil rights, represented a movement toward disorder and the destruction of culture. L. Nelson Bell, Billy Graham's father-in-law and founder of *Christianity Today*, would write an article denouncing the integration efforts as unnatural, immoral, and unchristian.[46] These claims arise from a direct appeal to the natural order and theology (Bell) and a covenantal understanding of American civil life and Scripture, as in minister Carl McIntire's critique of the civil rights of 1964. He writes that desegregation goes against the Bible's command to be born again and comes to this conclusion because of integration's false insistence, according to McIntire, on the shared "brotherhood" of all people. It was false because, as McIntire argues, the Civil Rights Act does not require all people to "have a new birth" to be siblings.[47] One must recognize the biblical codes and immutable principles at work here. Furthermore, McIntire utilizes the Ten Commandments to affirm personal property rights in the face of government overreach. He writes, "Man is responsible to God for his property, its use and its disposition. The entire private sector of our society with the individual capitalist and private owner is not to be subject to federal regulation and intervention which gives to the Government a responsibility in this field over private property."[48] Thus, fundamentalists relied on natural theology/order to form a literal interpretation of Scripture to fund their position, which maintained white privilege and segregation.

Fundamentalists failed to stop the Civil Rights Act of 1964, so they further entrenched themselves in a subculture. Many new academic and social institutions arose in the late 1960s and early 1970s to preserve segregation and the cultural ideology central to such a reading of Scripture. The universities would make a promise to their constituents to maintain

45. Du Mez, *Jesus and John Wayne*, 39.

46. Bell, "Southern Evangelical on Integration."

47. McIntire, "Minister Denounces the Civil Rights Act," 55.

48. McIntire, "Minister Denounces the Civil Rights Act," 55.

ideological purity while also protecting them from feminism, integrations, and the onslaught of progressive culture. Here, as many admissions strategies would suggest, fundamentalist kids would experience the old-time religion of a former, better golden age. However, this safety bubble would be short-lived as a federal law would prohibit any institution receiving federal funds to remain racially segregated. This event would cause a change in fundamentalists that would rivet them to a conservative political machine indefinitely, namely into the Moral Majority.

Most assume that the present alignment of evangelical Christianity and conservative politics over the issue of abortion predates the 1970s. However, this is a revisionist history. When fundamentalists lost the protection to segregate, they joined with a political group friendly to their cause that would give them access to a social influence beyond their wildest dreams. Not many fundamentalists would dare use racial segregation as a public platform after March 9, 1976, when George Wallace's presidential aspirations came to an end at the hands of Jimmy Carter. However, a sudden shift by leading fundamentalist pastors like Jerry Falwell Sr., pastor of Thomas Road Baptist Church and founder of Liberty University, would change the political landscape forever. The step from segregation to abortion would lead the subculture of fundamentalism out of the shadows to create a dominant political culture. Republican strategist Paul Weyrich utilized the vast network of fundamentalists and the public voices of figures like Falwell to widen the demographic for far-right conservative politics. The modern face of Christian nationalism grows from this moment.

Much more content remains on Christian nationalism, abortion, and the role of the Bible in the proceeding discussion on the distinct history of Christian nationalism. Though that history will include many similar moments and figures, the purpose of this section served as a crucial clarification on the precise use of Scripture that enlivens Christian nationalism. In short, the use of Scripture collapses the authority of God (the Word of God, John 1:1) into the authority of the Bible (the word of God as Bible). However, it keeps a hermeneutic of racial, extremist politics (i.e., a natural theology) as the central prism one must accept to read it. In other words, if one fails to read the Scripture through and toward this political and racial end, then one fails to pay proper respect to the Bible. The culture and rhetoric formed by this perspective allow for certain violence because of the sacred authority presumed here. However, Scripture is not God, and the recovery of this distinction will be a crucial task of this work.

How Fundamentalists Read the Bible

The historical analysis preceding this section locates the historical conditions that generated the movement known as fundamentalism. The inner logic of fundamentalism does not occur in a vacuum and serves the ends of Christian nationalism. It is, therefore, necessary to unpack this inner logic of fundamentalist readings of Scripture and not merely to identify from where it comes. Fundamentalism continues to drive contemporary debates around the status of Christianity's public role. Furthermore, the method by which the fundamentalist engages Scripture is an important tool in the hands of Christian nationalists. By discovering this hidden logic, one can begin to focus a critique of Christian nationalism to its heart.

As made clear by its history, fundamentalism is more than a literal or plain reading of Scripture. Theologians from Augustine to Barth comment on the biblical text's literal meanings. Rather, fundamentalism emphasizes one essential feature in its reading of the Scripture, namely inerrancy. The fundamentalist claim about Scripture is that it is without error and can be proven by empirical fact even when it directly contradicts other recognized empirical facts (e.g., young earth creation). This adherence to empirical fact does not abrogate human reason in favor of divine reason.[49] Rather, fundamentalists interpret everything in Scripture factually when possible and relinquish fact whenever necessary to maintain inerrancy.[50]

The language of inerrancy emerges in response to higher criticism. As stated at the outset, fundamentalism is thoroughgoingly antimodernist, and the advent of higher criticism serves as a crucial catalyst for its development. Higher criticism, as noted earlier, emerged from a desire to read Scripture more scientifically to glean true history from false. Higher criticism encourages a closer adherence to historical consistency, a closed account of nature that excludes the supernatural, and the construction of a moral core akin to contemporary social norms. Fundamentalists rejected this higher criticism and its reading of Scripture due to their conviction concerning the authority of the written text. To be clear, not all fundamentalists rejected higher criticism, but they used it for their own purposes. Rather, most merely desired that those who utilized the tools of higher criticism took the authority of the Bible seriously and recognized

49. See Harris, "Fundamentalist Readings of the Bible," 328.

50. Harris, "Fundamentalist Readings of the Bible," 328.

that criticism could not be neutral.[51] Thus, fundamentalists believed that higher criticism was a modernist threat to the sanctity and efficacy of the biblical text.

Though fundamentalists presented their position as antimodernists, they are nonetheless profoundly resonant with modernity and even the assumptions of higher criticism. Consider the insistence on inerrancy as a prerequisite to engagement with Scripture. Inerrancy is how one conceives of the biblical text and aligns with a modernist understanding of empirical fact. It is, in short, an epistemology. Thinking *with* the text's inerrancy resolves apparent conflicting interpretations and the dispute of conflicting facts. One can merely jettison any tension because the text must be inerrant and, thus, more *factual* than competing facts. As such, fundamentalists participate in a modernistic approach and Enlightenment rationality.[52]

The fundamentalist sympathies with the Enlightenment appear through three connected but distinct characteristics of inerrancy: 1) an empirical rationalist approach to the Bible where it is defined using reason for the evidence for reliability, 2) an assumption that readers of Scripture are reading direct reports of historical events and states of affairs, and 3) an inductive method of theology, according to which doctrines are inferred by gathering together biblical texts on any given topic.[53] Focusing on the first two characteristics, fundamentalists presuppose that the Bible expresses empirical fact. Again, fundamentalists will use natural theology for their own purposes and abandon it in the same moment. Faith itself is faith *in* the Bible primarily and God secondarily and only by extension. Furthermore, faith's content is assent to rational propositions and accompanying forms of life/moral code.[54] One can find this approach stated in the work of Princeton Theological Seminary professor B. B. Warfield, a proponent of inerrancy and the inductive approach to reading Scripture, who writes,

> We first prove [the Scriptures] authentic, historically credible, generally trustworthy, before we prove them inspired. And the proof of their authenticity, credibility, general trustworthiness

51. Harris, "Fundamentalist Readings of the Bible," 331.
52. Harris, "Fundamentalist Readings of the Bible," 336.
53. Harris, "Fundamentalist Readings of the Bible," 336–37.
54. Harris, "Fundamentalist Readings of the Bible," 337.

> would give us a firm basis for Christianity prior to any knowledge on our part of their inspiration, and apart indeed from the existence of inspiration.[55]

The efficacy of the Bible requires that I communicate true, empirically proven propositions. Faith, thus, only requires a recognition of reality as it is. The events of the Bible are historically exact accounts with verification independent of the biblical records. As such, *the Bible is inerrant precisely because it communicates historical, empirical fact.* Grounding Scripture in this way implicates fundamentalists in the logic they sought to avoid in their suspicion of higher criticism. Rather than rejecting aspects of the Scripture that do not align with historical scientific inquiry, fundamentalists bend empirical realities to emphasize that the Bible perfectly aligns with historical scientific inquiry. Any scientific or empirical claim that contradicts the Bible must itself be false. In short, higher criticism and fundamentalism practices operate from the same assumption in rationally verifiable, empirical fact but think from radically different starting points.[56]

The emphasis on fact arises in the unique context of the nineteenth-century collapse of truth into fact. The triumph of modern scientific inquiry, then, finds its way into all sectors of society. To claim it is a treasure because it has a clear, demonstrable method. The modern evangelicals shifted to modern science's depiction of reality and fell prey to its flattened account of the world. It is as if the empirical approach held them captive through a picture. Modern philosophy illustrates this, as Ludwig Wittgenstein writes a "*picture* held us captive. And we could not get outside it, for it lay in our language, and language seemed to repeat it to us inexorably."[57] Evangelicals, then, accepted a narrowed version of reality inside of a category error where the Bible is the object of worship. As Aristotle identifies, a category error refers to various ways a thing can be understood as the subject or predicate. Aristotle aids the modern reader in identifying the error in the fundamentalist reading of Scripture and how it worships the text alone. Aristotle unpacks his understanding of category errors in his *The Categories.* Aristotle helps readers answer

55. Warfield, *Inspiration and Authority of the Bible,* 210. Quoted in Harris, "Fundamentalist Readings of the Bible," 336–37.

56. Harris, "Fundamentalist Readings of the Bible," 337.

57. Wittgenstein, *Philosophical Investigations,* 41e (§115) emphasis original.

questions such as: What is a thing? How much is a thing? How is it constituted? Is a thing related to something else?

Aristotle's categories enable readers to recognize the errors of fundamentalism. For the fundamentalist, the ontology of Scripture sits within its ability to communicate fact. However, this is a categorical error. It inverts the status of a predicate into a subject. One can grasp Aristotle's theory of predication in the grammatical relation between subject and object. A relation occurs when two terms posit against one another where one is said (predicated) of the other. Beyond the grammatical, predication helps define a certain structure of reality. A category error occurs when one falsely assigns a predicate to a thing. For example, if one presents a number *as* a predicate of color (i.e., orange is five), one would commit a category error because that predicate cannot be said of a color. It belongs in a different category.

An example of a category error exists among the new atheist school that claims science disproves the existence of God. Since science deals with determining physical realities, it cannot comment on what is metaphysical or beyond the physical realities it observes. God belongs in another category. The same error occurs when fundamentalists collapse the authority of the text into the written words of the Bible and equate it with scientific fact. Fundamentalists claim the authority of the Bible arises from the written words themselves and a historical scientific world. However, this is not the category into which the Scriptures fit. Rather, the Bible is a predicate that states something about the subject, which is God. The Aristotelian categories help visualize the problematic structure of reality at the heart of the fundamentalist approach. Certainly, Aristotle recognizes the importance of the physical world and its study. However, Aristotle outlines a structure of the world that includes reality that embraces and exceeds it. Collapsing all reality into empirical fact means failing to recognize Scripture's predication on another reality, namely God.

In order to make this reading of Scripture, fundamentalists rely on a philosophical school of thought termed common sense realism, which allows them to collapse truth into empirical fact. First theorized by philosopher Thomas Reid, common sense realism proposed that humans naturally "have reliable accounts of actual states of affairs."[58] Rather than viewing the world through mediating ideas and principles, as did other philosophers, such as John Locke and David Hume, Reid theorized

58. Harris, "Fundamentalist Readings of the Bible," 338.

the opposite. This philosophical school enables fundamentalists to argue that the biblical texts communicate events themselves rather than interpretations of events.[59] Along these lines, James Machen insists that the "Bible is quite useless unless it is a record of facts."[60] Furthermore, it is precisely at the insistence on the reliability of facts and events that the laws of nature become most important for fundamentalists. Thomas Reid, for example, builds his account of common sense realism from the scientific, philosophical corpus of Francis Bacon, who wrote: "The true method of philosophising is this: from real facts, ascertained by observation and experiment, to collect by just induction the laws of Nature, and to apply the laws so discovered, to account for the phenomena of nature."[61] It becomes a matter of discerning the facts of the Bible to provide a systematic account of the general, observable truths involved in ascertaining those facts. Theologians like Charles Hodge and B. B. Warfield would use Reid and Bacon as the grounding framework for theological study, which is the basis for fundamentalism.

An example of this fundamentalist theology in the twenty-first century is most obvious in the theology of Wayne Grudem. Following theologians like Hodge and philosophers like Reid and Bacon, Grudem champions the inductive approach. Summarizing Grudem's inductive theology, Harris writes that in Grudem's work *Systematic Theology*,

> Biblical verses and passages are collected on a given topic and then the biblical position on that topic is inferred. The Bible comes to be seen as the textbook of theology, an image that owes little to Scripture itself, and which betrays an assumption that theology is simply "what the Bible says."[62]

There is no need to systematically understand doctrines other than to show the "shared rootedness [of theology] in Scripture."[63] In this way, inerrancy exists apart from doctrines such as the Holy Spirit, which means that the doctrine of the Spirit arises only from the reliability of Scripture. Theology must first assume the Bible's inerrancy and thus practice collecting verses and passages from the inerrant source to infer specific

59. Harris, "Fundamentalist Readings of the Bible," 339.

60. Machen, *Christian Faith in the Modern World*, 65. Quoted in Harris, "Fundamentalist Readings of the Bible," 339.

61. Bacon, *Works*, 271–72. Quoted in Harris, "Fundamentalist Readings of the Bible," 339.

62. Harris, "Fundamentalist Readings of the Bible," 339–40.

63. Harris, "Fundamentalist Readings of the Bible," 340.

doctrines. In short, fundamentalists find what they want in the Bible by selecting texts and inferring general theological truths.

Inerrancy concerns interpretation, theological method, and the doctrine of inspiration. For fundamentalists, Scripture's inspiration is, as Harriet Harris argues, "plenary and verbal." This means that "all of the words of Scripture are God's own words."[64] Thus, the Bible cannot err because God cannot err. Though one finds human literary styles and conventions, God preserves Scripture from error.

Fundamentalists use the doctrine of plenary inspiration for a deductive argument for inerrancy. If God inspires it and God does not err, then no error can be claimed in Scripture. It contains the very words of God fundamentalists posit. A crucial layer of defense exists for this understanding of inspiration and inerrancy: the original manuscripts may differ from the ones we presently possess. In short, the Scriptures are inerrant in the original manuscripts and the author's original intention. In this way, if scientific fact or available scientific reason disagrees with the texts, then it is either not an error in the original manuscript or the intended meaning is lost to us. One might assume the authority behind this text is God, but for fundamentalists the argument is circular, namely the Bible's authority is itself. As Wayne Grudem argues, "all arguments for an absolute authority must ultimately appeal to that authority for proof."[65] Thus, fundamentalists always find proof of inerrancy when searching for Scripture's inerrancy.

In sum, there are obvious tensions in the various strands of empirical and deductive/inductive approaches to Scripture. However, fundamentalists have isolated themselves from any critique against inerrancy. Again, one must see how the fundamentalists, who originally reacted against modernity, participated fully in the Enlightenment project of modernity. Harriet Harris summarizes the tensions and contradictions of fundamentalism well. She writes,

> By now it should be apparent why descriptions of fundamentalists as those who take the Bible literally, or as people who abrogate reason to divine revelation, fall wide of the mark. Fundamentalists are less interested in taking the Bible literally than they are in harmonizing apparent inconsistencies or inaccuracies in Scripture, and they will sometimes abandon a literal

64. Harris, "Fundamentalist Readings of the Bible," 341.

65. Grudem, *Systematic Theology*, 78. Quoted in Harris, "Fundamentalist Readings of the Bible," 342.

> reading in order to preserve a defense of inerrancy. In doing this, they are not simply abrogating reason to divine revelation. In some respects, they rest their verdicts about divine revelation based on their investigative reasoning. Frequently, this investigative reasoning is indeed performed in the context of an already accepted deductive argument that the Bible will not reveal any inconsistencies or inaccuracies because it is inspired by a God who does not err . . . But either way, the authority of Scripture is, ironically, made to rest upon reason: upon inductive or deductive arguments that justify the place of Scripture as the fundament of faith.[66]

Fundamentalists see what they want in Scripture. It is the highest authority, and it is impossible to err from fact, and one must reject any fact that does not agree. Thus, fundamentalists use the Bible to see what they want and order the world accordingly, but they fail to see how it only affirms their world.

Christian Nationalism

Though fundamentalism shares many key events and figures with the history of Christian nationalism, one must observe the distinct moments in the development of Christian nationalism. Though racial and religious privileges wed themselves to an inerrant Scriptural imagination in Christian nationalism, there remain specific moments in the nation's history worth examining. Like the fundamentalists, Christian nationalists will investigate the Scriptures and see only themselves. A natural theology of race, religion, and place are the crucial features of Christian nationalism. Fundamentalism will inform the Christian nationalist deployment of the natural. However, the singular desire of Christian nationalism is power.

Puritan Beginnings to Nineteenth-Century War

Christian nationalism lacks a clear point of origin as it intertwines the Bible, nation, and peoplehood, overlapping with fundamentalism. Samuel Perry and Philip Gorski propose three possible origins. The first is 1619, marking the arrival of the first enslaved Africans in Virginia, highlighting Christian Nationalism's Eurocentric bias and its historical

66. Harris, "Fundamentalist Readings of the Bible," 338.

erasure of Black Americans.[67] The second is in 1776, when myths about the United States' founding, such as George Washington's fervent prayer at Valley Forge, reinforced the idea that the nation was divinely ordained. This revisionist history, championed by figures like Mason Locke Weems and later popularized in school textbooks, shaped Christian nationalist ideology by portraying the founders as committed to Christian governance.[68] A third key influence is historian David Barton, who argues that Christian principles undergird the United States' founding and that the separation of church and state was never intended to be absolute. Barton's selective use of historical texts, including legal codes and early state constitutions, supports his claim that Christian morality was meant to guide public life.[69] However, scholars counter that the founders, while often personally religious, sought a secular government to protect religious freedom. Critics argue that Barton's claims conflate the Puritan vision of a theocratic society with the more pluralistic intentions of the founders, misrepresenting figures like Washington and Jefferson while ignoring the Puritan origins of the "city on a hill" ideal. Ultimately, Christian nationalism arose from a revisionist history, no doubt widely taught and believed, that seeks to merge faith and governance, despite the founders' more complex views on religious liberty.

1690: Beginnings of Christian Nationalism

Though many dates could be claimed for the beginning of Christian Nationalism, Perry and Gorski settle on another year: 1690. "For it was around 1690," they write,

> that racism, apocalypticism, and nationalism first fused into a deep story. It's important to emphasize that things could have turned out differently. You could say that in 1690 we lost an alternative vision for life in the New World: one in which the natives and the colonists would live in concord of even in community; one in which the line between white and Black did not yet fully and irrevocably correspond to that between freedom

67. See Hannah-Jones, ed., *1619 Project*, xvii–xviii.

68. For more on Weems see Seidel, *Founding Myth*, 26–27.

69. For a full account of this revisionist history, see Barton and Barton, *American Story*, 199–268.

> and bondage; and one in which there was room, not only for non-Protestants but also for non-Christians.[70]

The year 1690 comes amid a dominating Puritan influence in the colonies. As previously outlined, the Puritans arrived in the New World with the twin hopes of practicing their religion and living the political life envisioned *by* their religious beliefs. The Puritans took the Bible seriously, but they read themselves *into* it. They were the new Israel coming across the sea instead of the desert to their "promised land."[71]

The Puritans settled in the New World and thus played an instrumental role in developing the deep story of Christian nationalism. As already argued, the plain reading of Scripture deeply informed their experience. Furthermore, their role as new Christians required following this plain reading. Perry and Gorski write, "England would ultimately remain in the hands of the cooler sort of Protestants, the very sorts of the Puritans desperately sought to escape. If the Puritans were to have a Promised Land, it would have to be New England."[72] Puritans would create theocratic communities that obeyed a very disciplined adherence to a type of culture. The culture formed centered on creating a Christian vernacular that privileged certain people over others. This would lead to the privileging of religious, racial, and cultural posture.

The deep story of Christian nationalism finds its earliest roots in Puritan thought, particularly in the writings of Cotton Mather, whose vision tied religious purity to national identity. This perspective, which viewed religious dissent and ethnic differences as spiritual threats, set the foundation for a covenantal logic that justified violence as a means of preserving societal and theological order. This logic played out in events such as King Philip's War, where Puritans saw First Nation peoples as biblical "lost tribes" and justified their destruction in the name of covenant faithfulness. While some Puritans, like Roger Williams, advocated for religious tolerance and coexistence, the dominant view embraced exclusion, laying the groundwork for later racial and religious divisions.

Over time, this exclusionary vision expanded, incorporating racialized structures that privileged white Protestants and reinforced a rigid hierarchy of belonging. The emergence of racial slavery in the colonies intensified this framework, as theological arguments such as the "Curse

70. Gorski and Perry, *Flag and the Cross*, 47.

71. Gorski and Perry, *Flag and the Cross*, 50.

72. Gorski and Perry, *Flag and the Cross*, 50.

of Ham" provided theological justification for the enslavement of Africans. The growing American identity also dovetails into its understanding of warfare, from the French and Indian War to the Civil War, which reinforced the link between Protestantism, whiteness, and national destiny. The concept of Manifest Destiny further solidified this idea, casting westward expansion as a divine mission that demanded the subjugation of Indigenous peoples and non-Protestant immigrants.

By the nineteenth and early twentieth centuries, Christian nationalism became deeply entangled with movements resisting social and racial progress. The post-Civil War South recast its defeat theologically, merging eschatological hope with a longing for a resurrected Confederate order. This ideology fueled the rise of the Ku Klux Klan, which gained mainstream influence through cultural reinforcements like the film *The Birth of a Nation*, portraying white supremacist violence as a defense of Christian civilization against racial otherness. Although Christian nationalism and fundamentalism initially operated separately, their shared fear of diversity and moral decline brought them together, particularly as fundamentalists, retreating from public life after the Scopes trial, later found renewed political purpose in resisting the civil rights movement and cultural shifts of the mid-twentieth century.

Modern History: Twentieth- and Twenty-First-Century Christian Nationalism

Christian nationalism and fundamentalism surges in moments of cultural upheaval, driven by a reaction to perceived loss of privilege. The Civil War's defeat and its lingering mythology fueled a sense of lost power, which intensified after the Scopes trial and the civil rights movement, as racial and religious dominance over public space waned. Seeking to reclaim influence, Christian nationalists strategically aligned with fundamentalists in the mid-twentieth century despite their previous retreat from public life. This convergence, orchestrated by figures like Jerry Falwell Sr. and political strategist Paul Weyrich, transformed Christian fundamentalism into a political force. Weyrich used influential Christian scholars, such as Francis Schaeffer, to motivate fundamentalists like Falwell to join their cause.[73] Falwell initially focused on building a fundamentalist subculture, which was propelled into the public arena by Weyrich's efforts to mobilize

73. Balmer, "Historian's Pickaxe," 17–18.

evangelical resentment over cultural shifts, particularly the rise of civil rights and secularism. This alliance would reshape conservative politics, uniting Christian nationalists and fundamentalists in a shared mission to reassert their vision of a divinely ordained America.

For many fundamentalists, this affirmed their belief that the nation, by permitting civil rights and the lifestyle of LGBTQ individuals, disobeyed God's law and would reap punishment. One example is this statement by Jerry Falwell after 9/11:

> The pagans and the abortionists and the feminists and the gays and the lesbians who are actively trying to make that alterative lifestyle, the ACLU, People for the American Way—all of them who have tried to secularize America. I point the finger in their face and say, "you helped this happen."[74]

In this way, Falwell not only blames the attacks on minority communities, but also maintains that such events are, in effect, God's punishment on America. Falwell reflects the Puritan covenant theology: America must observe a series of covenants, or the nation will reap curses. The Puritan mentality is alive and well in *this* appeal to divine punishment in the twenty-first century. Furthermore, the covenant carries with it a white supremacist element that, along with fundamentalist Christianity, undergirds its assumptions. In short, among many groups of conservative, fundamentalist Christians, and, as we will see, Southern Democrats, there arose a majority that would reshape not only the Republican Party but also Christian history. Falwell would play a massive role in this history and recast an ideological net.

Lee Atwater

The first political figure to enable the rise of Christian nationalism through figures like Weyrich was Lee Atwater. Much like Weyrich, Atwater was a driving force behind the election of Ronald Reagan and the Bush family. However, Atwater's unique success arose from his ability to court a Southern white resentment that had existed since the Civil War loss.[75] His influence can be traced through various aspects of political campaigning, party dynamics, and the broader implications of his strategies on American political polarization.

74. Falwell, remarks on *The 700 Club*, quoted in Onishi, *Preparing for War*, 19.

75. See Maxwell and Shields, *Long Southern Strategy*.

Atwater's political campaigns used aggressive tactics and focused on appealing to the base of the Republican Party. He was instrumental in the 1988 presidential campaign of George H. W. Bush, where he employed strategies that emphasized negative campaigning (i.e., mudslinging) and the mobilization of conservative voters. This approach helped Bush win the presidency and set a precedent for future campaigns, emphasizing the importance of base mobilization and the use of media to shape public perception. Atwater's tactics reflected a broader trend within the Republican Party, where the need to cater to a diverse coalition of interests became less necessary, especially as the party sought to form a massive ideological base.[76]

Moreover, Atwater catalyzes a new phenomenon of political polarization in the United States. He contributed to the increasing divide between the two major political parties and effectively utilized media to amplify partisan sentiments. Various studies have documented this polarization, indicating that partisan media can push viewers toward more extreme positions, influencing candidates to adopt more radical stances.[77] Atwater's role in this transformation is significant. He exemplified the shift towards a more confrontational and polarized political landscape, which has continued to evolve in contemporary politics.[78]

The impact of these strategies can also be seen in the context of party dynamics and the evolution of the Republican Party. Atwater's tenure as the chairman of the Republican National Committee (RNC) marked a period where the party sought to redefine itself in the face of changing political realities. This included the challenge of maintaining unity among various factions within the party, as evidenced by the backlash Atwater faced from social conservatives during the Bush administration.[79] Tensions between different ideological groups within the party have only intensified in recent years, leading to a more pronounced polarization that can be traced back to the strategies employed by Atwater and his contemporaries.[80]

The impact of Lee Atwater's political strategies is most apparent in how he influenced party dynamics in the United States, particularly in

76. Galvin, *Party Domination and Base Mobilization*, 1–27.

77. See Levendusky, "Why Do Partisan Media Polarize Viewers?" See also Mason, "'I Disrespectfully Agree.'"

78. Lovett, "Ethics of Asymmetric Politics."

79. Galvin, *Party Domination and Base Mobilization*, 1–27.

80. Stanley and Niemi, "Partisanship and Group Support."

swaying Democrats to join the Republican Party. His tactics were characterized by a combination of aggressive campaigning, strategic messaging, and the exploitation of social issues, particularly around abortion and race, which resonated with certain voter demographics.

One of the key factors in Atwater's success was his ability to leverage social issues to create a sense of urgency and alignment among voters. During the late 1980s and early 1990s, the Democratic Party's stance on abortion became increasingly polarizing, particularly following landmark Supreme Court decisions like *Webster v. Reproductive Health Services* and *Planned Parenthood v. Casey*. These decisions not only solidified the Republican Party's anti-abortion platform but also prompted many moderate Democrats to reconsider their party affiliation, considering their personal beliefs on abortion.[81] Atwater's campaigns effectively framed the Republican Party as the defender of traditional values, appealing to those who felt alienated by the Democratic Party's evolving stance on social issues.

In sum, Lee Atwater's tactics were instrumental in swaying Democrats to join the Republican Party by strategically framing social issues and aligning party ideology with the evolving political landscape in the United States. His legacy is evident in the continued polarization of American politics, where party affiliation increasingly reflects deeper ideological divides. Thus, Atwater's role in American politics is marked by his innovative yet controversial strategies that have had lasting effects on the Republican Party and the broader political landscape. His legacy is evident in the ongoing polarization of American politics, the evolution of party strategies, and the increasing complexity of political campaigning in a diverse and divided electorate.

Barry Goldwater

A second contributing figure to the success of Atwater's campaigns and the rise of strategists like Weyrich is the illuminating 1964 presidential campaign of Barry Goldwater. This event is often cited in analyses of the rise of conservative Christian political involvement, marking a crucial point where the ideologies of white Christian nationalism began to intersect more visibly with mainstream politics. Goldwater presented himself as a rugged cowboy on a moral mission to restore a wayward nation.[82]

81. Killian and Wilcox, "Do Abortion Attitudes Lead to Party Switching?"

82. Onishi, *Preparing for War*, 36–37.

Furthermore, the language of frontier, conquest, and rugged individualism would drive the movement of Christian nationalism into the future.

In *Preparing for War*, Brad Onishi examines how Goldwater's campaign laid the groundwork for future Christian nationalist movements by mobilizing a conservative base that included white evangelical Christians and individuals opposed to civil rights advancements. Goldwater's staunch opposition to civil rights legislation, framed as a defense of state's rights and individual liberties, resonated with groups that held segregationist views, fueling a political strategy that appealed to white voters disillusioned with the direction of federal civil rights policies. Goldwater's stance established a precedent for the conservative Republican Party platform, setting up a legacy that would shape later campaigns, *particularly* those that sought to blend religious and political ideologies.

Goldwater's campaign rhetoric and policies appealed to a sense of threatened identity among white Christians, casting the federal government and progressive movements as threats to their way of life. By doing so, he catalyzed a shift where religious and cultural anxieties were increasingly aligned with conservative political agendas—a connection that would be amplified in later decades by figures like Ronald Reagan, Jerry Falwell Sr., and the Moral Majority.

Paul Weyrich

In the midst of this evolving dynamic, Paul Weyrich, a chief Republican strategist and key figure in the Goldwater campaign, would further shape this alliance, drawing Falwell and other influential figures like Pat Robertson into the public eye through a carefully crafted strategic plan for the conservative movement. After the election of Democrat Jimmy Carter in 1976 over Republican incumbent Gerald Ford as president of the United States, the political career of famed segregationist George Wallace ended. Carter, a committed Southern Baptist, would inspire a Christian following and illustrated the voting power that evangelical Christians possessed. Weyrich, wishing to reimagine the Republican Party, sought to draw on that same demographic under a new, publicly attractive agenda. Weyrich knew that the fundamentalist sector of evangelicalism, like Wallace, fought integration.

Recognizing the political potential of this stance, Weyrich would go on to become a central figure in the rise of the Christian Right, often considered one of the architects of the conservative Christian political movement that gained momentum after Barry Goldwater's 1964 campaign. Weyrich's influence appears in mobilizing Christian conservatives into a political force. This vision was partly inspired by Goldwater's campaign and solidified through strategic alliances and institutions designed to promote a socially conservative, religiously motivated agenda in American politics.

Weyrich notably formed key organizations like the Heritage Foundation in 1973 and, later, the Moral Majority with Jerry Falwell in 1979. These organizations aimed to consolidate Christian conservative political power, rallying around issues such as abortion, school prayer, and opposition to LGBTQ+ rights. Weyrich's work mobilized evangelical Christian voters by framing cultural and political battles as moral imperatives—much like the earlier rhetoric of Goldwater's campaign, which had linked conservative values to a broader sense of religious and moral duty.

One cannot state enough the influence of Puritan covenant theology on the approach outlined by Goldwater, Atwater, and Weyrich. They do not directly cite the Puritans in their work, but the posture created by the Puritans that develops into evangelical theology cannot be denied. Throughout the creation of the Religious Right, a constant appeal to a kind of "faithfulness" to God that Americans must follow will emerge repeatedly. Falwell, Weyrich, Goldwater, and many more will make such claims. Thus, one must see how this theology works even in Weyrich's political strategies.

Weyrich built upon Goldwater's legacy and Atwater's win-at-all-cost mentality, refining the political strategy of appealing to white Christian voters who felt alienated by social and political changes. While Goldwater was not particularly religious and later distanced himself from the Christian Right, his campaign tactics inspired Weyrich to recognize the untapped political potential of white evangelical Christians. Weyrich's approach cultivated deeply Christian nationalist ideologies by asserting that America was, at its core, a Christian nation under threat from secularism and liberal values, a sentiment one finds in contemporary Christian nationalism.

Evangelical Christian involvement in politics would intensify in the late 1970s. In 1978, the message resonated when Internal Revenue Service (IRS) clamped down on private schools that maintained segregationist practices, but this was not the first time a ruling would be made toward this end on segregation. To get the full picture, one must go back to 1971.

After the ruling in 1954 that required desegregation, many Christian parents sent their children to private Christian schools to avoid integration. Many of these private schools began around the year 1968, such as Liberty University and Bob Jones University, under the premise that they would protect the Caucasian children of fundamentalist families from the perceived secular shift in American culture. The potential loss of this privilege to segregate their institutions created a rage in fundamentalist circles that would bring them together with Republican leaders. As Weyrich admits,

> What galvanized the Christian community was not abortion, school prayer, or the ERA. I am witnessing that because I was trying to get those people interested in those issues and utterly failed. What changed their mind was [the IRS] intervention against the Christian schools, trying to deny them tax-exempt status based on so-called de facto segregation.[83]

Through this issue, Weyrich and other Republican leaders noticed the mass influence and power of fundamentalist congregations and believers to impact an election. Fundamentalists, as already argued, struggled through the civil rights movement and the eventual integration of schools. During this period, private education, both primary and secondary, would prove to be a haven for those seeking freedom from forced integration. However, the new law prohibiting tax-exempt institutions from segregation, which would threaten the tenability of these schools and institutions, radicalized evangelicals. The fundamentalists, embedded within evangelicalism, avoided direct political influence after the Scopes trial, but the events surrounding integration would lead many leaders to re-enter the political arena.

This shift in focus challenges the commonly held narrative that the *Roe v. Wade* (1973) ruling was the catalyst for the Moral Majority's political mobilization, as it does not align with the historical timeline of evangelical political engagement. As mentioned, Jimmy Carter became the thirty-ninth president in 1976, and in 1978, the IRS legislated against the tax-exempt status of segregated institutions. Falwell gave his first anti-abortion sermon the same year. This coincidence alone would not be sufficient to prove a connection. However, it does not stop there. As Weyrich himself admitted, integration was the issue. The *Roe v. Wade* decision occurred in 1973, but before that, the Supreme Court ruled to approve

83. Weyrich, quoted in Martin, *With God on Our Side*, 173.

the busing of students in 1971 in *Swann v. Charlotte-Mecklenburg* to uphold desegregation. After this point, fundamentalists would rely on their private institutions to maintain segregation. In a series of landmark cases (e.g., *Green v. Kennedy* 1970, *Green v. Connally* 1971, *Coit v. Green* 1971, *Bob Jones v. Schultz* 1971, *Bob Jones v. Connally* 1973, *Bob Jones v. Simon* 1974), the Supreme Court would extend desegregation to all institutions that receive tax-exempt status. Thus, large blocks of evangelicals and fundamentalists became a major voting block.

At this point, the political movement found its voice and target (i.e., the Supreme Court). Weyrich and other architects of the modern GOP needed a new issue to mobilize this large fundamentalist demographic in congregations like Thomas Road Baptist Church to make changes that would impact the Supreme Court. Abortion served that need. Unlike popular narratives, evangelicals and the GOP did not begin promoting anti-abortion legislation until the 1978 mid-term elections. Weyrich noted that since World War II, evangelicals, fundamentalists, and even Southern Democrats moved toward more interest in the Republican Party.[84] Strategists needed a new issue to mobilize their base as George Wallace illustrated segregation would not gain mass appeal. The issue that united Republican leaders and fundamentalist/evangelical leaders was desegregation, but promoting this platform became less and less popular, especially after George Wallace, who famously ran on this campaign, failed to achieve much support for his presidential bid. In the midterms, a noticeable victory occurred for Republicans over Democrats in New Hampshire, Iowa, and Minnesota. This drew the attention of Weyrich and other GOP officials. The sudden shift in these traditionally Democratic seats occurred due to a large push from Catholic anti-abortion activists that "leafleted church parking lots on the final week of the campaign . . . [for example] representatives of Iowans for Life (predominately Roman Catholics) distributed approximately 300,000 pamphlets in [evangelical] church parking lots."[85] It was at this point that Weyrich and fundamentalist leaders would barrage congregations with anti-abortion messaging to turn the tides in elections toward Republican candidates and, eventually, the election of President Ronald Reagan.

Historians widely acknowledge that abortion was not the initial catalyst for the political mobilization of the Religious Right, despite later

84. See Maxwell and Shields, *Long Southern Strategy*.

85. Balmer, *Bad Faith*, 53.

claims from figures like Jerry Falwell that *Roe v. Wade* (1973) had jolted evangelicals into action. In reality, Falwell did not preach against abortion until 1978, five years after *Roe*, and even then, his shift was a strategic move rather than a theological awakening. Before this period, evangelicals and fundamentalists were largely pro-choice, with groups like the Southern Baptist Convention (SBC) supporting abortion rights under certain conditions and major evangelical leaders expressing little concern over the issue. Instead, what mobilized them was the IRS revocation of tax-exempt status for segregationist Christian schools, particularly Bob Jones University, which became the defining issue for evangelical political engagement.

This shift marked a turning point for Paul Weyrich, who had long sought to mobilize evangelicals behind conservative causes. While his earlier efforts—focused on pornography, school prayer, and the Equal Rights Amendment—had failed to gain significant traction, this new issue ignited a more effective mobilization strategy. He needed an issue to unite evangelicals and fundamentalists into a cohesive political force. To accomplish this, he turned to Francis Schaeffer, a prominent Presbyterian theologian who had become increasingly vocal about *secular humanism*—the idea that American culture was being overtaken by a godless ideology threatening Christian civilization. Schaeffer's apocalyptic rhetoric about the dangers of secularism provided Weyrich with the perfect framework to radicalize Falwell and other evangelicals.

Schaeffer's 1979 film series *Whatever Happened to the Human Race?*, co-produced with C. Everett Koop, presented abortion as a symptom of a broader cultural collapse, linking it to euthanasia and even Nazi eugenics. This framing transformed abortion from a "Catholic issue" into an existential threat to Christian civilization, making it a rallying cry for fundamentalists. Weyrich strategically used Schaeffer's influence to persuade Falwell and other evangelical churches that abortion was the defining moral crisis of their time. Although Falwell had never previously spoken against abortion, he quickly adopted Schaeffer's rhetoric, aligning himself with the anti-abortion cause as part of a larger war against secularism. This move was not purely theological but a political strategy designed to consolidate evangelical political power under the Republican Party.

Ultimately, Weyrich's efforts were wildly successful. By the time of Ronald Reagan's 1980 presidential campaign, the Religious Right had fully embraced anti-abortion activism as a defining issue, even though many of its leaders had initially been indifferent to the topic. Schaeffer's war against secularism, reframed by Weyrich, provided the ideological foundation for a new fusion of fundamentalist Christianity and right-wing politics, cementing abortion as a central battleground in American evangelical activism.

Furthermore, after the decision of *Roe v. Wade*, W. A. Criswell, former president of the SBC and pastor of First Baptist Church in Dallas (a traditionally conservative, evangelical, and fundamentalist church), "expressed his satisfaction with the ruling. 'I have always felt that it was only after a child was born and had a life separate from its mother that it became an individual.'"[86] These positions and statements were clear and unanimous in most evangelical worlds. It was a dramatic shift, then, that occurred in 1975 when the abortion cause rose to the top of the messaging for these churches and among evangelical leaders. Why the shift, and what does this have to do with Christian nationalism? Weyrich himself explains:

> The new political philosophy must be defined by us [conservatives] in moral terms, packaged around non-religious language, and propagated throughout the country by our new coalition . . . When political power is achieved, the moral majority will have the opportunity to recreate this great nation . . . If the moral majority acts, results could well exceed our wildest dreams.[87]

The language of remaking here calls for a moment of reflection. The Moral Majority formed as a response to desegregation and utilized the new platform of anti-abortion. It arose from the convergence of a unique political moment, namely the re-imagining of the Republican Party and the disenfranchised fundamentalist movement afraid of losing its place in the culture war. Even though they were secluded away from culture, they would reemerge in order to reform it. As a result, success in the late seventies and early eighties would grant this new conglomerate of power a road to reconstruction.

Weyrich reached these conclusions in conversation with a Reformed philosopher, Rousas Rushdoony, who desired a more authoritarian government ruled by a populist leader who could conform the state to a vision of "biblical" law. This new vision would have a basis in divine command but function with more nationalist sympathies in that a nation must find its pride and perfection in its religious purity. Rushdoony writes,

86. Balmer, *Bad Faith*, 34.

87. Balmer, *Bad Faith*, 41.

> Where God's law is honored, no man can regard himself as meeting God's requirements of holiness who gives his children to a godless system [of] education, or who feels that a secular state is acceptable to a Christian. God's law requires obedience by all men and institutes at all times.[88]

To be holy, in Rushdoony's imagination, required a complete reform and control of society to a certain vision of the good and of Christianity. Such a posture impacted the work of Weyrich, who took a win-at-all-cost approach and desired a singularly "Christian" overturn of the state. Both Rushdoony and Weyrich would be in a small group of individuals who would influence then-President Ronald Reagan to kill a bill that would grant the state more control over religious educational institutions.[89] Weyrich and Rushdoony desired a greater authoritarian rule that could enforce a strict rule of law. Rushdoony believed that nothing less than allegiance to God is at stake. He wrote, "The world, moreover, cannot be surrendered to Satan. It is God's world and must be brought under God's law, politically, economically, and in every other way possible."[90] The degree to which this informs the specific nation's aims as a nation over and against the world creates the conditions of Christian nationalism.

With abortion as a rallying issue, Paul Weyrich spearheaded a reconstruction of both the GOP and the nation, not toward broad Christian principles but a narrow, Puritan-inflected vision of righteousness that privileged a specific way of life. Influenced by figures like R. J. Rushdoony, this movement framed political struggle in terms of divine blessing and curse—where failing to impose a strict moral order meant surrendering to Satan. Rather than moral persuasion, power became the vehicle for holiness, collapsing godliness into an immanent political structure. Over subsequent decades, this ideological shift reshaped the Republican Party, fueling far-right policies and increasing evangelical political engagement. Christian nationalist movements such as the Tea Party gained traction, leading to the erosion of civil rights advancements and culminating in a Supreme Court that not only overturned *Roe v. Wade* but also rolled back anti-discrimination protections. Redlining, voter suppression, and reactionary governance became hallmarks of this movement, which reached a flashpoint with the January 6, 2021 insurrection. Though unsuccessful,

88. Rushdoony, foreword to Bahnsen, *Theonomy in Christian Ethics*, x–xi.

89. McVicar, *Christian Reconstructionism*, 144–47.

90. Rushdoony, *Biblical Philosophy of History*, 16.

this event signaled the growing influence of Christian nationalists in mainstream politics, embedding their ideology within the highest levels of government.

Late-Modern Christian Nationalism: Whiteness

Though there are more events than one can cover in a single book that show the creeping authoritarianism of Christian nationalism, it is important for this text not merely to show what Christian nationalists do but how they think. The history and analysis of both fundamentalism and Christian nationalism merge into late-modern Christian nationalism. As illustrated, the two histories merged into one superpower in the United States around the 1960s and 1970s. Though this does not limit the connection between the two prior to these dates, the decades described here create the conditions of a superpower that reconfigures the conservative movement into what it is today.

The resurgence of Christian nationalism in the 1970s would emerge in response to questions of racial segregation and the cultural re-imagining of predominately straight, white, and male space. This leads many to describe Christian nationalism as White Christian nationalism. As Bradley Onishi argues, "By capitalizing White, we call attention to the specific racial category that has a particular history in the United States and beyond."[91] The central hermeneutic of Christian nationalism is the preservation of a specific cultural identity, allowing adherents to selectively apply or suspend biblical commands to maintain that identity. While some critiques rely on conjecture, scholars use empirical data to analyze the epistemic assumptions underlying this movement, particularly its connection to whiteness. This book shares the definition of whiteness offered by theologian Willie James Jennings, that whiteness "is not first a person or a people [but] it is a way of organizing life with ideas and forming a persona that distorts identity and strangles the possibilities of dense life together."[92] As Jennings defines it, it is not merely one's skin color that creates the conditions of whiteness, though they are not *finally* disconnected. Whiteness is the structuring structure that creates the conditions where some live and some die. It has many ideological companions, such as colonialism, and searches to afford authority to some and not others.

91. Onishi, *Preparing for War*, 4.

92. Jennings, *After Whiteness*, 8–9.

White, in this definition, would identify or support a system or structure that offers advantage to some rather than others. Thus, one theoretically could be Caucasian and not be white, even though they could benefit by identifying with and taking advantage of the system as it currently sits.

Christian nationalism, deeply intertwined with whiteness, operates as both a political ideology and a way of interpreting Scripture, privileging a narrow vision of religious and national identity. Perry and Gorski provide a statistical framework to analyze white Christian nationalism (WCN), categorizing supporters into Rejecters, Resisters, Accommodators, and Ambassadors, with the latter groups advocating for policies that reinforce Christian dominance in public life.[93] Their research highlights how WCN is predominantly embraced by white evangelical Protestants, particularly in conservative regions, and serves as a cultural defense mechanism against secularization and demographic change. This ideology influences voting patterns, policy preferences, and social attitudes, correlating with racial bias, anti-democratic sentiment, and authoritarianism.

The historical foundation of Christian nationalism and fundamentalism lies in Puritan theology, which framed America as a "new Israel" bound to uphold biblical literalism and covenantal obedience. This vision merged religious purity with social hierarchy, laying the groundwork for later fundamentalist movements that opposed modernity while paradoxically adopting a rationalist epistemology to defend biblical inerrancy. Over time, Christian nationalism evolved beyond theological commitments into a quest for power, using Scripture to legitimize racial and religious privilege. Through natural theology, both movements justified social stratification, treating the Bible as an authoritative tool to maintain control over public life.

Fundamentalism and Christian nationalism, though distinct, are ideologically linked by their literal reading of Scripture and their reliance on a natural theology that upholds white Christian hegemony. They do not simply interpret the Bible; they weaponize it to structure society in their image, shaping American politics by reinforcing exclusionary national and racial identities. This framework persists today, influencing legal decisions, public policy, and cultural narratives, ensuring that theological and political power remain deeply intertwined.

93. For a breakdown of the entire statistical structure of WCN see Gorski and Perry, *Flag and the Cross*, 13–45.

CONCLUSION

In conclusion, fundamentalism and Christian nationalism, while distinct, share a theological framework that elevates Scripture as a tool for power rather than a means of divine encounter. Their reliance on biblical literalism and natural theology reinforces social hierarchies and privileges their interpretation as absolute authority. The next chapter will explore how these movements, rather than critiquing modernity, embody their impulses by using Scripture to justify control, ultimately substituting biblical authority for divine transcendence in their pursuit of power.

2

The Secular Mysticism of Fundamentalist Christian Nationalism

"The change I want to define and trace is one which takes us from a society in which it was virtually impossible not to believe in God, to one in which faith, even for the staunchest believer, is one human possibility among others."

CHARLES TAYLOR

INTRODUCTION

This chapter explores the ideological foundations of Christian nationalism through its fundamentalist roots, emphasizing how it wields Scripture to maintain racial, religious, and social hierarchies. Christian nationalism, rather than simply defending the faith, operates as a political tool that privileges certain groups while masking its agenda under biblical authority. By examining its historical development, this chapter will show how white evangelicalism reinforces dominance through a theological framework that interprets Romans 13:1–7 as a justification for maintaining socio-political control.

Building on the Puritan legacy and fundamentalist tradition, this analysis highlights how Christian nationalism merges natural theology, secularism, and technique to solidify its influence. It valorizes the "common man" as a white Christian figure resisting progressive change, portraying secular shifts as existential threats to a divinely ordained order. The chapter will explore how this ideology functions through three key mechanisms: the use of secular rhetoric to frame fundamentalist beliefs as populist resistance, the application of biblical interpretation as a rigid technique rather than a means of divine encounter, and the role of theologians, politicians, and pastors in shaping this movement. Ultimately, it will argue that white Christian nationalism is not the antithesis of secularity but rather its fullest expression, collapsing divine revelation into the immanent frame to assert control over public life.

PART I: HOW ARE FUNDAMENTALISM AND CHRISTIAN NATIONALISM IDEOLOGICAL?

Individuals, academics, and others deploy the word *ideology* to critique positions that one does not prefer. That is not the intention here. Rather, *ideology* is a crucial term that illustrates how individuals or groups construct a world that creates certain moral and social imperatives. As such, ideology can be used to distort rather than illuminate the world around us. This practice is not new, but has an important history. The previous chapter and the emphasis on a "deep story" at the heart of fundamentalism and Christian nationalism serve as the history and content of cultural ideology. Ideology thus operates as a tradition with certain moral principles and structures. The success of the deep story of Christian nationalism is the way it has ideologically created a world and how that structure distorts and seduces a mass of people.

What Is Ideology?

Before showing *how* the "deep story" is ideological, I offer terms that will clarify what it means to term fundamentalist Christian nationalism (FCN) ideological in the first place. I turn to scholar and political scientist Jason Blakely, whose recent work provides an important account of ideology. Blakely's *Lost in Ideology* explores how ideologies shape our understanding of political and social realities. Drawing on Clifford Geertz's concept of ideologies as maps of problematic social reality, Blakely redefines ideologies as interpretive frameworks that help people make sense of a complex world but also obscure as much as they reveal.[1] However, it is for many a deeply important way to see the world. In short, ideologies are maps that help guide people in a specific direction. Blakely writes,

> Ideologies, for better or worse, are powerful sense-making aids. Often when someone adopts an ideology, they have a deep experience of something going "click" and might even feel a kind of exhilaration, as they think: "Aha! Now I finally understand politics! I know what steps to take and in which direction!"[2]

Contemporary disorientation in liberal democracies is largely due to these ideological factors, which makes it essential to understand how ideologies influence politics and shape individual identities and worldviews.

Blakely examines various ideologies, tracing their evolution over the past two centuries. This history arises from the conviction that each ideology must be understood on its own terms. Blakely posits that ideologies are not *merely* masks placed over reality but stories that construct worlds. As such they are traditions that clarify this orienting aim that presents ideologies as they develop over time. Blakely highlights how ideologies adapt and merge in response to changing social conditions. As traditions, they adapt and modulate over time, which Blakely describes as the process of hybridization. An example of hybridization is the combination of conservatism and libertarianism in the US, which combines a desire for traditional values with free-market principles.[3] As such, hybridization describes FCN well.

This hybridization is particularly evident in Blakely's observation that ideological tensions persist not merely because of intellectual differences, but because ideologies function as deeply affective frameworks, drawing followers through emotional resonance. He compares adherence to ideologies to religious conversions, suggesting that ideological commitment often transcends rational discourse. He writes that ideologies have "sensemaking and ethically magnetic powers," establishing a view of the world and a sense of self, often making it difficult for individuals to see beyond their ideological commitments.[4] According to Blakely, this dynamic can lead to internal contradictions and moral

1. Blakely, *Lost in Ideology*, 4–5.
2. Blakely, *Lost in Ideology*, 5.
3. Blakely, *Lost in Ideology*, 33–35.
4. Blakely, *Lost in Ideology*, 64.

blind spots, as ideologies claim to represent reality while shaping it according to their biases.

In sum, ideology is an orienting and disorienting structuring of life and mind. It is, in short, a map. Blakely argues that one must understand the traditions that guide ideologies to read the map of ideology in general, which we explored in chapter 1. The deep story orients Christian nationalists and fundamentalists to a world of white privilege while ignoring others. It mobilizes and enlivens an approach to political life that convinces its followers that certain structures are not only necessary but divinely mandated. Furthermore, for many, this deep story resonates and orients.

Mobilized Ideology: Propaganda

The way ideology spreads is just as important as the ideology itself. Thus, when I use the word *propaganda*, as with ideology, my intent is not merely to dismiss Christian nationalism and fundamentalism. Rather, ideology extends beyond itself through its mobilizing power. The term *propaganda* carries many popular and often negative connotations, but in this work, it serves as a crucial aspect of the technological system. It helps clarify how the Bible shifts from being a central document that participates in the revelation of the triune Lord to a self-enclosed divine authority used to justify and reinforce power structures.

To articulate the connection between ideology and propaganda, I turn to Jacques Ellul, whose central argument is that propaganda is not merely a tool used by specific individuals or groups but an intrinsic element of modern technological societies. He posits that propaganda thrives in environments characterized by rapid information flow, mass media saturation, and the normalization of conformity. In short, ideology forms the content of the FCN position, but propaganda is how it saturates culture. Ideology is the *message*, and propaganda is the *messaging*. Propaganda shapes individual attitudes through overt lies, half-truths, and strategic omissions that align with preexisting beliefs and societal currents. The emphasis on inerrancy and literal reading specializes in these strategic omissions and half-truths that align with pre-existing beliefs. The coding of reality exists at this site. For example, during World War II, Nazi propaganda effectively used societal myths about national pride and racial superiority to mobilize public support for its agenda, demonstrating Ellul's concept of propaganda as a *sociological* phenomenon that integrates with cultural symbols and social myths.

Ellul identifies several types of propaganda, including political propaganda, which seeks to direct public behavior toward specific political objectives, and sociological propaganda, subtly reinforces ideology's orienting and disorienting work. A contemporary example of sociological propaganda is how social media algorithms amplify content that confirms users' biases, thus fostering conformity and reducing critical engagement. Ellul's analysis shows that propaganda aims to cultivate orthodoxy and orthopraxy, meaning it seeks to dictate beliefs and actions, thus making it an essential tool for maintaining order in modern societies.[5]

Ellul's work sets the groundwork for the connection to ideology. However, in *How Propaganda Works,* Jason Stanley emphasizes propaganda's dual function in democratic societies: it can both support and undermine democratic ideals. Stanley provides a crucial insight for this study of Christian nationalism and fundamentalism. At once, Christian nationalists and fundamentalists will use Romans 13:1–7 as a defense of their structure of government but will abandon that defense with a claim about the evil nature of government when addressing a structure they disapprove. Stanley argues that propaganda often defends democratic values, such as freedom or equality, while advancing unjust hierarchies or discriminatory policies. He writes, "Supporting propaganda aims to promote false beliefs or distort facts by appealing to widely accepted ideals."[6] If the ideal is central to Christian nationalism, one can pivot one's position based on the system's needs. Such propaganda appears in historical campaigns like McCarthyism in the United States, where the rhetoric of national security was used to justify witch hunts against alleged communists, effectively stifling free speech while claiming to protect it.

The propaganda that supports sits alongside what Stanley terms "undermining propaganda," which erodes (read disorients) democratic ideals by creating division or fear.[7] He uses contemporary illustrations like "fake news" campaigns that exploit existing social biases or ideological beliefs, making it harder for the public to discern fact from fiction. Such propaganda blurs the line between genuine democratic debate and deceptive rhetoric, thus making citizens more susceptible to manipulation.[8]

5. Ellul, *Propaganda*, 47.

6. Stanley, *How Propaganda Works*, 45.

7. Stanley, *How Propaganda Works*, 57.

8. Stanley, *How Propaganda Works*, 73.

As such, when one considers the role of Scripture, one finds a new kind of propaganda: a way to package ideology within a certain grammar. The Bible, for fundamentalists especially, provides a ready-made excuse to ignore fact. FCN extends the biblical inerrancy to the Constitution; it too is divinely inspired and without error so long as it promotes what is necessary. Propaganda can co-opt theological and religious language to conceal its real intent, a tactic visible in modern political discourse where populist leaders use rhetoric about "the people's will," or Christian nationalists use the language of "God's will" to mask authoritarian aims.

Ellul and Stanley help illustrate that propaganda is a pervasive, multifaceted force that adapts to society's technological conditions and democracy's rhetoric. Both authors agree that propaganda is most effective when it aligns with existing social beliefs and prejudices, leveraging cultural symbols and language to achieve its goals. While Ellul highlights the sociological integration of ideology into everyday life through propaganda, Stanley emphasizes its strategic use within democratic discourse to maintain or undermine power structures.

Before turning from propaganda, it is important to emphasize its formative nature. One of the crucial elements that one must recognize about propaganda is that it normalizes certain words and phrases that otherwise would feel out of place. As Bonhoeffer biographer Laura Fabrycky writes about the propaganda of Nazi Germany,

> The most powerful effect of Nazism upon German life . . . did not come through the grandiose speeches and torchlit rallies, nor from the posters, fliers, or other overt forms of propaganda. Rather, the party spread its ideas in the beguilingly commonplace ways that Nazi terms became everyday terms . . .[Nazi] language burrowed deep into minuscule adjustments in language to the subtle buildup of arsenic in a body. One is hardly aware of its deadly work when it's introduced in small doses, and that is its unique power.[9]

The formative work of FCN is its profound ability to whittle away at the moral conscience of the public, especially those in the faith community, by suspending the ethical. Normalizing certain behaviors and words leads to the undercutting work that Stanley presents. It leads to the false belief in Christian nationalism. As such, the Christian faith is a tool to suspend one's ethical commitments that one would otherwise practice.

9. Fabrycky, *Keys to Bonhoeffer's Haus*, 45.

PART II: THE SECULAR

I define fundamentalist Christian nationalism as secular, technological, and rooted in natural theology. First, its secularity is evident in its reliance on the immanent frame, as Charles Taylor describes—a social order where meaning is confined to human agency and historical development rather than divine transcendence. Though these movements claim a sacred vision, their religious practice functions within a secular age, offering a mysticism limited to the immanent rather than openness to the divine mystery. Their theology aligns more with natural theology than revealed faith, constructing divine order from historical and cultural givens rather than God's self-disclosure in Christ. They ultimately mirror modern rationalism by rooting Christian faith in national identity, cultural heritage, and moral absolutism, presenting not revelation but a "this-worldly" certainty disguised as faith.

This analysis of secularism is not to suggest that the secular is inherently immoral or opposed to faith but rather to highlight how FCN misunderstands its position. In waging a battle against "the secular," it fails to recognize that it, too, is a secular movement—one that operates within the same framework it claims to resist. Its conflation of cultural dominance with divine authority reveals a fundamental contradiction: in seeking to preserve a Christian order, it relies on the very secular mechanisms and ideological structures it denounces.

Charles Taylor and *A Secular Age*

To fully understand secularity, we begin with Charles Taylor's *A Secular Age*, which explores how Western societies have shifted from when belief in God was almost universal to one where it is one among many options.[10] Taylor asks a central question: how did Western culture go from one where belief was natural to one of almost universal rejection? To answer this question, Taylor distinguishes three forms of secularity. Secular one refers to separating religion from public spaces, such as government, law, and institutions. Taylor provides a more classic definition understood in the popular imagination. The secular, in short, is distinct from the secular. For example, clergy serve the sacred realm while the butcher serves the secular. On the other hand, secular two focuses on the

10. Taylor, *Secular Age*, 1–2.

modern condition. In secular two, the secular is the areligious, neutral, and objective. In other words, it is the shared public space of neutrality and objectivity.

These two accounts contrast with Taylor's most detailed contribution, secular three, which emphasizes how the broader cultural conditions of belief have changed and are now contested. This form does not simply refer to the separation of church and state or the decline of religious observance but rather to a transformation in the conditions of belief, where religious faith is no longer a default position but one possibility among many. In Taylor's framework, secularity three consists of a societal shift from a world where it was "virtually impossible not to believe in God" to one where faith is just one option in a pluralistic landscape.[11] In this modern context, belief is fragile. Taylor means that even the most committed believers know their faith is one of many possible interpretations of reality. Thus, space is contested and must be won. Taylor explains that we now live in the "immanent frame," a conceptual space where natural explanations of the world dominate, and transcendence is not a given. This frame is not necessarily closed to spiritual beliefs. However, it is oriented toward life's material and human-centered aspects, making religious belief a conscious choice rather than an assumed reality.[12]

A key aspect of secular three is the experience of "cross-pressure." Charles Taylor uses this term to describe the tensions between belief and unbelief that characterize modern life. Under these conditions, individuals feel pressure from competing spiritual options, even as they are caught in what Taylor calls an "echo of transcendence." This echo persists in the face of an overwhelming cultural drive toward "immanentization."[13] These pressures arise because, within the immanent frame, individuals encounter moments of existential uncertainty that challenge a purely materialistic understanding of life. At the same time, belief in the transcendent is not automatically persuasive, leaving believers and nonbelievers in a state of "fragilization," where their convictions feel less secure.[14] Taylor argues that even deeply religious individuals are secular in the sense that their faith is aware of its optionality and often coexists with doubt.[15] This

11. Taylor, *Secular Age*, 3.
12. Taylor, *Secular Age*, 539–540.
13. See Smith, *How Not to Be Secular*, 140.
14. Taylor, *Secular Age*, 304, 331–32.
15. Taylor, *Secular Age*, 595.

dynamic creates a more complex environment for faith, as believers must navigate their convictions amid diverse, often contradictory, worldviews.

Taylor further describes how the immanent frame fosters "expressive individualism," where personal fulfillment and authenticity become central cultural values. In short, great pressure exists to remain only within the "human domain."[16] This development is part of the age of authenticity, a stage in modern culture where individuals are encouraged to pursue self-realization as the highest good, often without reference to external or transcendent norms. In this environment, religious belief is often reframed as a personal spiritual journey rather than adherence to a collective dogma.[17]

Even religious individuals, such as Christian nationalists and fundamentalists, appeal to *secularity* (specifically secular three). They, too, practice their faith in a context where it is not assumed. Taylor points out that believers must justify their faith to others and themselves, as they know the plausibility of alternative perspectives. This move leads to a more reflective and individualistic faith, often focused on personal spirituality rather than communal religious practice.[18] Thus, the fragility of belief is a hallmark of the secular age, affecting both religious and nonreligious people.

Christian nationalism and fundamentalism participate in expressivism.[19] Both groups sense and feel that there is a right fulfillment of human identity and that there must be a strong central value. Taylor writes,

> It seems that that fusion of faith, family values, and patriotism is still extremely important to one-half of American society, that they are dismayed to see it challenged, both in its central values (e.g., the fight over abortion or gay marriage) and in the link between their faith and the polity (fights over school prayer, the phrase "under God," and the like).[20]

These groups shape their faith expression by defense of key elements of their ideological lens in ways that create a distinctly nationalistic feel. Even though expressive individualism wants only the desire to see the individual express their fulfillment, the expressive elements of Christian

16. Taylor, *Secular Age*, 727.
17. Taylor, *Secular Age*, 473–74.
18. Taylor, *Secular Age*, 530.
19. Taylor, *Secular Age*, 527–30.
20. Taylor, *Secular Age*, 527.

nationalism lie in institutions. The institutions, for FCN, must express the *true* (i.e., Puritan) fulfillment of the United States. Taylor continues,

> Issues like the banning of school prayer, abortion, and, more recently, homosexual marriage become highly charged. I spoke above of a "culture war," but another analogy might be "la guerre franco-française," two strong opposed ideological *codings* of the same nation's identity, in a context where nationalism (not to say great power chauvinism) remains powerful. This is the recipe for bitter struggles.[21]

The language of coding is essential here. Taylor recognizes that the same expressive feature of expressive individualism exists in the expressivist position of Christian nationalism in the age of authenticity as FCN seeks a collective identity that *codes* (i.e., writes) itself into all its assumptions about society, law, and order. As already argued, the predominately Eurocentric person is coded into the assumptions of the organization of the state.

Taylor illustrates that the struggle for expression leads to the contested space within which nationalism thrives. Christian nationalists and fundamentalists, due to nostalgia, feel that the public space is increasingly cross-pressured. The anxiety (fragilization) leads to greater intensification of nationalistic ideology. Thus, it also leads to a greater battle for immanent space. Faithfulness is not undergirded or secured by God but rather must *be* secured by Christians *for* God.

In sum, Christian nationalism and fundamentalism are secular. They collapse all meaning into the present through the collapse of God into the Bible and the Christian life as principles. Furthermore, the fundamental posture of Christian nationalists (and fundamentalists) is the conquering of public space and securing a particular expression of the nation and Christianity through law. Through the experience of fragilization in a cross-pressured world, only the achievement of power that secures by force the compliance of the world will do.

Secular Political Action: Acceleration

Taylor's insights illustrate the nature of secularity and the novel Christian social responsibility within the immanent frame alone. However, the domination and accumulation of this space is a crucial aspect of this understanding of secularity. Sociologist Hartmut Rosa utilizes Taylor's

21. Taylor, *Secular Age*, 528. Emphasis mine.

work to tease out this element of possession of social space as the goal of secularity. In *Social Acceleration*, Rosa presents a compelling analysis of Taylor's work and how the ever-increasing pace of life reshapes personal and societal dynamics. Rosa's theory categorizes social acceleration into technical acceleration, acceleration of social change, and acceleration of the pace of life, arguing that these forms profoundly impact cultural stability, personal relationships, and political processes. Rosa posits that the relentless push for efficiency and speed leads to a state of "frenetic standstill," where individuals feel alienated from themselves, others, and the world around them.[22] His analysis extends into democracy and religion, suggesting that both areas suffer in a high-speed society lacking the listening heart necessary for meaningful engagement. Rosa illustrates Taylor's point that the increasing speed of social processes defines the modern experience of time and fundamentally alters individual and collective life. He argues that social acceleration is not merely about moving faster; it reshapes cultural structures, personal experiences, and political processes. Again, Rosa categorizes acceleration into three interrelated processes: technical acceleration, acceleration of social change, and acceleration of the pace of life.

The first category, technical acceleration, refers to the speeding up of goal-oriented processes, especially through technological advancements.[23] Rosa notes that economic imperatives, such as the maxim "time is money," drive this acceleration, resulting in rapid transportation, communication, and production improvements.[24] This relentless push for efficiency has profound implications on one's time.

The second process, accelerating social change, describes the increasingly brief lifespan of cultural norms, social institutions, and personal relationships.[25] Rosa calls this phenomenon the "contraction of the present," in which once-stable beliefs and practices quickly become outdated.[26] This creates a situation where contemporary social expectations and cultural knowledge continuously shift, reducing their relevant period.

This constant flux not only reshapes societal norms but also feeds into what Rosa identifies as the acceleration of the pace of life—a paradox in which technological advancements, instead of increasing leisure,

22. Rosa, *Social Acceleration*, 15.

23. Rosa, *Social Acceleration*, 97–107.

24. Rosa, *Social Acceleration*, 161–73.

25. Rosa, *Social Acceleration*, 108–19.

26. Rosa, *Social Acceleration*, 76–77.

intensify the demands of everyday activities.[27] The pressure to complete more tasks in shorter periods creates a frenetic standstill and a completely rigid state.[28] Rosa links the experience of rushing without a clear direction leads to alienation, as individuals struggle to form stable relationships with themselves, others, and the world due to the rapid tempo of life. Acceleration is not merely about moving faster but expanding one's presence across more spaces in less time—what Rosa describes as the need to accumulate spatial reach at an ever-increasing rate. Specifically it is the ever-increasing occupation and possession of the immanent frame. In this framework, authentic existence becomes equated with constant movement, maximizing opportunities, and occupying more domains of life at once. However, this demand for rapid expansion comes at the cost of depth and reflection. Efficiency precedes contemplation, leaving individuals with little time to engage meaningfully with their experiences or critically assess their trajectories. In this way, acceleration fosters alienation and a pervasive sense of disorientation, as the pursuit of "keeping up" overrides the possibility of genuine connection and purposeful direction.

Rosa's concept of social acceleration also has significant political implications. He suggests that the rapid pace of change undermines democratic decision-making, which requires time for reflection and deliberation. For example, political responses to technological innovations often become reactive rather than thoughtful, as seen in policy debates on issues like cloning or data privacy.[29] Rosa uses Max Weber's metaphor of the "iron cage" to describe the experience of being trapped within modernity's relentless pursuit of speed and efficiency, which dominates personal, social, and political life.

The entrapment of secular space and acceleration is not just about how one navigates secular space, but about how life within the immanent frame is structured by speed, expansion, and control rather than depth or reflection. Social acceleration operates similarly to insights in Erich Fromm's work, which provides a careful nuance to both Taylor and Rosa's account of secularity.[30] Fromm presents and critiques modern capitalist society's focus on possession, or what he calls the "having mode," with the "being mode" that emphasizes presence, creativity, and genuine

27. Rosa, *Social Acceleration*, 78–80.

28. Rosa, *Social Acceleration*, 56.

29. Rosa, *Social Acceleration*, 263, 268.

30. I want to thank Andrew Root for establishing the connection between Taylor, Rosa, and Fromm. See Root, *Churches in the Crisis of Decline*, 124–28.

connection. Fromm argues that the obsession with ownership leads to a crisis of identity, environmental degradation, and social inequality, instead advocating for a shift toward meaningful existence over material accumulation.

One must explore the contrast between the having and being modes to truly grasp Rosa and Fromm's significance in connection to Taylor. The *having mode* centers on possession, where individuals define themselves by what they own, whether material goods, social status, or knowledge.[31] According to Fromm, this orientation is prevalent in modern capitalist societies, emphasizing acquisition and consumption as key indicators of success. He describes it as a mode in which people seek security and identity through what they possess. For example, Fromm writes, "If I am what I have and if what I have is lost, who then am I?"[32] This illustrates how individuals' identities become bound to their possessions, leading to anxiety and a constant drive for more as the fear of loss threatens their sense of self.

In contrast, the *being mode* focuses on genuine engagement and active presence. Fromm argues that the *being mode* is characterized by expressions of love and a sense of joy that are not dependent on external possessions. Rather than having, being rests in the *is-ness* of existence. In contrast, the *having mode* leads to alienation and a lack of fulfillment. The relationships and experiences in this mode are objects to be controlled or owned rather than those we enjoy or connect to.[33]

The analysis provided by Rosa and Fromm complements Taylor's work. Christian nationalists and fundamentalists seek to dominate the immanent frame. But domination is not alone in the method. Rather, as Rosa suggests, there is acceleration and speed to move efficiently to take control. Spiritual practices, sermons, and religious language are all coopted to cultivate the most loyal political base *for* the immanent frame.

Furthermore, acceleration exists entirely within the having mode. The more space, offices, and laws, the more faithful the Christian nationalists have become. Though the secular world is not entirely corrupt, the way that the secular encourages acceleration and possession in Christian nationalism forms the crux of its ideological force. Thus, Christian nationalism and fundamentalism are fully secular, seeking the accelerated path to having as much space as possible. They seek the most efficient capture of the immanent frame.

31. Fromm, *To Have or To Be?*, 22–23.

32. Fromm, *To Have or To Be?* 44.

33. Fromm, *To Have or To Be?*, 98–101.

Secular Mysticism: Religion Inside the Immanent Frame

Rosa argues that the politics of the secular age require accelerated possession of the immanent frame, including religious practice. Theologian Andrew Root calls this spirituality secular mysticism. For Root, the mystical is "a spirituality that seeks to overcome our impediments (even our guilt) by drawing us into a spiritual union."[34] However, in *secular* mysticism, union is not with God but shifts to other sites of meaning, such as the self or, as with fundamentalism and Christian nationalism, political parties. In this secular mysticism, Scripture plays a role in developing a grammar of personal transformation that entails a political reorganization of the self inside of society. The catalyst for such transformation is not God but the Bible and political ideology. Furthermore, the transformation does not require a transcendent experience but merely an adoption of present categories in a certain political system and, thus, an all-or-nothing type of political activity centered on politics of means.

Utilizing the work of Taylor, Root argues that the church operates with secular presuppositions. As Taylor illustrates, the secular is a contested space that must be won. For the fundamentalists and Christian nationalists, the Bible efficiently wins that space by converting conservative ideology into God-ordained order. This posture also explains how one could no longer "maintain biblical values" while holding nonconservative positions. Secular mysticism, as Root argues, "looks sideways and skeptically at any definition or articulation of human experience that draws on anything other than the immanent."[35] When transcendence is refused in this way, political and national identities are easily elevated to bear ultimate meaning, which helps explain why Christian nationalism can appear as a fulfillment of this logic within fundamentalist readings of Scripture.

Root clarifies distinct features of the new secular mysticisms in our secular age. There are two predominant postures within secular mysticism: exclusive humanism and counter-enlightenment. The former encourages transformations that help humans become their more authentic selves. The latter comprises rejection, transcendence, and the present moral order.[36] These two postures within secular mysticisms exist on a continuum but in a triangular relationship with what Root terms

34. Root, *Church in an Age of Secular Mysticisms*, 7.

35. Root, *Faith Formation in a Secular Age*, 110.

36. Root, *Church in an Age of Secular Mysticisms*, 90.

beyond.[37] The *beyond* of the beyond is not metaphysical or transcendent, but rather what lies "beyond exclusive human flourishing" in order to challenge the everyday assumption that "nothing lies beyond death."[38] Exclusive humanists and counter-enlightenment individuals exist in this triangular relationship, sliding up and down a scale relative to this third point. Root locates the political climate of Christian nationalism within the counter-enlightenment side of the triangle, as they crave heroic boldness in opposition to the moral order of the day.[39] This boldness couples with beyonders in that the opposition takes shape as a heroic action. As Root illustrates, heroism is why so many individuals could be convinced of election fraud and seek to storm the Capitol to overthrow the election. These actions provide a means to inhabit the heroic in their minds. It is beyond their selves while remaining in the immanent frame. Every mystical practice and experience cultivate this heroism, which clarifies why many who stormed the Capitol carried signs emblazoned with Scripture, crosses, and other Christian symbols.

Conclusion: Secular, Accelerated, and Possession

This section explored the secular aspect of fundamentalist Christian nationalist ideology. It concerns the domination of the immanent frame in a way foreign to ages past. Instead of being secured by divine order, humans must secure political space either for God or not. In the case of Christian nationalism, it is the former. Furthermore, since this immanent frame contains cross-pressures and fragilization, one must secure the space to prove one's faithfulness and true faith. This leads to acceleration and the dominance of the having mode of being. Thus, the direction of ideology motivates the capture of this space, and propaganda is how it spreads. Religious practices and expression are co-opted in this mode. The only correct practice or even moral framework is *winning*. The messaging of propaganda is the win-at-all-costs mentality, namely that one must win an election *for* God. Furthermore, the right ordering secures the right covenant.

37. See Root, *Church in an Age of Secular Mysticisms*, 91–96.

38. Root, *Church in an Age of Secular Mysticisms*, 92.

39. Root, *Church in an Age of Secular Mysticisms*, 91.

PART III: THE BIBLE AS TECHNOLOGY

The goal of Christian nationalism is the accelerated possession of the immanent frame to resist the anxiety of fragilization. This drive is not simply ideological but deeply technological—where technology is not just machinery but a relentless pursuit of efficiency, optimization, and control over social space. The logic of Christian nationalism follows this technological imperative: to dominate the secular sphere not through theological reflection or moral persuasion but through streamlined, highly effective means of cultural and political acquisition.

The key question is how this ideological framework can so efficiently and seamlessly take over the immanent space. The answer lies in its relationship to the Bible—not as a text that invites ongoing revelation and engagement with divine transcendence, but as a technological instrument wielded for social and political consolidation. In its ideological function, the Bible is an efficient mechanism for structuring authority, legitimizing power, and rapidly expanding Christian nationalism's influence within the immanent order. Rather than offering a space for divine encounters, it becomes a closed system that stabilizes identity, wards off pluralism, and mechanizes belief into a tool of cultural warfare. In this way, FCN does not merely seek a sacred order within the secular but operates within the logic of modern technological systems, where accumulation and control replace openness and reflection.

In order to illustrate this, I turn to a 2010 film, *The Book of Eli*, which follows a lone traveler, Eli (Denzel Washington), who journeys across a postapocalyptic wasteland carrying a sacred book, the Christian Bible, that he believes holds the key to humanity's survival. Along the way, he faces ruthless enemies, including a power-hungry warlord (Gary Oldman) who seeks to possess the book for his control, leading to a revelation about faith, resilience, and the power of the written word. After a particularly difficult attempt to secure this book, one of his soldiers asks him about its importance. Oldman's character states, "It's not just a book. It's a weapon. A weapon aimed right at the hearts and minds of the weak and the desperate. It will give us control of them. If we want to rule more than one small f*ing town, we have to have it. People will come from all over. They'll do exactly what I tell them if the words are from the book."[40] This quote and scene summarize well the technological mentality concerning Scripture by Christian nationalists and why

40. Hughes and Hughes, dirs., *Book of Eli*.

fundamentalism is such an appealing interpretation of the Bible. When authority is located absolutely within the written words of the text alone, as interpreted through a narrow and culturally specific lens, interpretive flexibility collapses. It makes very efficient, as Oldman expresses, the means to dominate and control a lot of space.

One must locate Romans 13:1–7 readings within this technological efficiency. In short, the way that FCN secures the immanent frame is a fundamentalist reading of Scripture because it is efficient. Fundamentalism provides this avenue because it boils Scripture down to an interpretation technique. One must merely adopt the fundamentals and an extremist conservative ideological mindset to understand the Bible and *be* Christian. The key to an efficient political life is a tool that demands authority and streamlines obedience. This is the secular collapse of meaning into the immanent frame that replaces God with the Bible. The following chapter will highlight the theological connection between God and Scripture. However, for now, it is important to highlight how the Bible serves as a tool (or technology) for Christian nationalists, and the fundamentalist method of reading is the technique that serves that technology.

Technological Society

This technological use of the Bible transforms it from a site of divine encounter into a mechanism for ideological control. By reducing interpretation to a rigid technique, fundamentalism ensures that Scripture functions as an efficient tool for securing authority within the immanent frame. This practice raises a crucial question: How does this transformation reflect broader technological and secular dynamics? To answer this, we turn again to Jacques Ellul's critique of technology, illuminating how Christian nationalism's use of the Bible mirrors the logic of technological systems—prioritizing efficiency, predictability, and control over mystery, revelation, and genuine faith.

Ellul's work provides a crucial framework for understanding this dynamic, particularly his distinction between technology and technique. Ellul explains how technique—systematic methods of efficiency and control—becomes autonomous and ultimately dominates human life. Technique is not just about machines or tools but represents the overarching drive for efficiency, rationalization, and optimization in all areas of life. Ellul argues that this autonomous drive for efficiency shapes social, economic, and political structures, often sidelining human values and creativity. Thus, technology births the idea of technique. As Jacob van Vleet and Jacob Rollison summarize, technology "describes an ensemble of means striving toward calculated efficacy in all sectors of society, a search for one mathematically best way to do things."[41] As with the reality of computers, one need not master subjects such as mathematics but merely the skills or techniques necessary to run the computer system that will do the work. Learning a tradition of thought is no longer prized but instead a pragmatic knowledge that merely achieves an end. There is no room for knowledge or an education that forms the individual, only the skills to achieve a goal. Ellul writes, "Technique has penetrated the deepest recesses of the human being. The machine tends not only to create a new human environment, but also to modify man's very essence."[42] The self-reinforcing nature of technique means it perpetuates itself beyond the intentions of its creators, thereby reducing human freedom and agency.

Ellul provides three characteristics of technique and the technological society itself. First is automatism or technological rationality.[43] Ellul defines automatism as,

> There is not personal choice, in the respect to magnitude, between say 3 and 4; 4 is greater than 3; this is a fact that has no personal reference. No one can assert the contrary or personally escape it. Similarly, there is no choice between two technical methods. One of them asserts itself inescapably; its results are calculated, measured, obvious, and indisputable.[44]

In this respect, automatism is the process by which a group claims a certain technique as absolute. Once a group decides on the most efficient way, it becomes the only way to achieve a goal or perform an action. Key to automatism is the emphasis on quantifiable and measurable consequences.

Second to automatism is self-augmentation, which relies on the recruitment of the greatest number of people to a favored way of thinking. In short, once more people find themselves devoted to technique and efficiency, it creates a consciousness that attracts others. The ideological

41. Van Vleet and Rollison, *Jacques Ellul*, 88.

42. Ellul, *Technological Society*, 52.

43. Van Vleet and Rollison, *Jacques Ellul*, 90.

44. Ellul, *Technological Society*, 80.

content is that the Bible is tantamount to scientific and historical fact because it is the Word of God. The technique is more efficient than any alternative. There is no authority outside of it; thus, more people defend this approach to Scripture when more people adopt it. Ellul writes: "Modern humans are so enthusiastic about technique, so assured of its superiority, so immersed in the technical milieu, that without exception, they are oriented toward technical progress."[45] Because fundamentalism creates an authority that is its authority, *and* that authority guarantees a certain order of power, it marshals a lot of interest and investment. It is attractive, easy to understand, and manipulable. This desire for efficiency means that the most efficient practices will inevitably grow and, thus, expand. Furthermore, as Ellul understands, self-augmentation creates even more efficient techniques.

The last feature of the technological society is monism, namely the collapse of all systems into one. This collapse is most clear in the combination of fundamentalism into Christian nationalism. Once these systems become dependent on one another, as with fundamentalism and Christian nationalism in the 1970s, they must continually sync toward the most efficient ends. As such, "There is no foreseeable limit to the spread of technology that has entered on the path of complete ingestion of natural resources, of nature itself, of human beings and everything in existence."[46] In short, the goal of the technique is for nothing to exist outside of it. Just as no authority exists outside of the Bible, the move of monism secures that the Bible's meaning will not exist outside of conservative politics.

The technological society complements the secularism portrayed by Taylor well. As Ellul understands, the techniques create an inner circle of meaning outside of which no reality can exist. Thus, naturally, the Bible becomes the highest authority in the secular age because it exists *within* the immanent frame. Literal readings champion everything we need, and the correct interpretation secures the interpreter's immanent frame. For our purposes, the interpreter is the FCN. Thus, the interpretation that cultivates privilege for this group must prove correct.

For those not familiar with the work of Ellul, it is important to note that he does not merely mean technology as a machine or greater computational devices. This is, no doubt, an aspect of his work. However, he

45. Ellul, *Technological Society*, 85.

46. Ellul, *Living Faith*, 194.

is more concerned with the form of the world created by the existence made possible *by* technological advancement. Ellul rightly recognizes that the efficiency created by such a reality changes the human approach to everything. Therefore, a posture toward realities occurs where an item's importance becomes its ability to efficiently bring about a desired end. The Bible becomes a technology and interprets a certain technique that serves a certain end. As we discovered, in a secular age, the expressive nature of secular institutions—like fundamentalism and Christian nationalism—codes certain forms of life into authentic embodiments of humanity. As such, the Bible, as we found in chapter 1, serves merely to secure power and influence for a certain group over another.

PART IV: NATURAL THEOLOGY IN FUNDAMENTALIST CHRISTIAN NATIONALISM

The final ideological component of fundamentalist Christian nationalism is its reliance on natural theology, particularly to secure power within the immanent frame. While natural theology historically refers to the use of reason to discern God's existence and moral law, the version embraced by white Christian nationalism distorts this tradition. Drawing on literalist interpretations of Scripture and natural observations, it justifies a socio-political order that privileges specific racial, religious, and national identities. This ideological framework positions white Christians as defenders of divine moral authority, portraying cultural shifts and secularization as existential threats to God's ordained social structure. Nostalgic appeals to a "Christian America" reinforce this vision, framing political engagement as an effort to reclaim a divinely sanctioned past. In this way, Christian nationalism merges religious identity, racial politics, and national supremacy into a seamless theological justification for exclusionary policies and authoritarian governance.

Theological Misuse of Natural Theology

Not every natural theology leads to fascism, and many theologians—from Thomas Aquinas to Emil Brunner—have argued that reason alone is insufficient without God's special revelation in Jesus Christ. However, white Christian nationalism severs natural theology from revelation, transforming it into a self-contained system that sacralizes cultural norms and human power structures rather than pointing toward divine transcendence. By collapsing divine revelation into immanent reality, fundamentalist Christian nationalism equates its ideological constructs with God's will, treating political and social hierarchies as eternal truths. This theological misstep allows Christian nationalists to sanctify their biases under the guise of biblical fidelity while rejecting the corrective function of divine revelation. Consequently, faith becomes a mechanism for power rather than a call to transformative, relational discipleship.

Infallibility, Political Power, and Scriptural Control

At the heart of fundamentalist Christian nationalism is the doctrine of biblical infallibility, which serves as a tool for legitimizing political and social control. By treating Scripture as an inerrant, closed system, fundamentalists enforce a literalist interpretation that affirms racial hierarchies, American exceptionalism, and patriarchal authority. This closed interpretive loop extends beyond theology, as Christian nationalists elevate the US Constitution to the same infallible status, positioning it as a divinely inspired document. This rhetoric reinforces white supremacy and nationalist ideology, which ensures that any critique of established power structures is reframed as an attack on divine order itself. In this context, passages like Romans 13:1–7 are weapons in the hands of the powerful to demand unquestioning submission to a government authority, provided that authority aligns with Christian nationalist interests. The fusion of infallibility, natural theology, and political dominance creates a framework where the Bible is no longer a site of divine revelation but a technological instrument for securing ideological control.

Example of Natural Theology: Governmental Authority and Romans 13:1–7

An example of this natural theology of governmental authority comes from fundamentalist pastor Mark Driscoll, who argues that God ordains all authority along these fundamentalist lines. He frames resistance to governing authorities as equivalent to rebellion against God.[47] Driscoll argues that governmental authority derives from God's sovereignty, suggesting that compliance with laws, regardless of their nature, is a

47. Driscoll and Breshears, *Vote Like Jesus*, 11–22.

fundamental expression of Christian obedience. Similarly, former advisor to President Trump and pastor of Dallas First Baptist Church Robert Jeffress asserts that governing authorities are extensions of God's rule.[48] By quoting Romans 13:1–2, Jeffress reinforces that the state is a *minister* of God, celebrating God's justice and morality. In short, it is the church's role to legitimize government structures as reflections of divine will.

The central object of the text is that the governing authorities punish on God's behalf. Those punished are those who threaten the established racial hierarchies naturally ordained by God. For fundamentalists and Christian nationalists, these hierarchies and governmental systems are those, not ironically, controlled by the Christian nationalists. A central theme to these interpretations is that the governing authorities match a radically conservative agenda, which is God's law, and must punish other forces that threaten it. For example, in 2018, former Attorney General Jeff Sessions cited Romans 13 to defend the Trump administration's zero-tolerance immigration policy, which led to family separations at the US-Mexico border. Sessions claimed that obeying the laws of the government was a biblical imperative, reflecting the belief that God establishes authority and that resistance to it constitutes rebellion against divine order.

However, when social and political structures fail to organize themselves to Christian nationalism, then it is false, evil, and corrupt. Because the Bible is infallible, any interpretation that critiques governing authorities should be dismissed, as Driscoll and Jeffries argue. However, here fundamentalists betray their commitment to infallibility and pivot to confess that if the governing authorities enforce laws against Christian nationalism or the conservative agenda, it is fallen. For example, during the COVID-19 pandemic, evangelical leaders revoked their allegiance to Romans 13 to oppose restrictions like mask mandates and church closures. They argued that while submission to the government is typically required, any mandate perceived as infringing on religious freedom is invalid, suggesting selective obedience based on perceived divine priorities. As Driscoll recounts,

> The COVID season, where the demonic spirit of fear ruled the planet and closed churches at Easter for the first time in world history, caused many, if not most, pastors to become cowards, surrendering their flock to Fauci as the new global pope. Locking the church doors when people needed to worship most, demanding they get a vaccination, and mandating everyone

48. Jeffress, *How a Christian Should Vote*, 9–10.

> wear a mask to worship felt a lot like the early Church, when the controlling, religious bureaucrats forcing masks became the new circumcision debate between the clean and unclean.[49]

Thus, for fundamentalist Christian nationalists, Romans 13 is conditional. It only serves as a theological mandate to preserve a certain status quo of specific social structures—such as racial hierarchies or traditional gender roles—that are divinely sanctioned. Christian nationalists, through *this* literal reading, argue that since God establishes authority, even racial segregation and patriarchal structures fall under God's ordained social order. Thus, resistance to these structures is a political act and a rebellion against God's established hierarchy.

Within this framework, Christian nationalists argue that Romans 13:1–7 validates a vision of governance where laws and policies must align with biblical principles to secure divine favor. For example, in his book *Politics According to the Bible*, Wayne Grudem defends significant Christian influence in politics, portraying government as a mechanism for promoting *divine* justice. He emphasizes that laws opposing abortion or same-sex marriage, for instance, are divinely sanctioned and necessary for the moral governance of society.[50] Similarly, Jeffress equates voting for candidates who uphold godly principles (i.e., conservative) with supporting God's divine plan.[51] Leaders who fail to align with these principles invite divine wrath, reinforcing that Christian morality should shape the nation's laws and policies. This interpretation frames American governance and the Constitution as sacred, portraying the United States as a city on a hill with a divine mission.

This reading of Romans 13 also affirms specific social and racial hierarchies as part of God's divine order. Returning to Driscoll, he argues that God ordains authority in a hierarchical structure, beginning with the family and extending to government, as a reflection of God's natural order.[52] This interpretation legitimizes traditional social structures, such as patriarchy and racial segregation, as divinely sanctioned and resistant to critique. Resistance to these hierarchies is not merely a political dissent but a rebellion against God's established order. Grudem echoes this sentiment by emphasizing that governments must maintain a moral compass

49. Driscoll and Breshears, *Vote Like Jesus*, 9–10.
50. Grudem, *Politics*, 30–33.
51. Jeffress, *How a Christian Should Vote*, 16.
52. See Driscoll and Breshears, *Vote Like Jesus*, 1–10.

rooted in *biblical* principles, directly opposing progressive reforms that challenge traditional social norms.[53] Jeffress further critiques what he calls "secular" influences, portraying efforts to remove God from public life or promote civil rights movements as rebellious acts threatening divine order.[54] He calls for Christian political engagement to resist these secular and progressive agendas, framing them as antithetical to God's will.

Furthermore, the fundamentalist Christian nationalist interpretation of Romans 13:1–7 often incorporates an apocalyptic dimension, which suggests that submission to authority is crucial for averting divine judgment. Jefferies frames political engagement as spiritual warfare, arguing that rejecting Christian nationalism is akin to opposing God's sovereignty. He describes such resistance as part of a broader demonic assault on divine authority, tying compliance with biblical (again, read conservative) governance to national survival. Jeffress similarly warns that leaders who promote secular or progressive agendas risk inviting divine judgment upon the nation. He calls on Christians to elect leaders who enact biblically aligned policies to stave off societal collapse and ensure God's continued favor.[55]

Overall, the FCN interpretation of Romans 13:1–7 portrays the passage as a foundational text for legitimizing a certain kind of American governance as divinely ordained. This reading reinforces traditional hierarchies, opposes progressive reforms, and advocates for Christian dominance in politics. Treating the passage as infallible, proponents argue that aligning political power with biblical principles is necessary and divinely mandated. Consequently, resistance to the state is equated with rebellion against God, solidifying the role of Christian nationalism in shaping American political and social landscapes.

Conclusion: Natural Theology

In sum, the natural theology within Christian nationalism and fundamentalism merges racial hierarchies, efficient techniques, biblical authority, nostalgic longing for a divine past, and an apocalyptic urgency to legitimize a specific socio-political order. This framework aims to restore what adherents believe is a divinely sanctioned American identity

53. Grudem, *Politics*, 19.

54. See Jeffress, *How a Christian Should Vote*, 4–6.

55. Jeffress, *How a Christian Should Vote*, 5.

marked by racial, religious, and national superiority. Natural theology shapes religious beliefs and drives political strategies that align with a vision of America as a new "holy nation."

CONCLUSION

Christian nationalism and fundamentalism operate within an ideological framework shaped by natural theology, nostalgia-driven social ideology, and a critique of secularism and modernity. FCN advocates for a Christian-infused nationalism, claiming divine sanction for specific social and political structures while promoting a covenantal vision of America as a "chosen nation." This theology, rooted in Puritan influences and biblical inerrancy, frames secularism and progressive movements as existential threats. Jacques Ellul's critique of technological society reveals a paradox within this movement, as figures like Greene use technology to disseminate ideological messages, reinforcing power structures through simplified, uncritical narratives. Hartmut Rosa's concept of social acceleration further explains how rapid cultural shifts fuel reactionary responses, with fundamentalists using biblical certainty as an anchor against perceived instability. Similarly, Charles Taylor's "secular three" highlights how modern believers experience fragilization, leading figures like Grudem to double down on scriptural inerrancy as a defense against doubt. Finally, Jason Blakely's analysis of ideology reveals how Christian nationalism constructs rigid interpretive frameworks that map reality through exclusionary politics, securing the immanent frame through the technique of infallibility and advancing a natural theology of whiteness. This discourse ultimately reflects a tension between preserving a unified national identity and confronting modern society's pluralistic, secular, and accelerated conditions.

3

The Word of God and the Primal Narrative

Literary Theology as Resistance

"For that reason, at every decisive point we took our answer to the question of revelation from the Bible. And the Bible has given us the answer. It has attested to us the lordship of the triune God in the incarnate Word by the Holy Spirit."[1]

KARL BARTH

INTRODUCTION: MOVING BEYOND FUNDAMENTALIST CHRISTIAN NATIONALISM

The Word of God is a dynamic and transformative reality, not confined to static interpretations or ideological distortions. It cannot be collapsed into Scripture alone. However, fundamentalism and Christian nationalism frequently reduce Scripture to a tool for wielding power, stripping it of its relational and living power. This chapter challenges such misuses by drawing upon theological insights, literary imagination, and narrative frameworks to propose a different understanding. To clear the

1. Barth, *Church Dogmatics I/2, Study Edition* 5, 1.

slate, one must consider important theological insights. The theology of Karl Barth, Justin Martyr, and John Webster will aid a relational, Spirit-guided, and communal interpretation of Scripture. The chapter will also articulate a literary theology and imagination in conversation with works of the literature of Toni Morrison and W. E. B. Du Bois, and others, which unveil divine beauty and confront systemic injustice through storytelling. We will also rely on René Girard as an interpretive guide. Additionally, as articulated by Walter Brueggemann, the primal narrative introduces the foundational thread of God's redemptive acts that shape the communal identity of God's people. The chapter concludes with reflections on Robert Jenson's theology of narrative and Flannery O'Connor's exploration of grace and beauty, each providing unique insights into how stories reveal the ongoing presence and work of the triune God.

SCRIPTURE AND THE WORD OF GOD: KARL BARTH WITH JUSTIN MARTYR

This section explores the complex and multifaceted understanding of the Word of God as presented in the work of theologian Karl Barth. Each theologian considered offers a distinct perspective that, when combined with others, provides a comprehensive theological framework that emphasizes the relational, dynamic, and transformative nature of divine revelation. Karl Barth's theology of the Word of God articulates a rooted Christocentrism in a threefold form—revelation, Scripture, and proclamation—emphasizing the dialectical tension between divine transcendence and human participation. Webster's Trinitarian approach nuances Barth and situates Scripture within the divine economy, emphasizing that the Bible serves as a witness to the triune God rather than being the Word itself. Together, these insights invite a broader understanding of the Word of God that transcends a merely textual interpretation, encouraging believers to encounter the living God through an active and Spirit-guided faith.

PART I. KARL BARTH ON THE WORD OF GOD

A new understanding of Scripture and the Word of God is essential for any theological critique of FCN. For Karl Barth, the Word of God is divine speaking, not a static text but a living and active event. Barth's theology of the Word is fundamentally Christocentric, dynamic, and relational, shaped by his conviction that God's self-revelation is not an object fixed within human control but a free, sovereign act of divine self-disclosure. While Barth affirms that the Bible can be known as the Word of God, he does so with a crucial qualification: Scripture is not inherently the Word but becomes the Word as God chooses to speak through it. The authority of Scripture, therefore, does not rest in its infallibility as a text but in its witness to the living Christ, the true and ultimate Word of God. This distinction is essential in resisting fundamentalist claims that conflate the Bible with divine revelation itself, reducing it to a static repository of absolute propositions rather than a means of encounter with the triune God.

In Barth's theology, revelation is fundamentally both an unveiling and a veiling. This paradox maintains divine freedom and prevents humans from claiming mastery over God's self-disclosure. Barth articulates that revelation occurs in the person of Jesus Christ but retains an element of hiddenness to uphold divine transcendence. He emphasizes that the Word of God "remains veiled even as it reveals," demonstrating that God's self-disclosure occurs solely by divine initiative.[2] The hiddenness of revelation ensures that it is not reducible to human knowledge or control but remains an act of divine grace.

Revelation, for Barth, takes place in three primary forms: the incarnation of Christ, the witness of Scripture, and the proclamation of the church. However, Barth is clear that Scripture and proclamation do not, in themselves, become divine.[3] Instead, they are instruments through which God speaks. The Bible, therefore, does not constitute revelation but is a witness to revelation. As Barth states, "The Bible is the concrete means by which the Church recollects God's past revelation, is called to expectation of His future revelation, and is thus summoned and guided to proclamation and empowered for it."[4] However, the Bible is not revelation in the same way that church proclamation is not future revelation; Scripture becomes revelation if God speaks *through* it.

This distinction is central to Barth's doctrine of the Word of God. Revelation, in his view, is not a static possession of the church or statistically in the Bible but an *event*—it is something that happens when God freely chooses to reveal. Thus, while the Bible "bears witness to past revelation" and church proclamation "promises future revelation," both

2. Barth, *Church Dogmatics*, Vol. I.1, *Study Edition* 1, 108.

3. Barth, *Church Dogmatics*, Vol. I.1, *Study Edition* 1, 108.

4. Barth, *Church Dogmatics*, Vol. I.1, *Study Edition* 1, 108.

derive their significance from God's active decision to make them God's Word in the present.[5] This understanding safeguards against a static doctrine of scriptural authority and resists the tendency to equate the text of Scripture with revelation. Instead, revelation is God speaking anew through Scripture, a truth that "rests on faith in that which has taken place once and for all."[6]

The Nature of Witnessing in Revelation

A key feature of Barth's theology of the Word of God is his doctrine of witnessing—the biblical text functions as an attestation to revelation rather than being revelation itself.[7] As Barth states, "Witnessing means pointing in a specific direction beyond the self and on to another."[8] The Bible does not establish its authority but derives it from the event of revelation itself, which alone grants it meaning and power. The biblical authors do not write to offer personal religious experiences or individual theological insights but rather to testify to the event of God's self-revelation.[9] They "do not speak and write for their own sakes, nor for the sake of their deepest inner possession or need; they speak and write, as ordered, about that other."[10] Barth's insight aligns with John the Baptist's role as a witness to Christ, who pointed away from himself toward the light.[11] In this regard, Barth insists on the difference between an apostle and a genius. In short, a genius originates truth, and a biblical witness only attests to the truth already given in divine revelation.[12]

Therefore, the authority of the biblical witness does not rest in the authors' personalities or insights but in their function as instruments of God's self-disclosure.[13] "We thus do the Bible poor and unwelcome honour if we equate it directly with this other, with revelation itself."[14] This

5. Barth, *Church Dogmatics*, Vol. I.1, *Study Edition* 1, 108.
6. Barth, *Church Dogmatics*, Vol. I.1, *Study Edition* 1, 108.
7. Barth, *Church Dogmatics*, Vol. I.1, *Study Edition* 1, 108.
8. Barth, *Church Dogmatics*, Vol. I.1, *Study Edition* 1, 109.
9. Barth, *Church Dogmatics*, Vol. I.1, *Study Edition* 1, 109.
10. Barth, *Church Dogmatics*, Vol. I.1, *Study Edition* 1, 109.
11. Barth, *Church Dogmatics*, Vol. I.1, *Study Edition* 1, 110.
12. Barth, *Church Dogmatics*, Vol. I.1, *Study Edition* 1, 110.
13. Barth, *Church Dogmatics*, Vol. I.1, *Study Edition* 1, 110.
14. Barth, *Church Dogmatics*, Vol. I.1, *Study Edition* 1, 110.

distinction protects God's sovereign activity and ensures that revelation remains an act of divine grace rather than human possession.

The Event of Revelation and the Role of the Bible

For Barth, the Bible becomes revelation if God speaks through it. This movement is not a given but occurs only in God's freedom.[15] "It takes place," Barth argues, "as an event when and where the biblical word becomes God's Word."[16] Barth likens this to the role of John's finger pointing to Christ—it is not the finger itself but the reality it signifies that matters.[17] This event-character of revelation means that Scripture cannot be automatically identified with God's Word; rather, it must be used by God in the moment of divine address.[18] Barth draws on Luther's understanding of biblical preaching, where it is not the words themselves but God's action that makes them revelation: "For 'tis all the same if thou hearest or readest this preaching as if thou hadst heard it from the angel himself."[19] The distinction between revelation and Scripture is not just a formal distinction but a theological necessity. Revelation is an event, not a static text. Barth explains, "Formally, the revelation to which the biblical witnesses direct their gaze is to be distinguished from the word of the witnesses in exactly the same way as an event itself is to be distinguished from even the best and most faithful account of it."[20] The ultimate reality of revelation is Jesus Christ, God's Word spoken by Godself.[21]

Barth insists that revelation precedes and establishes the authority of Scripture. The Bible does not validate itself but is validated only through the event of revelation.[22] As Barth states, "Revelation engenders the Scripture which attests it."[23] The prophets and apostles did not make themselves witnesses; their authority derives from the divine event that preceded them.[24] Thus, Scripture's authority is not self-evident—it is not

15. Barth, *Church Dogmatics*, Vol. I.1, *Study Edition* 1, 110.
16. Barth, *Church Dogmatics*, Vol. I.1, *Study Edition* 1, 110.
17. Barth, *Church Dogmatics*, Vol. I.1, *Study Edition* 1, 110.
18. Barth, *Church Dogmatics*, Vol. I.1, *Study Edition* 1, 110.
19. Barth, *Church Dogmatics*, Vol. I.1, *Study Edition* 1, 110.
20. Barth, *Church Dogmatics*, Vol. I.1, *Study Edition* 1, 112.
21. Barth, *Church Dogmatics*, Vol. I.1, *Study Edition* 1, 113.
22. Barth, *Church Dogmatics*, Vol. I.1, *Study Edition* 1, 111.
23. Barth, *Church Dogmatics*, Vol. I.1, *Study Edition* 1, 111.
24. Barth, *Church Dogmatics*, Vol. I.1, *Study Edition* 1, 112.

a sacred book with inherent divine power but a witness that becomes authoritative only as God uses it in revelation. Barth states, "What makes [the authority of Scripture's words] . . . is the occurrence of God's revelation itself apart from their own existence."[25] The truth of Scripture is not an inherent property but a function of its relationship to revelation.

The Unity of Revelation, Scripture, and Proclamation

For Barth, revelation, Scripture, and proclamation are distinct yet unified. Revelation is the event in which God speaks; the Bible attests to this event, and proclamation is the church's response. "Revelation is originally and directly what the Bible and Church proclamation are derivatively and indirectly."[26] The freedom of God's grace governs this relationship, ensuring that Scripture and proclamation become the Word of God only when God acts in them.

This dynamic relationship challenges static understandings of biblical authority and subjective interpretations of revelation. The Bible's authority is not conditioned by human belief but by God's free action.[27] Barth maintains that "The reference is to the freedom of God's Word," ensuring that the church's proclamation remains dependent on God rather than itself.[28]

Conclusion: The Living and Active Word of God

Barth's doctrine of the Word of God is a dynamic, event-driven divine speech act that resists static and human-centered interpretations of revelation. His insistence that revelation remains God's free act ensures that the Word of God is always a living and active reality rather than a fixed doctrine or a possession of the church. The authority of Scripture is found not in its words alone but in the event in which God speaks through them.[29]

Ultimately, Barth's theology challenges the church to remain open to the living voice of God, recognizing that faithfulness to Scripture is

25. Barth, *Church Dogmatics*, Vol. I.1, *Study Edition* 1, 112.
26. Barth, *Church Dogmatics*, Vol. I.1, *Study Edition* 1, 113.
27. Barth, *Church Dogmatics*, Vol. I.1, *Study Edition* 1, 113.
28. Barth, *Church Dogmatics*, Vol. I.1, *Study Edition* 1, 113.
29. Barth, *Church Dogmatics*, Vol. I.1, *Study Edition* 1, 113.

not about control but openness to divine encounter. "The 'God with us' becomes actual for us here and now as the promise received and grasped in faith."[30] Thus, the Word of God is not merely written or spoken—it is revealed, and in being revealed, it remains free.

The Triune Lord: Scripture and the Divine Economy

Close readers of Barth will recognize his insistence that the Word of God cannot be reduced to Scripture itself but must be understood in its proper relation to divine speech. For Barth, the Word of God is not a static text but a dynamic event, the *Deus dixit*—God's self-communication, which takes place supremely in Jesus Christ. The Scriptures are not themselves the Word of God but bear witness to it; they are an attestation to the living speech of the triune God.[31] Barth's distinction between the Word of God and the text of the Bible is essential in resisting any theological framework that collapses divine revelation into human possession, including the theological foundations of Christian nationalism. The Word of God remains wholly other, an act of divine sovereignty humans cannot wield for their ends. The proper function of the Bible is to direct its readers toward this *krisis*—the inbreaking judgment and mercy of God, which disrupts human structures, including distorted readings of Romans 13:1–7 that seek to absolutize earthly authority.

John Webster, following Barth, develops a theological account of Scripture that deepens this understanding. He asserts that Holy Scripture must be ontologically located in its attestation to the triune Lord:

> To talk of the biblical writings as Holy Scripture is ultimately to refer to more (but not to less!) than those writings . . . in light of their origin, function and end in divine self-communication, and, on the other hand, to make recommendations about the kinds of responses to these texts which are fitting in view of their origin, function and end.[32]

Scripture is not merely a static deposit of divine speech but is integrally bound to the life of God, the church, and the believer's encounter with divine reality. Webster critiques a static or objectified understanding of the Bible, arguing instead that its authority derives from its *function*

30. Barth, *Church Dogmatics*, Vol. I.1, *Study Edition* 1, 119.

31. Barth, *Epistle to the Romans*, 91–106.

32. Webster, *Holy Scripture*, 5.

as a medium of God's self-communication: everything about Scripture is "subservient to the Self-presentation of the triune God."[33] The Bible does not possess an autonomous status apart from the God who speaks through it.

For Webster, this view requires reforming the doctrine of inspiration to avoid objectifying and spiritualizing errors: "Scripture is revelatory because it is inspired."[34] Scripture's inspiration is not a mechanical process of divine dictation, nor does it mean that the biblical text itself is inherently divine. Instead, inspiration signifies that the biblical texts are taken up into the sanctifying work of the Spirit, serving as a means by which God speaks. Webster warns against an improper approach to divine action that objectifies revelation as a fixed possession or abstracts it into an inaccessible spiritual realm: "Inspiration is a mode of the Spirit's freedom, not its inhibition by the letter."[35] Instead, Scripture's authority is bound to its role within the divine economy, particularly in the work of sanctification and regeneration.

This theological understanding of Scripture has profound implications for hermeneutics and Christian practice. Webster emphasizes that reading Scripture is not a neutral or purely intellectual act, but a spiritual practice deeply intertwined with the human condition. He states, "to read Holy Scripture is to participate in the history of sin and its overcoming to encounter the *clear* Word of God; and to be a pupil in the school of Christ." He means that interpretation is never a purely objective endeavor but always takes place within the reality of human fallenness.[36] The act of understanding Scripture is, therefore, not merely a technical or historical task but one that requires the transformation of the reader:

> Reading Scripture is thus best understood as an aspect of mortification and vivification: to read Scripture is to be slain and made alive. And because of this, the rectitude of the will, its conformity to the matter of the gospel, is crucial so that reading can only occur as a kind of brokenness, a relinquishment of willed mastery of the text, and through exegetical reason's guidance towards that encounter with God of which the text is an instrument.[37]

33. Webster, *Holy Scripture*, 7.
34. Webster, *Holy Scripture*, 31.
35. Webster, *Holy Scripture*, 33.
36. Webster, *Holy Scripture*, 87.
37. Webster, *Holy Scripture*, 89.

This regeneration is made possible through the work of the crucified and risen Christ, who enables readers to perceive and respond rightly to the divine Word.

Furthermore, Webster underscores the ecclesial nature of Scripture's authority. The Bible is not an isolated text interpreted apart from the church's communal life. Rather, it interrupts and speaks to the church through challenge, meaning that Scripture continually confronts and reshapes the church's understanding, calling it back to faithfulness in its proclamation and practice.[38] This dynamic understanding resists any reduction of the Bible to a mere repository of doctrinal correctness or moral instruction. Instead, it emphasizes that Scripture functions as a living witness active in the church's ongoing life.

In summary, Webster's theology of Scripture builds upon Barth's insights by articulating a framework in which the authority of the Bible is inseparable from the self-revelation of the triune God. Scripture is not autonomous or self-validating but derives meaning and function from its role in divine self-communication. This approach ensures that the authority of the Bible remains a dynamic and relational reality in which God, through the Spirit, speaks afresh in the life of the church. When read alongside Barth's theology, Webster's perspective reinforces that Scripture is not simply the Word of God but a sanctified medium through which the triune God reveals and addresses humanity.

PART II. SCRIPTURE, NARRATIVE, AND THE LITERARY IMAGINATION

The authority of Scripture is not an abstract or self-contained textual integrity but in its role as a vehicle of divine communication. If Scripture is fundamentally a means by which God speaks, then its meaning cannot be reduced to static propositions or detached historical claims. Instead, it must exist within the dynamic narrative through which God reveals himself—one that unfolds across the biblical canon and culminates in Christ. This perspective necessitates a shift from viewing Scripture as an inert repository of doctrinal statements to recognizing it as a cohesive and dramatic witness to God's redemptive work. Such an approach invites a reading strategy that prioritizes narrative coherence, allowing the biblical

38. Webster, *Holy Scripture*, 106.

text to remain a collection of individual truths and a unified theological vision that draws readers into the reality it proclaims.

A New "Literal" Reading: Hans Frei and Narrative Coherence

Narrative coherence is the foundation for a literary imagination because it situates the text within the larger unfolding of divine revelation rather than reducing it to an isolated or self-contained authority. Suppose Scripture possesses an intrinsic authority apart from its narrative context. In that case, it risks becoming a static document rather than a dynamic witness to God's redemptive action. Instead, its literal meaning must work within the broader rhythm of the biblical story, where the unfolding relationship between God and humanity shapes meaning. This shift moves beyond an empirical defense of inerrancy, which often seeks to verify the text through historical or scientific measures. Instead, it allows Scripture to function as a theologically rich and literarily imaginative work that draws the reader into the drama of salvation. By embracing narrative coherence, the reader can move beyond prooftexting or doctrinal rigidity and instead perceive the interconnected themes, symbols, and theological movements that define the Bible. The narrative coherence provides the rhythm of past revelation in order to learn the pattern for future recognition. This narrative approach does not dismiss the significance of historical accuracy. However, it recognizes that the authority of Scripture exists in its participation in divine revelation, where meaning emerges through the interplay of text, tradition, and the living voice of God.

To unpack this new literal meaning, I turn briefly to Hans Frei's classic *The Eclipse of Biblical Narrative*. Frei's understanding of the literal reading of Scriptural narratives emphasizes the primacy of the narrative form of Scripture in conveying theological meaning. For Frei, the literal sense is not reducible to a simplistic or purely historical interpretation; rather, it involves reading the biblical text as a coherent narrative that presents the identity and activity of God in history. This approach insists that the meaning of Scripture is in the narrative itself, not in external frameworks such as historical-critical reconstructions, empirical fact, or abstract theological systems.

Frei critiques both pre-modern allegorical readings and modern historical-critical methods for distorting Scripture, arguing that the biblical text should be read on its terms rather than through imposed symbolic or historical frameworks.[39] He emphasizes that narratives, particularly those about Jesus Christ, reveal God's identity through their internal logic rather than as mere records of events. For Frei, the literal sense of Scripture is not historical verifiability but how the story portrays reality and shapes the reader's perception of truth.[40] Lamenting the shift from narrative-centered readings toward doctrinal abstraction or historical analysis, Frei calls for a recovery of Scripture's plain sense that respects its theological and literary integrity.[41] In contrast to fundamentalism, which treats the Bible as a repository of verifiable facts, Frei insists that Scripture's coherence lies in its depiction of God's saving action, from the exodus to Christ's resurrection. He argues that readers can fully grasp its meaning and significance only by patiently inhabiting the biblical narrative.

In summary, Frei's concept of the literal reading of Scripture emphasizes a theological hermeneutic that is faithful to the narrative's form and function, seeing the story itself as the primary vehicle for meaning through which readers encounter the God revealed in Christ. By prioritizing narrative coherence over historical verifiability and allegorical abstraction, Frei moves beyond simplistic literalism while maintaining the integrity of the biblical text. His rejection of fundamentalism challenges the notion that Scripture's authority depends on its factual accuracy, instead locating its meaning in how the narrative mediates divine self-revelation. However, his critique of allegorical readings—particularly their tendency to subordinate the text to external theological systems—also problematizes Scripture's ability to communicate the triune Lord beyond the immediate contours of its narratives. Frei limits how Scripture can be drawn into broader theological synthesis by resisting allegorical interpretation, out of concern that unbounded allegory can constrain the church's ability to articulate the full depth of God's self-disclosure in Christ. Nevertheless, his focus on the narrative's internal logic seeks to re-center the church's engagement with Scripture as a living witness to God's redemptive activity, calling readers to inhabit its world with patience and attentiveness.

39. Frei, *Eclipse*, 31.

40. Frei, *Eclipse*, 11–12.

41. Frei, *Eclipse*, 280–81.

Excursus: Critique of Postliberalism and the Limits of Narrative Coherence

Frei's emphasis on narrative coherence offers a crucial corrective to fundamentalist readings of Scripture, which rely on historical verifiability and external theological frameworks. By prioritizing the internal logic of Scripture, Frei preserves its theological and literary integrity, positioning it as a witness to God's redemptive activity. However, Frei resists allegorical and other types of readings because of his emphasis on the singularity of meaning that arises from the text. Kathryn Tanner critiques this aspect of Frei's postliberal approach, arguing that while narrative theology preserves the distinctiveness of Christian discourse, it can inadvertently isolate it from broader cultural and ethical engagement.

Tanner challenges the assumption that religious traditions, including biblical interpretation, function as self-contained systems. She emphasizes their dynamic, contested nature, suggesting that a theology shaped by narrative coherence must remain open to adaptation and ethical responsiveness.[42] Frei's approach, which treats Christianity as an internally coherent framework, risks limiting its openness to new interpretations.[43] Tanner contends that religious traditions, including scriptural narratives, are not monolithic but evolve over time. She critiques the static portrayal of tradition in postliberal thought and calls for a theology that remains responsive to historical and cultural shifts. Additionally, Tanner highlights the exclusionary tendencies in traditional readings of Scripture, noting that power dynamics shape who controls biblical interpretation. She offers an alternative model in which Christian theology, including its engagement with Scripture, remains adaptable and capable of interacting with external intellectual and ethical frameworks. Ultimately, while Frei's insistence on narrative coherence challenges fundamentalist readings, Tanner underscores that the authority of Scripture cannot be limited to a singular insistence on internal logic, which could merely be cultural interpretation projected as a universal; it must remain open to allegorical expansion, theological synthesis, and ethical critique.[44] A richer engagement with Scripture necessitates an approach that honors the biblical story's integrity while remaining open to broader theological and cultural perspectives.

42. Tanner, *Theories of Culture*, 103.

43. Tanner, *Theories of Culture*, 112.

44. Tanner, *Theories of Culture*, 117.

Walter Brueggemann on the Primal Narrative

Just as narrative coherence frees Scripture to be a unified theological drama rather than a fragmented collection of texts, the concept of a primal narrative provides the central gravitational force that holds this drama together in revelation of past events. Suppose the integrity of Scripture is found in its participation in divine revelation rather than in empirical inerrancy. Identifying the fundamental story that animates and orients the biblical witness becomes essential. This story is where the crucifixion and resurrection of Christ emerge as the primal narrative—the definitive event that reinterprets all other scriptural narratives and theological themes. Much like how Hans Frei emphasizes the necessity of reading the Bible through its narrative structure, the concept of the primal narrative ensures that this structure has a clear center, preventing interpretive fragmentation. By recognizing the death and resurrection of Jesus as the climax of God's redemptive story, we can better understand how Scripture's literary imagination is shaped—not simply by historical events or moral teachings but by the transformative rhythm of divine action.

Brueggemann articulates the concept of the primal narrative as a foundational element in understanding the biblical text and its implications for contemporary faith and practice.[45] This narrative serves as a lens through which believers can interpret their experiences of the Bible and the world around them. Such an approach to the Bible emphasizes, as does the literary imagination, the importance of storytelling in shaping identity, community, and theological understanding, particularly within the context of the Hebrew Bible.

Brueggemann defines the primal narrative as "the consistently believed in and recited root story that a community relies upon in crisis and the one by which the truth or falseness of every other story is judged."[46] It is not a collapse of the entire Bible into a fundamentalist code. It does not rely on a modern understanding of the sciences as its ground. Rather, this narrative begins with the creation account in Genesis, where God establishes a relationship with humanity and the world, which is not merely a historical event but a profound theological statement about God's intentions for humanity and the cosmos. Such a statement of faith affirms an act of God that changes the recipients of said action. As such, it "becomes the grammar of biblical faith [that] presents an active verb

45. See Brueggemann, *Bible Makes Sense*, 33–38.

46. Brueggemann, *Bible Makes Sense*, 34.

with God himself as the subject and the church or world as the object."[47] As such, they "are statements of confession or assertion that make no attempt to explain or prove. They are bold, primitive affirmations of faith stripped of every ornamentation or justification."[48] The events confessed by the biblical figures are arresting and reality-changing. Even though they arise from a specific event (e.g., a birth or healing), they possess a "universal significance."[49] In other words, these events "dismantle" the old arrangements of the world and the shape that life can take.[50] For this reason, the primal narrative will be passed down from generation to generation, eventually culminating in Scripture.

An emphasis on the primal narrative highlights the significance of memory and tradition in shaping communal identity. There is more to Scripture than the primal narrative. Brueggemann identifies the first material order beyond the primal narrative as the expanded narrative. According to Brueggemann, the expansion of the primal narrative by the biblical authors is not "careful or disciplined."[51] The confessions of faith made by the authors and characters of Scripture echo throughout history as the promise of God's activity. As Brueggemann argues, these other materials are "pressed" into service of the primal narrative.[52] The expanded narrative represents the encounter of other narratives as they become arrested by the central story. Brueggemann gives the example of Genesis 12–50, which expands on the promises made to Abraham. As such, this expanded narrative in the Hebrew Bible is not static but dynamic, allowing communities to engage with their past while addressing contemporary challenges. This engagement with narrative serves as a means of fostering resilience and hope, particularly in times of crisis or dislocation. For Brueggemann, remembering these stories is crucial for communities seeking to navigate the complexities of modern life while remaining anchored in their faith.

As the communities grow and retell this primal narrative, new stories emerge as subsequent generations encounter the God of the primal narrative. Brueggemann continues, "the *old primal story* was supplemented

47. Brueggemann, *Bible Makes Sense*, 36.
48. Brueggemann, *Bible Makes Sense*, 36.
49. Brueggemann, *Bible Makes Sense*, 36.
50. Brueggemann, *Bible Makes Sense*, 36.
51. Brueggemann, *Bible Makes Sense*, 38.
52. Brueggemann, *Bible Makes Sense*, 38.

by an *ongoing tradition.*"[53] Brueggemann argues that God's presence has ongoing significance in the lives of the people who live into the ongoing significance of the primal narrative. These derivative narratives concern "the power of God's word to work its will, that is, to keep the promises announced earlier . . . [and] at work in a new way."[54] The primal story locates the present newness of the primal story and the ongoing acts of God.

Brueggemann's work underscores the transformative power of narrative in shaping ethical and moral frameworks. From the derivative narratives, Brueggemann argues that institutionalization (history), mature theological reflection (theological teaching), and instruction/vocation (prophecy) all emerge. The latter categories that emerge from the primal narrative emanate from a central thread as concentric circles into expanded histories and theological teachings. Brueggemann contends that the biblical narratives provide a foundation for understanding justice, mercy, and community responsibility. Individuals and communities can discern their roles within the larger narrative of God's redemptive work by engaging with these stories. This perspective challenges believers to move beyond individualistic interpretations of faith and to consider the communal implications of their beliefs and actions.

Brueggemann's approach to the primal narrative also emphasizes the role of imagination in theological reflection. He suggests engaging with the biblical stories requires a creative and imaginative response, allowing individuals to envision new possibilities for their lives and communities. This imaginative engagement with the text encourages believers to see themselves as active participants in the ongoing story of God's work in the world rather than passive recipients of religious tradition.

Before moving from the primal narrative, I want to give an example that will help initiate readers into a more nuanced understanding of its workings. Brueggemann presents Joshua 24:1–13 as a primal narrative. Here, Joshua gathers the national assembly to set the boundary for the covenantal life of Israel. In all accounts, this primal story gives guidance in times of crisis and confusion. Most of these texts reflect the structure of Exodus 15, which tells of God's deliverance of Israel out of Egypt. This narrative will shape and form the people as a consistent story that will organize and guide the life of Israel. In Joshua, the call to remember God's deliverance weds itself to a call to leave other gods and serve the one God

53. Brueggemann, *Bible Makes Sense*, 40. Emphasis original.

54. Brueggemann, *Bible Makes Sense*, 41.

of their ancestors. It is a normative statement of faith responding to an event that causes jubilation.

Joshua's expression of the primal narrative will be an example for future generations of faithfulness. Judges, prophets, and even kings will appeal to this story of God's faithfulness to their ancestors. It will be the pattern by which other generations will expect the gift of God. As Brueggemann writes, this primal narrative calls the people

> to leave what is organized against the promises of God and to be on the way to the place where God's purposes have power. It is a call that takes the form of demand because such leaving is abrasive and painful. It is a call that takes the form of a gift, because the place of promise is never invented by us. It is always given by God in ways we cannot imagine or control.[55]

In this quote, Brueggemann outlines a crucial difference between the primal narrative and fundamentalist, Christian nationalist readings of Scripture. The primal narrative need not fit in empirical ways but is proclaimed in faith and is never under human control or imagination. Furthermore, the content of the narrative should clue in the types of faithful responses from future generations. The primal narrative tells of a "covenanting God who brings slaves out of bondage and who brings life out of death."[56] The material life commanded in response to this primal narrative receives instruction from this view from the bottom. It is not a recipe for power, and faithfulness to the narrative takes shape in material solidarity with the outcast, the enslaved person, the orphan, the widow, and the ones who bear a countercultural witness.

In summary, Walter Brueggemann's articulation of the primal narrative serves as a vital framework for understanding the biblical text's theological, ethical, and communal dimensions. His emphasis on storytelling as a means of shaping identity and fostering resilience invites believers to engage deeply with their faith and the world around them. By reimagining their lives considering the primal narrative, individuals and communities can find hope, purpose, and direction in their spiritual journeys.

55. Brueggemann, *Bible Makes Sense*, 47.

56. Brueggemann, *Bible Makes Sense*, 45.

The Primal Narrative: The One Who Raised Jesus from the Dead

Utilizing Brueggemann's key insight on the primal narrative, one must see the lyrical themes in the primal narrative that should appear across every aspect of the interpretive life of the Christian community, namely in the exaltation of the lowly and the mighty ripped from their thrones. (Luke 1:52) Like the primal narrative, it will provide the imagination for the future expectation of God's activity.

The primal narrative plays a crucial role in helping us identify God. I propose that Robert Jenson rightly identifies the primal narrative of the Christian faith when he writes that, "God is whoever raised Jesus from the dead, having before raised Israel from Egypt."[57] For the Protestant church, God's identifiability connects to God's self-revelation. Central to that continuing work of revelation is the witness of Scripture. In short, the ongoing work of Holy Scripture in the life of Christian community must take account of this one God who raises Jesus from the dead. Barth's theology performs such a function as he intricately weaves together the Word of God and Scripture concepts while maintaining a clear distinction between the two. The Word of God in Barth's framework is not limited to the written text of Scripture but refers to the self-revealing action of God, who speaks in various forms. Barth identifies three interconnected forms of the Word of God: revelation, Scripture, and proclamation.

Revelation is the foundational and ultimate form of the Word of God, the act by which God makes himself known to humanity. Barth insists that revelation is not a static deposit of truth but the dynamic presence of God in the person of Jesus Christ. This revelation is God's free and sovereign self-disclosure, an event in which God communicates Godself without being reducible to human comprehension or mediation. Barth explains, "It is because God has revealed Himself, and as He has done so, that there is a Word of God, and therefore Holy Scripture and proclamation as the Word of God."[58] In Barth's understanding, Scripture is the second form of the Word of God. It is not identical to revelation but serves as a *witness* to it. This distinction highlights that the Bible, though divinely inspired, remains a human product—words written in human language by individuals in specific historical contexts. Barth writes, "A

57. Jenson, *Systematic Theology*, 1:63.

58. Barth, *Church Dogmatics I/2, Study Edition* 5, 1.

witness is not absolutely identical with that to which it witnesses."[59] Yet, through the work of the Holy Spirit, Scripture becomes more than a mere historical document; it becomes the living Word of God to the church, conveying the reality of divine revelation. Barth calls Scripture "holy and the Word of God" because "by the Holy Spirit it became and will become to the Church a witness to divine revelation."[60] This dual character of Scripture—human and divine—requires careful theological and historical engagement. It ensures that its human dimension is fully appreciated without diminishing its divine significance.

The third form of the Word of God, proclamation, refers to the church's preaching and teaching. Proclamation becomes the Word of God when it faithfully aligns with the biblical witness and is empowered by the Holy Spirit. Barth emphasizes that the Word of God is always active and relational, meeting believers in Scripture and proclamation but always pointing back to its source in the revelation of Jesus Christ.

By distinguishing between the Word of God and Scripture, Barth preserves the sovereignty and transcendence of God's revelation while honoring the unique role of Scripture in mediating this revelation. He writes, "When we have to do with the Bible, we have to do primarily with this means, with these words, with the witness which as such is not itself revelation, but only—the witness to it."[61] This perspective ensures that Scripture is not venerated in isolation or mistaken for revelation but understood as the medium through which the living God speaks.

In Barth's view, the authority of Scripture does not rest in its infallibility or human constructs, such as church tradition or doctrinal systems. Instead, its authority lies in its ability, through the Spirit, to bear witness to God's revelation. Barth insists, "If we have really listened to the biblical words in all their humanity, if we have accepted them as witness, we have obviously not only heard of the lordship of the triune God, but by this means it has become for us an actual presence and event."[62] Thus, the transformative encounter with the living God occurs through the mediation of the human words of Scripture, empowered by the Spirit.

Barth's theology calls for a posture of obedience and humility toward Scripture. The church must continually test its proclamation against Scripture's witness to ensure alignment with God's revelation. This

59. Barth, *Church Dogmatics I/2, Study Edition* 5, 6.

60. Barth, *Church Dogmatics I/2, Study Edition* 5, 1.

61. Barth, *Church Dogmatics I/2, Study Edition* 5, 6–7.

62. Barth, *Church Dogmatics I/2, Study Edition* 5, 7.

underscores the dynamic interplay between the Word of God, Scripture, and the church, emphasizing the active role of the Spirit in ensuring Scripture's efficacy as the Word of God.

Ultimately, Barth's theology challenges readers to approach Scripture as a space where divine revelation is uniquely encountered while maintaining a distinction that ensures God's Word remains free and sovereign, not confined to any human artifact, even Scripture itself.

Jenson's work, when read in concert with Barth, locates Scripture back in its proper place to aid in the disclosure of divine identity. The Word of God, namely divine speech, is God's speaking to humanity and is not exclusively found in the pages of Scripture. The primal narrative locates this identity within God's activity that forms human imagination to receive divine speaking. The importance of the primal narrative, then, is its ability to name the central divine activities and narratives in Scripture that identify divine speech.

The central activity of the primal narrative is to help reveal divine identity. To narrow the language of the primal narrative, I borrow a summary from Jenson's theology. As noted, he writes, "God is whoever raised Jesus from the dead, having before raised Israel from Egypt."[63] The primal narrative of Joshua 24 names God as the one who raises Israel from Egypt. God casts the horse and the rider into the sea and makes Israel walk safely on dry ground. (Exod 15:1) As Jenson stipulates, God's identity as this one who raises Jesus from the dead after first raising Israel out of Egypt performs a crucial work. He writes, "these statements *identify* God, they have a specific status among true statements about him. The way or ways in which they fit him display how he is a this one who is not that one, how he has identifiable particularity; they display what we may call his hypostatic being."[64] The fact that God is identifiable through this primal understanding allows humans to inquire about God and construct ways of living. The most interesting aspect of this identity is how it connects to the other contingencies of the larger biblical narrative. Jenson argues that "before each decisive event we cannot predict it, but afterwards see it was just what had to happen."[65] God is ancient and foretold but also eternally new, albeit almost impossibly so. It would follow, naturally, that the God who delivered Israel from Egypt would identify with the crucified of the world and usher them out of the slavery of death.

63. Jenson, *Systematic Theology*, 1:63.

64. Jenson, *Systematic Theology*, 1:63.

65. Jenson, *Systematic Theology*, 1:64

The dramatic coherence of a God who frees the enslaved people and raises the dead victim provides a consistent means to wait in hopeful expectation. As Jenson continues, this story and primal narrative also includes the assumption of humans' rejection of God, specifically God with us. The nation of Israel rejects God by enslaving, and when God incarnates, humanity crucifies that same God.[66] Jenson argues that this point cannot escape our ability to discern history and Scripture, namely that when humans attempt to build anything on their own, it inevitably turns into a rejection of God with us.[67] God must remain a great danger to Israel and the Christian community. Unlike other gods, God precisely does not guarantee their future. Jenson argues, "The archetypically established order of Egypt was the very damnation from which the Lord released her into being, and what she thereby entered was the insecurity of the desert. Her God is not salvific because he defends against the future but because he poses it."[68] The goal of Israel is not to build and establish an order like Egypt (which they do attempt by rejecting God over them in favor of a king) but to remain in their desert-like insecurity. This political posture is because Israel, and by extension the Christian community, knows they exist not by necessity but only through divine gift.[69]

The primal narrative must guide the interpretive meaning of our biblical texts. As Stanley Hauerwas argues, the gift of this primal narrative, summarized by Jenson, is that its form and content exist inseparably.[70] Hauerwas goes on to clarify that this theological sentence, in its narrative form, shapes Christian speech and life. The confession "Jesus is Lord" finds its center in the primal narrative. Through these sentences, which are no less a part of the primal narrative, the believer learns the Christian faith and the imagination to live it. Hauerwas adds a sentence that clarifies and extends the primal narrative into an extended narrative: "the first task of the church is not to make the world more just, the first task of the church is to make the world the world."[71] By extending the primal narrative to include this statement, Hauerwas performs a necessary extension to envision the moral life. He recognizes, with Jenson, that the human history of *God with us* entails a rejection of God. Hauerwas continues that

66. Jenson, *Systematic Theology*, 1:72.

67. Jenson, *Systematic Theology*, 1:72.

68. Jenson, *Systematic Theology*, 1:67.

69. Jenson, *Systematic Theology*, 1:67.

70. Hauerwas, *Work of Theology*, 137.

71. Hauerwas, *Work of Theology*, 138.

what "makes the world the world is its refusal to acknowledge that Jesus was raised from the dead. So the world turns out to be that which takes the time of God's patience not to live in the light of the resurrection."[72] Hauerwas does not intend to set up a dichotomy between the world God loves and the one condemned by God. Rather, his distinction names how humans interact with God's presence in history and how God desires through the events culminating in the primal narrative. To live in light of the one who raises Jesus from the dead after first raising Israel out of Egypt means "to refuse to use the powers that crucified Jesus in the name of achieving justice."[73] What makes this statement intelligible is the primal narrative that identifies God with the crucified and resurrected Christ.

The preceding analysis of the primal narrative—that God is the one who raises Jesus from the dead after first raising Israel out of Egypt—illustrates the literary character of the narrative that is the account of past revelation. The narrative, as Jenson summarizes it, illustrates the interconnectivity of the narrative in its relationship to Israel through the new community of Christianity. It locates all the extended and derivative narratives in connection to this singular narrative of God with the crucified and enslaved people of the world. One must locate the events of resurrection and exodus within a universal symphony of care for the poor and oppressed against the organizing powers and human cooperation in organizing against God. Furthermore, there emerges a moral posture toward the world that believers must take up. This posture knows that God cannot be foreknown but only anticipated.[74] Jenson summarizes, "God is not eternally himself in that he persistently instantiates a beginning in which he already is all he ever will be; he is eternally himself in that he unrestrictedly anticipates an end in which he will be all he ever could be."[75] In short, the primal narrative cultivates a particular palate for God, for God is the God of resurrection and exodus.

The Moral Horizon of the Primal Narrative

Before turning from the primal narrative and the moral horizon that it creates, I draw out the moral implications of the God who raised Jesus

72. Hauerwas, *Work of Theology*, 139.

73. Hauerwas, *Work of Theology*, 139.

74. Jenson, *Systematic Theology*, 1:66.

75. Jenson, *Systematic Theology*, 1:66.

from the dead after first raising Israel from Egypt. To summarize, in the crucifixion of Jesus Christ, believers find a divine solidarity with the poor, marginalized, and crucified of the world. God, out of this solidarity, creates a way out of no way and challenges the structuring structures of the humanity that create and organize oppression. There is much more to be said, but I will briefly outline how the primal narrative extends the moral imagination in the resurrection.

I turn to Sarah Bachelard and her *Resurrection and Moral Imagination*, which profoundly explores how the Christian understanding of the resurrection informs and transforms the moral imagination.[76] The resurrection provides an alternative horizon to that dominated by mortality. Through her theological engagement with philosophical and biblical thought, Bachelard articulates how resurrection reshapes human subjectivity, expands moral horizons, and fosters a radical openness to love, justice, and creativity.

Like Jenson and Hauerwas, Bachelard recognizes the reality of human sinfulness and its impact on human action. As Bachelard argues, mortality and death form the backdrop of the ethical imagination. Theologian John Milbank summarizes this idea well. Communities judge virtue by the sacrifice it requires, namely the rejection of other goods in favor of the virtuous choice.[77] For example, in defending those against the threat of death, the virtue of just war is measured "by a willingness to die. Death for death to *secure* life against death: this is morality."[78] This complicity with death gives life in sacrifice to secure a greater good. Milbank writes, "Virtue is what holds death back, inhibits death, protects people from death, even though, from a Christian point of view, death is also remedy and mercy."[79] Thus, the limiting of death is a measure of morality.

Like Milbank, Bachelard recognizes that death's inevitability shapes the contemporary moral imagination. In this framework, morality often becomes a defensive act aimed at negotiating the challenges of mortality rather than transcending it.[80] Philosophies rooted in secularity frequently abandon the notion of the Good, viewing life as governed by randomness, necessity, and finitude.[81] The fixation with death creates a

76. See Bachelard, *Resurrection and Moral Imagination.*

77. Milbank, *Word Made Strange*, 223.

78. Milbank, *Word Made Strange*, 223.

79. Milbank, *Word Made Strange*, 224.

80. Bachelard, *Resurrection and Moral Imagination*, 58.

81. Bachelard, *Resurrection and Moral Imagination*, 10.

moral imagination focused on survival and self-preservation, limiting the human capacity for generosity and creativity.

Bachelard presents resurrection as an event to be acknowledged and a transformative moral horizon that reorients human existence toward hope, love, and engagement with vulnerability. Rather than framing morality as denying death, she envisions it as an openness to life's frailties and uncertainties, shaped by trust and responsiveness to suffering.[82] This resurrection ethic disrupts conventional moral reasoning tied to rigid laws or mortality-driven fears, instead fostering a dynamic encounter with divine grace. Engaging with philosophers like Iris Murdoch and Raimond Gaita, Bachelard critiques their secularized visions of transcendence, arguing that true moral goodness is not an abstract ideal but lives in the person of the risen Christ.[83] By placing Christ in the role traditionally held by Plato's Form of the Good, she integrates Christian theology with ethical philosophy, grounding moral life in divine forgiveness, solidarity with the vulnerable, and radical compassion.

Bachelard's resurrection ethic calls for contextual and relational discernment rather than rigid moralism, advocating an ethical approach open to the Spirit's guidance in ever-changing circumstances. She critiques dualistic moral systems that divide good and evil into fixed categories, warning that such frameworks often create victims of their logic. Instead, she emphasizes forgiveness, solidarity, and a courageous hope that emerges from confronting death and loss.[84] This hope is neither sentimental nor naive but empowers the moral imagination to embrace vulnerability, inspiring acts of justice, creativity, and compassion that transcend self-interest. Ultimately, Bachelard's vision of Christian ethics, rooted in the resurrection, challenges rigid doctrinal or legalistic moralities, offering a framework for engaging life's complexities with courage, love, and an openness to divine transformation.[85]

82. Bachelard, *Resurrection and Moral Imagination*, 51–52.

83. Bachelard, *Resurrection and Moral Imagination*, 74–84.

84. Bachelard, *Resurrection and Moral Imagination*, 43–44, 47–50.

85. Bachelard, *Resurrection and Moral Imagination*, 95–96, 117, 123–30.

PART III. THE LITERARY IMAGINATION AND THE PRIMAL NARRATIVE

Reading the Bible in light of the primal narrative should cultivate the palate of the literary imagination—in other words, a longing anticipation for the transcendent Lord. This longing approaches the Scripture with an eye toward this narrative of God with us that brings life out of death and releases enslaved people from their bondage. Furthermore, the formation of the believer is that they reject the forces that enslave and crucify. The God of the primal narrative disrupts the story as each believer finds themselves and forms their mind according to different patterns. Thus, the literary imagination forms the present community through the faith expressions of the past that press the present into service of the transcendent, triune Lord.

Beauty Ever Ancient, Ever New: Theological Aesthetics and Literary Imagination

The triune God is the living Lord, not held prisoner in the pages of Scripture. Yet, Scripture participates in the triune divine economy through its unique place in relationship to the living Lord, free from all human aspirations but their one true goal. As such, one must not approach Scripture as a code book that sources a technological society. Resisting the inerrant interpretations of Scripture and the mutilated way that FCN uses it to achieve their ends, a radical shift in approach to Scripture must occur. This requires a new imagination focused on beauty that frees the mind so that Scripture can participate in the divine economy of the triune Lord. Beauty moves our engagement with Scripture from the immanent frame and technique into a unique posture of engagement that looks for reality beyond its pages.

David Bentley Hart's theological aesthetics serves as a rich resource for an exegesis that aligns with Webster's theology of Scripture by emphasizing the role of beauty in revealing God and drawing believers into a transformative encounter with the divine. Webster's theology of Scripture is fundamentally Trinitarian, seeing Scripture as ontologically situated in its role of pointing to the triune God. The Bible exists, for Webster, within the divine economy of revelation and serves as a vital conduit through which God engages humanity relationally and communally. Thus, Scripture is not merely a collection of texts but a dynamic,

Spirit-infused medium through which God reveals Godself. An ecclesial context and a dependence on divine illumination characterize it.

Hart emphasizes that beauty is not an aesthetic addendum to truth but a fundamental aspect of reality that shapes ethical life and spiritual perception. Hart argues that beauty is a guiding principle that draws individuals toward divine life. He critiques modern ethical theories that have alienated the ethical from the aesthetic, arguing that such division has impoverished moral understanding. Instead, he sees beauty as "the very splendor of purpose, the fulfillment that makes the good the ultimate repose of the will and mind, in perfect concord."[86] This understanding of beauty as an attractive force that harmonizes and fulfills resonates with Webster's view that Scripture participates in an encounter that draws believers into communion with God's triune life.

Hart's approach offers a path for engaging with Scripture that does more than seek doctrinal clarity or ethical guidance; it invites readers to behold the beauty of God within the text, much as Webster emphasizes the importance of reverence and communal engagement in interpreting Scripture. For Hart, beauty is not merely an intellectual concept but something that "elicits only our delight" and evokes an aesthetic transport that brings the soul into contact with the divine.[87] In applying this aesthetic vision to Scripture, believers approach the text not as a mere repository of divine commands or truths but as an *entry point* into an encounter with God's beauty. In short, Scripture's significance exists in its role within the life of the church as a means through which God continues to speak.

Hart's integration of beauty and ethics advances Webster's view by offering a deeply relational and affective way to read Scripture. Hart suggests that beauty compels us toward a life that imitates Christ, calling it a "sense of style" that expresses the attractiveness of a Christ-shaped life.[88] This sense of style is not a superficial adornment but a moral and spiritual disposition that reflects God's beauty in one's character and actions. In an embodied exegesis that incorporates Hart's aesthetics, reading Scripture becomes a practice of discerning theological truths and cultivating a desire to reflect divine beauty in one's life. This echoes Barth and Webster's belief that the Holy Spirit is crucial in enabling believers to read and interpret Scripture faithfully, as the Spirit's work is essential for experiencing Scripture's transformative power. Just as Hart sees beauty as

86. Hart, "Sense of Style," 244.

87. Hart, "Sense of Style," 244.

88. Hart, "Sense of Style," 248.

a force that naturally draws people toward the good, Webster and Barth understand Scripture as a means through which the Spirit draws believers toward the divine life.

Hart's assertion that beauty is inseparable from truth and goodness offers a corrective to interpretations of Scripture that may focus narrowly on doctrinal precision or moral duty. Hart critiques the modern tendency to separate the ethical from the aesthetic, arguing that "ethics is in many respects a matter of cultivating good taste" and that this taste is an "indication of one's moral aptitude for the splendor of the good."[89] When applied to Scripture, this aesthetic dimension suggests that proper engagement with the Bible requires intellectual rigor and a cultivated sensitivity to the beauty of God's revelation in Christ's charity, which also presents a moral ontology.

Hart's insights thus invite a form of exegesis that seeks to understand Scripture intellectually and to encounter it aesthetically, cultivating a vision attuned to God's beauty. Hart argues that "Christian aesthetics . . . enjoins us not only to seek but ultimately to find the beautiful in those very regions of reality from which a conventional scale of appreciation would exclude it."[90] This aesthetic openness to the beauty of God's revelation, even in the brokenness and humility represented in Scripture, resonates with Webster's call to approach Scripture with reverence and to see it as an instrument of divine self-disclosure within the life of the church. It also supports a communal approach to reading Scripture, where the church collectively seeks to discern the beauty of God's presence within the text, guided by the Spirit and grounded in a shared commitment to embodying Christ's love.

In her moral philosophy and aesthetics, Iris Murdoch sharply distinguishes between true art and what she might call selfish art, which merely gratifies the artist's ego. For Murdoch, true art is an exercise in counseling—it directs the viewer (or the artist) away from the self and toward reality, truth, and the good.

She criticizes art as merely an extension of the artist's "fat relentless ego," meaning art that serves only self-expression, self-aggrandizement, or personal gratification without engaging with moral and aesthetic reality.[91] Murdoch argues that great art helps us overcome the distortions of

89. Hart, "Sense of Style," 244.

90. Hart, "Sense of Style," 246.

91. Murdoch, *Sovereignty of Good*, 51.

our selfish desires and illusions by orienting us toward something beyond ourselves—whether it be beauty, truth, or the complexity of human life.

Selfish art, in contrast, is solipsistic; it turns inward rather than outward. It reflects the artist's ego, reinforcing self-centeredness rather than challenging it. Murdoch is wary of modern tendencies toward self-indulgence in art, where personal expression is mistaken for artistic or moral greatness. She believes that true artistic engagement should involve disciplined attention to the world, much like the moral life itself, which requires overcoming the self's temptations and seeing others with clarity and compassion.

Fundamentalist Christian nationalists often approach the Bible in a manner akin to what Iris Murdoch critiques as the selfish art that serves only to reinforce the ego. Their reading is not an act of moral attention but of domination—seeking to impose their desires, political ambitions, and cultural anxieties onto the text. Like the self-indulgent artist who bends reality to fit their mythology, they engage in a technological and secular reading of Scripture, reducing it to a tool for power, control, and self-justification. Murdoch helps uncover an instrumentalized approach that treats the Bible as a mechanism for securing certainty and authority rather than as a space for genuine encounters with the divine. In this sense, their reading is profoundly secular, even when cloaked in religious language, because it prioritizes human sovereignty over divine transcendence. It turns the text into a reflection of the fat relentless ego, distorting it into an ideological weapon rather than allowing it to call the self into question.

In contrast, reading Scripture as true art—akin to Murdoch's vision of real artistic engagement—requires an unselfing, an openness to being transformed by the text rather than using it as a means of self-assertion. This kind of reading is an act of attention, where one does not impose a preordained meaning but instead allows the text to reveal something beyond the self. Like true reading, true art does not provide easy answers but invites the reader into mystery, complexity, and discomfort. Artistic encounters are where real freedom is found not in the rigid certainties of fundamentalist nationalism but in the liberating encounter with a reality that resists control. A reading of Scripture that is attentive, loving, and self-effacing—one that does not seek to co-opt God into human schemes—opens new possibilities for justice, grace, and transformation. It allows the reader to see beyond their narrow concerns and enter a fuller vision of truth, which, like all great art, refuses to be possessed but invites participation instead.

In conclusion, Hart and Murdoch articulate an account of beauty that enriches Webster's theology of Scripture by offering an aesthetic framework that emphasizes the beauty of God's self-revelation as encountered through Scripture. For Hart, beauty is the splendor of divine reality, which attracts and transforms believers into communion with God. When applied to Webster's theology, Hart's aesthetics suggest that Scripture should be read not only as a source of doctrine or moral instruction but as a means of encountering God's beauty and being drawn into the divine life. Through this aesthetic lens, Scripture becomes a practice of beholding, a way of cultivating the "eye of charity" that discerns divine splendor even in humility and suffering. In the communal and Spirit-led reading of Scripture, believers approach the text with a cultivated sensitivity to beauty, allowing the Spirit to guide them into a deeper understanding of God's love, presence, and glory.

Apocalypse of Scripture: Flannery O'Conner and the Literary Imagination

Transitioning from the theological aesthetics of David Bentley Hart and the moral vision of Iris Murdoch to Flannery O'Connor's fiction requires an exploration of how beauty, grace, and disruption manifest within the literary imagination. If, as Hart argues, beauty is not an ornamental aspect of truth but its very splendor—an attractive force that draws one toward divine reality—then literature becomes a vital medium through which one encounters beauty. However, as Murdoch reminds us, true art does not flatter the ego but confronts and disorients, demanding an unselfing that allows one to see beyond personal illusions. This intersection of beauty and disruption finds its most profound expression in O'Connor's fiction, where grace often arrives not as a gentle illumination but as a violent upheaval, stripping away the protagonist's carefully constructed self-image and forcing them into an encounter with the divine.

O'Connor's work embodies the theological and aesthetic vision articulated by Hart and Murdoch but in a form that is uniquely grotesque, ironic, and unsettling. Her characters, like those shaped by Murdoch's moral and aesthetic framework, are often trapped in self-serving narratives—stories that reinforce their illusions of control, righteousness, and superiority. Whether it is Ruby Turpin in "Revelation" or the grandmother in "A Good Man Is Hard to Find," O'Connor presents figures who initially resist the counseling that Murdoch sees as central to the moral vision. Their self-conceptions are rooted in rigid social hierarchies, nostalgia, and religious platitudes that serve more as instruments of self-justification than as paths to divine encounter. However, through shocking and often violent moments of grace, these characters are wrenched out of their moral blindness and confronted with a vision of reality that is both beautiful and terrifying.

Hart's aesthetics advocate for a heightened sensitivity to divine beauty that surpasses mere moralism, while Murdoch's philosophy emphasizes an engagement with art that disrupts the perpetual cycle of self-absorption. O'Connor provides a literary demonstration of how these principles unfold in narrative form. Her fiction does not merely illustrate theological concepts; it performs them, enacting the unsettling yet redemptive work of grace on both the character and the reader. In doing so, O'Connor's work aligns with Hart's assertion that Christian aesthetics must seek beauty in unexpected places, even in "those very regions of reality from which a conventional scale of appreciation would exclude it."[92] In O'Connor's world, the grotesque, the violent, and the absurd become the means through which beauty and grace erupt into human experience.

Thus, moving from a discussion of narrative coherence in Scripture and theological aesthetics to an analysis of O'Connor's fiction requires an acknowledgment of literature's role in shaping the moral imagination. Like Scripture, O'Connor's stories are not ideological affirmations or mere moral instruction; they are artistic encounters that challenge, disturb, and ultimately transform. If reading Scripture rightly requires a cultivated sensitivity to beauty, as Hart suggests, reading O'Connor's fiction demands a similar openness to the unexpected ways grace manifests in the world. This sets the stage for exploring "Revelation" and "A Good Man Is Hard to Find," where O'Connor dramatizes the moment of divine disruption and its consequences for human pride, perception, and salvation.

First, "Revelation" centers on Mrs. Ruby Turpin, a self-assured, middle-aged white woman sitting in a doctor's office waiting room whose moral and social superiority form the foundation of her worldview. Ruby views the world through a rigid hierarchy, ranking people based on class, race, and appearance. As her internal monologues reveal, she is deeply grateful to God for placing her near the top of this hierarchy: She is neither "white trash" nor Black, and she believes this makes her a good

92. Hart, "Sense of Style," 246.

Christian.[93] Ruby's place in the doctor's waiting room metaphorically suspends her between the world she controls and the divine encounter she cannot escape.

The inciting moment of disruption comes through Mary Grace, a college-aged girl whose disheveled and acne-ridden appearance contrasts sharply with Ruby's obsession with social order.[94] Mary Grace, who endures Ruby's polite but condescending conversation, suddenly snaps. After hurling a book at Ruby and physically attacking her, Mary Grace delivers the pivotal line: "Go back to hell where you came from, you old wart hog!"[95] This violent, grotesque moment serves as a breaking point in Ruby's narrative, thrusting her into an existential and theological crisis.

The arc of Ruby's transformation unfolds gradually. Back on Ruby's farm, Mary Grace's words haunt her, dismantling her self-image and forcing her to confront the reality of her pride. Standing in the pig pen, she has a mystical vision of the heavenly procession, which is the story's climax. In this vision, those she deems inferior—poor people, Black people, and "white trash"—lead the way to heaven, joyfully ascending while the "respectable" people like Ruby are last in line, their faces contorted with resentment.[96] At the climax of "Revelation," Mrs. Turpin has a vision in which she sees the social order she has always upheld radically overturned. The very people she had looked down upon—the poor, Black people, and "white trash"—are at the front of a procession entering heaven, while the respectable, churchgoing people like herself come last. As they ascend, she sees that "even their virtues were burned away," suggesting that entry into God's kingdom requires a purification that extends beyond sin to include even the qualities in which people like Ruby take pride.[97]

This moment encapsulates O'Connor's theological vision, in which grace is not a confirmation of one's righteousness but a force that disrupts human illusions. Mrs. Turpin believed that her virtues—her hard work, respectability, and public gratitude to God—were evidence of her moral superiority. Yet, in this final revelation, even these must be burned away, as they have been tainted by pride, self-righteousness, and a hierarchical view of others. In O'Connor's world, virtues are not inherently good if they serve as a means of self-congratulation rather than true humility before God.

93. O'Connor, "Revelation," 491, 499.

94. O'Connor, "Revelation," 490–91.

95. O'Connor, "Revelation," 500.

96. O'Connor, "Revelation," 508–9.

97. O'Connor, "Revelation," 508.

This purification imagery echoes biblical themes of divine refinement, such as in 1 Corinthians 3:13–15, where works are tested by fire, and Isaiah 6:5–7, where the prophet's lips must be burned before he can speak for God. O'Connor suggests that virtue, when funded by pride, can become an obstacle to grace, requiring painful purification before one can enter God's presence. This challenges fundamentalist notions of faith that equate righteousness with outward moral behavior, revealing that true salvation demands a deeper transformation that dismantles not just sin but the illusions of self-earned goodness.

Ultimately, Mrs. Turpin's vision is not just a moment of personal reckoning but an indictment of the racial and social hierarchies that undergird Christian nationalism and fundamentalism. Her entire worldview is shaped by the assumption that faith and moral worth are inseparable from whiteness, social status, and respectability—a logic that mirrors the ideological foundations of Christian nationalism, where theological authority is often weaponized to uphold systems of racial and cultural dominance. In Ruby's vision, the very people she has viewed as inferior—the poor, Black people, and "white trash"—are the first to enter heaven, while those who, like herself, saw their whiteness and social standing as marks of divine favor are pushed to the back. That "even their virtues were burned away" signals that the metrics of goodness constructed within white Christian nationalism—respectability, moral discipline, economic success—are themselves tainted by the sin of racial superiority and exclusion. O'Connor's radical reversal exposes the myth of divine favoritism that has long justified racial and social hierarchies, revealing that God's justice is not about preserving white cultural power but about dismantling it, reordering the world in ways that disrupt the very structures fundamentalism seeks to protect.

"Revelation" traces the slow unraveling of Ruby's pride over time, but "A Good Man Is Hard to Find" delivers its transformation with sudden violence. The grandmother, a self-righteous and manipulative figure, insists on presenting herself as a paragon of virtue. Her superficial religiosity manifests in her constant appeals to politeness, nostalgia, and moral superiority over others. Like Ruby, the grandmother's worldview is self-serving, reinforcing her sense of control and status. However, O'Connor wastes no time placing the grandmother in a situation where this control is stripped away.

The story's inciting incident occurs when the family's car crashes on a remote road after the grandmother's scheming detour. Their encounter with the Misfit, an escaped convict, brings her carefully curated moral facade into sharp relief. As her family members are taken into the woods and executed, the grandmother desperately appeals to the Misfit, calling him a "good man" and insisting that he has the capacity for redemption.[98] These pleas, rooted in her manipulative tendencies, initially reflect her shallow understanding of morality and grace.

The grandmother's transformation occurs in a moment of startling clarity. As she confronts her imminent death, she recognizes her shared humanity with the Misfit, calling him "one of my own children."[99] This gesture, while brief, represents a moment of divine grace breaking into her life. The grandmother's face, described as smiling up at the sky after she is shot, signals a profound but incomplete transformation—a realization of grace that transcends her lifelong pride. In contrast to Ruby's extended vision in "Revelation," the grandmother's transformation is abrupt, underscoring the fragility of human constructs in the face of divine disruption.

"Revelation" and "A Good Man Is Hard to Find" explore the themes of grace, pride, and divine disruption. However, they do so in different ways, each illustrating the role of the literary imagination in unmasking self-deception and reorienting moral vision. In "Revelation," Ruby Turpin's vision does not merely critique social and racial hierarchies; it forces her into a moment of unselfing, where the fat, relentless ego that had shaped her understanding of faith is violently stripped away. Her realization that those she deemed inferior lead the way to heaven aligns with James Cone's theology of the cross, which identifies Christ with the marginalized and oppressed, disrupting the false piety of those who equate faith with status and power.

However, the two stories differ in their pacing and scope, affecting how their protagonists experience grace. "Revelation" allows Ruby time and space to grapple with her pride, gradually unraveling the illusions she had built around herself, ultimately offering her a glimpse of redemption, even if it is painful. By contrast, "A Good Man Is Hard to Find" offers no such process; the grandmother's moment of grace is abrupt, violent, and unresolved. She is arrested by grace in a single instant, her final words to the Misfit—calling him "one of my own children"—marking a sudden, profound shift in her perception. Yet, unlike Ruby, she is given no time to reflect or change; her death cuts short any possibility of transformation.

98. O'Connor, "Good Man Is Hard to Find," 127.

99. O'Connor, "Good Man Is Hard to Find," 132.

This contrast mirrors Murdoch's understanding of how literature reshapes moral perception. In both stories, O'Connor uses grotesque, unsettling encounters to strip away self-satisfaction, but the process unfolds differently. In "Revelation," Ruby's transformation is slow and painful, allowing the literary imagination to function as a moral discipline, forcing her to look at herself with increasing clarity. In "A Good Man Is Hard to Find," the grandmother's change is sudden and ambiguous, leaving her fate open-ended, much like the destabilizing power of divine grace described by Barth. Both stories reveal how the literary imagination, when used as a tool of moral perception, ruptures self-satisfaction and invites a painful yet necessary confrontation with truth—whether over time, as with Ruby, or in an instant, as with the grandmother. As the Misfit reflects, "She would have been a good woman . . . if it had been somebody there to shoot her every day of her life."[100] These differences reflect how O'Connor engages with beauty and the theological: Ruby's vision is cathartic, while the grandmother's death is unsettling, leaving readers with a sense of grace and mystery.

Through these short stories, O'Connor presents complementary explorations of divine grace and disruption. Both stories critique the self-serving distortions of faith and reveal the transformative power of God's grace to shatter human pride and reorient lives toward the divine. Whether through Ruby's extended journey or the grandmother's abrupt moment of clarity, O'Connor's narratives invite readers to confront their assumptions and encounter the unsettling yet redemptive nature of grace. In either case, the works each depict a reality to which one is attracted.

Toni Morrison and the Literary Imagination

If, as Murdoch argues, the literary imagination is a discipline of attention that resists self-serving illusions and reveals reality more truthfully, then Toni Morrison extends this insight by demonstrating how literature can also serve as an act of historical recovery and cultural reckoning. While Murdoch's moral vision focuses on individual unselfing, Morrison's literary imagination insists that entire societies must confront their collective fantasies—particularly those that justify racial and historical oppression.

Morrison's vision of the literary imagination as a means of truth-telling, liberation, and cultural preservation resonates deeply with

100. O'Connor, "Good Man Is Hard to Find," 133.

Murdoch's belief that literature disciplines us to see more clearly and love more justly. However, Morrison expands this vision by showing that literature is a means of individual moral refinement and a tool for dismantling historical amnesia. In novels like *Beloved* and *Song of Solomon*, storytelling is an act of cultural resurrection, ensuring that the voices of the enslaved, the dispossessed, and the marginalized are not lost to history. Morrison's work aligns with Murdoch's view that moral progress depends on resisting self-serving distortions, but Morrison sharpens this insight by exposing how societies construct myths that sustain oppression and how literature must disrupt them.[101] Much of Morrison's work seeks to fill the gaps left by historical narratives that have marginalized or erased Black voices, reclaiming agency over these stories and bringing them to life.

For Morrison, the literary imagination is an inherently political force because language itself is a site of struggle. In her essays, lectures, and interviews, she repeatedly insisted that storytelling is not neutral—it shapes how reality is perceived and whose lives are deemed worthy of remembrance. For Morrison, language is a living force capable of oppression and liberation, which parallels Murdoch's belief that good literature breaks down self-serving fantasies, compelling readers to encounter the world with greater clarity and moral seriousness. Morrison's insistence that the artistic quality of literature is inseparable from its ethical weight echoes Murdoch's critique of the "fat relentless ego," which distorts reality through personal or cultural self-interest.

Morrison's aesthetic approach also resonates with Robert Jenson and Walter Brueggemann's vision of the biblical narrative as a dynamic, generative force. Just as Morrison saw storytelling as a way to retrieve suppressed voices and challenge ideological structures, Jenson and Brueggemann argue that the biblical narrative actively reconfigures human understanding of history, identity, and divine reality. The poetic and dramatic quality of Scripture—what Brueggemann calls its "world-making" capacity—parallels Morrison's belief that literature does not merely depict reality but reshapes the reader's perception of what is possible.

Morrison's work also intersects with René Girard's scapegoat mechanism, particularly in how literature exposes the hidden structures of power that sustain cycles of violence and exclusion. Just as the biblical text, in Girard's view, unveils the innocence of the victim and God's

101. See Morrison, *Goodness and the Literary Imagination*, 13–22.

solidarity with the outcast, Morrison's novels disrupt historical myths that justify oppression. *Beloved*, for example, refuses to allow the reader to view enslaved people as passive victims or to accept a narrative that sanitizes the horrors of slavery. Instead, Morrison forces the reader into a position of moral witness, much like Murdoch insists that great literature compels us to see beyond ourselves.

In this way, Morrison's literary imagination becomes a vehicle for individual moral transformation and a challenge to entire systems of meaning. This force exposes the myths that sustain oppression and invites readers to inhabit an alternative moral world. Morrison also aligns with Brueggemann's notion of Scripture as a counter-narrative that resists the dominant cultural scripts of empire and exclusion. Morrison, like Brueggemann, understands the literary imagination as a prophetic act that calls forth a vision of justice beyond what the present world allows.

Murdoch's view of the literary imagination as a means of moral vision and selfless attention is powerfully expanded in Morrison's work, which insists that truth-telling is a communal, historical, and political act. While Murdoch focuses on literature as a means of individual moral clarity, Morrison demonstrates that this clarity must also be applied to historical memory and cultural identity. Her work reinforces Murdoch's belief that fantasy and self-deception must be resisted. However, she further shows that entire societies construct myths that justify their violence and that literature must actively transcend and disrupt these narratives.

Thus, Morrison's literary imagination does not simply align with Murdoch's; it radicalizes it. By making storytelling a means of historical reckoning, Morrison shows that literature does not only unself the individual but can unself an entire culture, forcing it to confront its buried truths. In this way, Morrison enhances Murdoch's account of the literary imagination, demonstrating that its purpose is to see reality more clearly and redeem what history sought to erase.

Beyond preserving history, Morrison saw the literary imagination as a tool for interrogating power. She believed that writers are responsible for questioning and deconstructing dominant ideologies, particularly those related to race, gender, and class. Literature, for Morrison, fulfilled what Hart understands as the connection between the beautiful and the good—an art form that should challenge oppressive systems while revealing the complexities of human existence. At the same time, she viewed storytelling as a profound means of fostering empathy. Through richly drawn characters and deeply immersive narratives, she believed literature could bridge divides and allow readers to step into perspectives different from their own.

Essential to Morrison's literary vision was the idea of freedom—both creative and personal. Her writing resisted conformity to Western literary traditions, instead prioritizing an authentic portrayal of African American life, spirituality, and cultural heritage. In her Nobel Prize lecture (1993), Morrison described language and storytelling as living forces, warning against how language can be deadened through lies, violence, and oppression.[102] Instead, she celebrated the literary imagination as a means of liberation, a way to sustain life by fostering critical engagement, truth-telling, and hope. Ultimately, for Morrison, the literary imagination is a transformative force that illuminates the human condition, challenges injustice, preserves cultural identity, and reaffirms the enduring power of language.

This transformative power is vividly embodied in *Beloved* through the character of Baby Suggs, a spiritual and communal restoration figure. As the narrative describes her, she is "an unchurched preacher, one who visited pulpits and opened her great heart to those who could use it."[103] She is a powerful character who speaks to many people like Sethe, who seek their agency. In one of her open-air sermons, Baby Suggs declares,

> Here, in this here place, we flesh; flesh that weeps, laughs; flesh that dances on bare feet in grass. Love it. Love it hard. Yonder, they do not love your flesh. They despise it. They don't love your eyes; they'd just as soon pick 'em out. No more do they love the skin on your back. Yonder they flay it. And O my people, they do not love your hands. Those they only use, tie, bind, chop off and leave empty. Love your hands! Love them. Raise them up and kiss them. Touch others with them, pat them together, stroke them on your face 'cause they don't love that either. You got to love it, you![104]

Suggs preaches to those who feel lost in their agency to love the things that a broader world might reject. She wants her listeners to take her literally here—that these appendages and hands are beloved. Yet, her sermon is more than an act of self-affirmation; it is a radical theological and political claim against the dehumanization imposed by the institution of slavery. In declaring that "we flesh," Suggs refuses the false dichotomy between Spirit and body that has often justified oppression. Her call to "love it

102. Morrison, *Nobel Lecture.*

103. Morrison, *Beloved,* 87.

104. Morrison, *Beloved,* 88.

hard" is not merely a sentimental plea but a subversive demand in a world that seeks to commodify, brutalize, and erase Black bodies. The repetition of "they do not love your flesh" underscores the systemic violence enacted upon Black existence, from physical mutilation to psychological subjugation. However, her response is neither despair nor resignation—it is reclamation. By urging her people to love their hands, raise them, and use them for touch, she reorients their sense of worth away from how they are seen and used by others and back toward their own embodied dignity. This sermon is a form of resistance deeply tied to Morrison's literary imagination, which insists on the necessity of self-definition in the face of external narratives of erasure. Suggs's sermon thus functions as a re-narration of the self, a communal liturgy that transforms suffering into sacred affirmation, insisting that love—particularly self-love—is both an act of defiance and a condition for survival.

Suggs's sermon is not merely an individual call to self-love but a communal act of restoration, affirming the collective worth of those stripped of their agency. Thus, Morrison's literary imagination includes a necessary exploration of community, as she portrays relationships of care, solidarity, and shared memory as essential to healing and survival in the face of historical and ongoing violence.

One of the most poignant ways Morrison explores this is through the idea of beauty, particularly how racial hierarchies and social conditioning shape it. Morrison also engages directly with the concept of beauty. In *The Bluest Eye*, she examines the internalized racism that often plagues marginalized communities. The character Pecola Breedlove's desire for blue eyes symbolizes a yearning for acceptance and validation in a world that devalues her existence. Morrison poignantly states, "Beauty was not simply something to behold; it was something one could *do*."[105] This assertion reveals her commitment to redefining what is included in the public understanding of beauty. As such, Morrison advocates for a more inclusive understanding of identity.

Beyond metaphor, *Beloved* underscores the literary significance of exorcism, not merely as a supernatural event but as an act of communal reckoning. The novel's climactic exorcism of Beloved is not about rejecting the past but confronting it, naming it, and ultimately seeking liberation from its grip. Morrison positions this act as an essential function of storytelling itself: literature, like the ritual of exorcism, forces hidden

105. Morrison, *Bluest Eye*, xi.

wounds into the open, demanding that they be seen, acknowledged, and, perhaps, healed. This underscores her belief that the literary imagination is a conduit for reckoning with history, offering a space where suppressed voices—whether literal ghosts or the spectral presence of historical trauma—can speak, be heard, and be transformed. Through *Beloved*, Morrison demonstrates that remembering is both painful and necessary and that true healing requires a communal effort to confront the ghosts that linger in the present.

Apart from this spectral exploration, Morrison's work is known to interrogate the intersections of race, gender, and class, revealing the multifaceted nature of oppression. In *Sula*, she presents the lives of two women navigating a patriarchal society that seeks to confine them. This assertion reinforces her belief that literature can empower individuals to reclaim their narratives and assert their identities. Furthermore, Morrison's literary imagination is deeply rooted in communal storytelling, resisting white supremacy. Returning to *Beloved*, she illustrates how storytelling within the Black community rebuilds cultural solidarity and fosters a sense of belonging. This perspective aligns with her broader vision of literature as a means of cultural reclamation and empowerment. Moreover, Morrison's exploration of maternal love and its complexities is a recurring theme in her work. For example, Sethe's character embodies the sacrifices and struggles of motherhood in the context of slavery. This exploration of maternal love serves as a lens through which Morrison examines the broader implications of identity, agency, and resilience.

Toni Morrison's literary imagination is a powerful exploration of identity, history, and community, particularly within the African American experience. Her works use storytelling as resistance and healing, redefining beauty, belonging, and utopia while reclaiming history and asserting identity. Through her engagement with trauma, resilience, and the strength of marginalized communities, Morrison illuminates pathways toward justice and collective belonging. This literary imagination also offers valuable tools for reading Scripture, highlighting storytelling as a means of reclaiming identity and fostering community. Just as Morrison's characters navigate histories of suffering and redemption, biblical figures like Ruth, Hagar, and Mary embody perseverance and divine grace. Morrison's emphasis on the ethical significance of storytelling may encourage readers to engage Scripture as a set of moral directives and as a living narrative that invites empathy, reflection, and transformation. By incorporating Morrison's imaginative approach, readers can uncover new ways to encounter Scripture as a source of healing, justice, and communal belonging.

PART IV. LITERARY THEOLOGY: JAMES CONE AND FCN

At the heart of this chapter is the claim that the Word of God, the primal narrative of Scripture, and the literary imagination converge in an aesthetic reading of Scripture that reshapes vision and calls forth new ways of being. Theologically, Karl Barth's doctrine of the Word of God, Walter Brueggemann and Robert Jenson's account of the biblical narrative, and Iris Murdoch and Toni Morrison's literary imagination all participate in a shared concern: how revelation, story, and language function as transformative encounters with truth and, thus, God. Barth insists that God's Word is not merely text but an event that disrupts and reorients. Brueggemann and Jenson show how Scripture is not a static document but a dynamic, generative narrative that reconfigures history and identity. Murdoch and Morrison extend this by demonstrating that literature is a moral and aesthetic act that disciplines vision, resists ideological distortion, and preserves truths that would otherwise be erased.

At this intersection stands James Cone's theology, which fuses these insights into a radical vision of the Word of God as a living, aesthetic, and liberating event. Cone insists that the Word of God is not an abstraction but a spoken reality that takes root in the suffering and resistance of the oppressed—an insight that not only deepens Brueggemann's primal narrative and Barth's revelation but also aligns with Morrison's insistence that language creates and reclaims history. Reading Scripture is not a neutral act but a transformative engagement with a living Word that demands a response. The primal narrative of Scripture, like great literature, does not merely inform but re-forms, shaping a new moral imagination and calling the reader into a reality where old hierarchies, false securities, and distorted desires are undone.

In this way, Cone's theology provides a bridge toward a literary theology, an approach that sees revelation as an aesthetic, narrative, and imaginative encounter—one that resists control, reshapes perception, and calls the reader or hearer into a new world of meaning and justice. To read Scripture rightly is to enter into its dramatic and poetic unfolding, allowing it to unsettle, convict, and invite the reader into the alternative world it proclaims. A literary theology insists that Scripture is not simply to be studied but inhabited; its story is not merely analyzed but lived.

Cone and the Word of God

If the Word of God, as Karl Barth argues, is not a static set of doctrines but a living event in which God speaks, then James Cone extends this understanding by placing Barth's description of the Word of God squarely within the historical struggle of the oppressed. As Cone writes,

> The theologian is *before all else* an exegete, simultaneously of Scripture and existence. To be an exegete of Scripture means that the theologian recognizes the Bible, the witness to God's Word, as a primary source of theological discourse. To be an exegete of existence means that Scripture is not an abstract word but a rational idea. It is God's Word to those oppressed and humiliated in this world.[106]

For Cone, the Word of God is revealed in Scripture and Jesus Christ and actively disclosed through the lived experience of Black people fighting for liberation. Furthermore, Cone argues, "the truth of the Bible is the story of the call of God's people from slavery to freedom."[107] Here, one witnesses the wisdom at the heart of the primal narrative and its connection to divine speech. The God who resurrects Jesus from the dead and liberates from slavery in Egypt is the one who speaks in the biblical account of past revelation and the lens *through which* one hears the Word of God speaking today. This means that biblical attestation to the Word of God is inseparable from the struggle for justice in history. As with Barth's rejection of natural theology, Cone resists any attempt to reduce the Word of God to abstract principles, insisting that it speaks in the concrete, lived reality of the poor and the marginalized.

By locating the Word of God within the lives of the oppressed, Cone aids in recognizing the truth of the primal narrative and the literary imagination. As Cone argues, "The Word is more than *words* about God. God's Word is a poetic happening, an evocation of an indescribable reality in the lives of people."[108] The Word of God as a "poetic happening" recognizes that revelation is not a fixed deposit of truths but a dynamic and disruptive

106. Cone, *God of the Oppressed*, 8. Emphasis original.

107. Cone, *God of the Oppressed*, 84.

108. Cone, *God of the Oppressed*, 17.

event that resists control and demands participation. Cone insists that "the Word . . . transcends conceptual analysis and becomes a liberating event wherein the people are moved to another level of existence, and they are permitted to experience a foretaste of the New Jerusalem."[109] The Word is spoken *in* history and *through* history, taking shape in the lived realities of those struggling for freedom. The scriptural narrative, then, points to a reality that transcends. If the Word is truly poetic, it does not function merely as doctrine or law but as aesthetic and dramatic speech that breaks open new worlds. It is an encounter where history, theology, and beauty converge to reorient perception and call forth new ways of being. In this way, Cone's theology is deeply aesthetic: the Word is not merely conceptualized but embodied in rhythm, language, and communal experience, where speech itself becomes an act of creation and resistance.

James Cone's understanding of the Word of God resists the collapse into immanentism that characterizes FCN. While FCN distorts divine revelation into a closed ideological system, reducing theology to political power, cultural identity, and nationalistic myth, Cone insists that the Word of God remains transcendent even as it speaks through history, particularly in the cries of the oppressed. The Word of God is not merely an idea or historical phenomenon; rather, it is a liberating event that preserves Barth's insistence that it is a dynamic divine speech that calls people into another level of existence. In this way, Cone's theology avoids the secularizing impulse to confine truth to history alone while simultaneously refusing the escapist spirituality that neglects the world's suffering.

For Cone, to be an exegete of both Scripture and existence means holding together the radical particularity of history and the irreducible transcendence of God. The Bible is not merely a static record of past events nor a system of theological propositions; it is the witness to God's active Word, which disrupts, liberates, and draws people toward the eschatological reality of the new Jerusalem. This means that the suffering of the oppressed is not merely a social or political issue—it is the very location where God's speech breaks into history. However, this is not to say that suffering itself is divine or that history, in its immanent form, contains the fullness of redemption. Rather, the liberating Word of God pierces through the conditions of history without being contained by them—it is always oriented toward the eschaton, toward something beyond the present world order.

109. Cone, *God of the Oppressed*, 18.

In his understanding of the Word of God, Cone's theology resists secular modernity's confinement of meaning *to* the immanent frame and FCN's instrumentalization of faith *for* earthly power. The Word of God cannot be co-opted into a national identity, an ideological program, or a political platform because it always retains its character as a living event. The divine happening unsettles rather than secures, liberates, and justifies the present order. In contrast, FCN attempts to collapse theology into a closed system, where Scripture is reducible to a set of absolute principles and techniques that reinforce the status quo. In doing so, FCN strips theology of its eschatological horizon, confining divine action to national destiny, moral legislation, or cultural supremacy.

Cone's emphasis on the transcendent Word disrupts this closure. When he says that the Word transcends conceptual analysis and becomes a liberating event, he argues that God's revelation is not reducible to human language, doctrinal systems, or ideological control. The Word cannot be exhausted by theological formulations or contained within any given historical moment. It is always ahead of us, calling the oppressed into new possibilities and summoning the powerful to account. Thus, theology must be dynamic, poetic, and disruptive—it cannot be a repetition of the past but must attune to how God speaks in the present.

Thus, Cone's literary theology protects the Word of God from secularism and ideological capture. It resists the modern tendency to enclose meaning within human frameworks while rejecting any attempt to make divine revelation serve earthly empires. The Word remains rooted in history yet irreducible to it, always speaking through the suffering of the world but never confined by the limits of human vision. This theological force keeps Christian faith from collapsing into either political ideology or secular historicism, ensuring that the gospel remains what it has always been—a liberating event that breaks open the world, revealing the inbreaking reality of God's justice, beauty, and love.

Cone and the Primal Narrative

The poetic happening of the Word does not function as static doctrine but as a living, improvisational event, shaped by the people who proclaim it and the contexts in which it is spoken. This dynamic interplay between text, voice, and historical reality resonates with Brueggemann and Jenson's understanding of Scripture as a generative and dramatic narrative—not a rigid system of truths but a world-making event that draws its hearers into an alternative reality. Just as Brueggemann speaks of the primal narrative as the gravitational center that orients the biblical witness, Cone's vision of the Word of God resists fragmentation, preventing Scripture from being reduced to isolated propositions, doctrinal proof texts, or ideological weapons. The primal narrative ensures that Scripture is not merely an anthology of moral teachings or historical accounts but an active, unfolding drama that demands participation.

If, as Brueggemann argues, the primal narrative is "the consistently believed in and recited root story that a community relies upon in crisis and the one by which the truth or falseness of every other story is judged," then Cone's theology situates this primal narrative within the concrete historical realities of the oppressed. The exodus of Israel and the resurrection of Christ form the primal pattern that shapes all derivative narratives, revealing God's unwavering solidarity with the crucified of history. This narrative coherence refuses to let Scripture be read as an abstract theological system divorced from the realities of suffering and liberation. Instead, it insists that the meaning of Scripture is only truly grasped when the reader stands in solidarity with the world's exiles, the enslaved and the lynched. Cone's insistence that the Word of God is a happening rather than a static text means that to read Scripture rightly is not merely to interpret but to become implicated in its unfolding drama. As a poetic happening, the Word does not passively confirm human structures but collapses them, reconstructing the world according to God's justice.

This understanding of the Word as an event resists the fundamentalist and Christian nationalist impulse to fix meaning within rigid ideological frameworks. Such frameworks, as Cone critiques, often remove the living, disruptive force of Scripture by treating it as a closed system—whether as a divine legal code that upholds the status quo or as a repository of prooftexts marshaled in service of political power. Christian nationalism, in particular, severs Scripture from its primal narrative by aligning it with the structures of empire rather than with the God who delivers enslaved people and raises the dead. FCN offers precisely the kind of ideological misreading that Cone warns against: a reading that subordinates divine revelation to the demands of nationalism, capitalism, or white supremacy, rendering the Word inert and domesticated.

By contrast, the literary imagination—whether in Morrison's fiction or Cone's theology—refuses a neutral language. If, as Cone argues, the Black sermon is a poetic happening—an event where rhythm, repetition, and storytelling reconstitute identity and reimagine history—then Morrison's literary imagination functions similarly. Both expose the hidden structures of power that shape perception and demand that language become an instrument of truth-telling, resistance, and new creation. Morrison's fiction, much like the prophetic imagination in Scripture, unsettles the dominant narratives of history, lifting the voices of the forgotten and unveiling the deep wounds beneath the veneer of national mythology. Likewise, Cone's theology refuses to let the Word of God be spoken in a way that does not liberate; for him, the Word is always bound to the cries of the oppressed, shattering the illusions of power and calling the world into a new moral imagination.

This connection between Cone's theology and Brueggemann's primal narrative underscores the vital role of memory in shaping faithful interpretation. Just as Israel was commanded to remember its deliverance from Egypt and the early church confessed the resurrection of Jesus as the decisive act of God, so does the Black theological tradition root itself in the memory of suffering and liberation. This is why Cone insists that theology must be a poetry of resistance rather than a mere intellectual exercise. Like the biblical witness itself, it must be a mode of proclamation that interrupts the world's assumptions about power, justice, and beauty.

By grounding the Word in the primal narrative, Cone ensures that divine speech does not collapse into the immanent frame of secular history. While the Word speaks through history, through the cries of the oppressed, it remains irreducible to history. Like Barth and Jenson, Cone maintains that divine revelation is an event that breaks into time without being confined to it. The God who raised Israel from Egypt and Christ from the grave continues to speak, not as an echo of the past but as the living voice that calls forth new futures. The primal narrative does not merely recall what God has done; it invites hearers to anticipate what God will do. This eschatological orientation ensures that theology remains open, dynamic, and resistant to ideological captivity. It is not a closed system but a drama still unfolding, drawing its hearers into the freedom of God's new creation.

Cone and the Literary Imagination

The aesthetic and transformative nature of the Word of God connects Cone with Toni Morrison's literary imagination and Iris Murdoch's moral vision. Morrison and Murdoch understand storytelling as a means of truth-telling that resists fantasy and self-deception. Just as Morrison argues that narrative preserves the memory of those erased by history, Cone asserts that the Word of God in Black theology must be a liberating word that exposes hidden power structures and refuses ideological distortions. He warns that "ideology in the context of biblical revelation is interpreting Scripture from an axiological perspective that contradicts the divine will to liberate the poor and the downtrodden."[110] This insight aligns with Murdoch's critique of the "fat relentless ego," which distorts the truth by filtering it through self-interest, power, and cultural supremacy.

To say that the Word of God is poetic also affirms its aesthetic, embodied, and communal nature, echoing David Bentley Hart's understanding of beauty as a revelation that resists commodification and control. In Cone's account, the poetic happening of the Word does not occur in isolation but within the living speech of a people, where biblical storytelling and Black cultural expression merge in aesthetic defiance of oppression. Here, revelation does not merely inform—it disrupts, enlivens, and summons the hearer into a new reality. If the Word of God moves through poetry, rhythm, and story, reading Scripture is not about mastering a text but surrendering to an encounter.

Furthermore, Cone's aesthetic theology compliments, extends, and radicalizes David Bentley Hart's theological aesthetics. Just as Hart insists that beauty is not an object of control but a divine disclosure that resists commodification, Cone presents Black preaching, music, and storytelling as spaces where the Word of God breaks into history, disrupting the status quo and making new futures possible. He writes, "The black sermon arises out of the totality of the people's existence—their pain and joy, trouble and ecstasy."[111] This echoes Morrison's belief in language as a living force that shapes reality rather than simply describing it.

Taken together, Cone's theology of the Word expands the literary imagination described by Morrison and Murdoch, grounding it in the biblical witness to liberation. His account of revelation reinforces the claim that Scripture is not merely a set of ancient texts but an active and aesthetic force that transforms perception, history, and human desire. Whether through Morrison's fiction, Murdoch's ethics, or Cone's

110. Cone, *God of the Oppressed*, 84.

111. Cone, *God of the Oppressed*, 18.

theology, the Word—when rightly heard—liberates, unsettles, and reorients the imagination toward justice and beauty.

Cone's account of the Black literary imagination is intricately woven into the fabric of his theological and philosophical explorations. Cone's perspective on the Black literary imagination is not merely an aesthetic consideration but a profound engagement with the historical and cultural realities of Black life in America. James Cone's recognition of the literary and artistic imagination as a more theologically perceptive witness than traditional theology speaks to his conviction that beauty and truth are bound together in the experience of suffering. Cone writes,

> black poets, novelists, painters, dramatists, and other artists saw clearly what white theologians and clergy ignored and what black religious scholars merely alluded to: that in the United States, the clearest image of the crucified Christ was the figure of an innocent black victim, dangling from a lynching tree.[112]

Cone draws attention to the aesthetic dimensions of theological truth—that sometimes the clearest articulation of the gospel is not found in doctrinal systems but in the visual, narrative, and poetic expression of trauma and transcendence. The lynching tree, as Cone famously argues, is America's cross. It is the central symbol by which the crucified Christ can be rightly discerned in the history of American racial violence. This is not merely a historical analogy but a theological claim grounded in the literary imagination that identifies divine presence in the most forsaken places.

Cone's insight highlights the capacity of the literary imagination to bear theological weight, especially in contexts where traditional theology has failed to speak the truth. Through their poetry, stories, paintings, and plays, Black artists enacted a kind of theology from below. This theology told the truth about the American cross and exposed the deep contradictions of a Christian faith aligned with white supremacy. Figures like Billie Holiday, Langston Hughes, Toni Morrison, and even anonymous blues singers did not require a seminary education to grasp the christological meaning of black suffering. Their art becomes a form of theological resistance, unmasking the idolatries of Christian nationalism and insisting that any theology worth its name must find God not in the cathedrals of empire but in the bodies hung from lynching trees.

112. Cone, *Cross and the Lynching Tree*, 93.

In Cone's vision, the literary imagination is not ornamental but revelatory. It does not decorate theology with emotional color; it opens theology to realities that cold reason or systematic formulations are too timid to name. The image of the lynched Christ refuses abstraction. It forces theology to be embodied, historical, and particular. It reorients Christian aesthetics away from sanitized depictions of glory and toward a cruciform beauty—one that, as Balthasar suggests, embraces "the most abysmal ugliness of sin and hell by virtue of the condescension of divine life."[113] In this way, the literary imagination narrates suffering and dares to reveal God's presence within it.

This aesthetic theology, born from the underside of American history, disrupts both liberal optimism and conservative moralism. It insists on a Christ who does not merely suffer for the world but suffers with the world—especially with those cast out by it. In making this claim through literature and art, Black artists perform the very kind of theology Cone calls for: a theology that begins not in abstraction but in the flesh and blood of real history, a theology that listens to screams, sees scars, and sings laments. This theology—cruciform, literary, and liberating—reveals the gospel anew, not as a system to be believed but as a story to be inhabited, a drama in which the crucified still speak.

Cone's interpretation of Scripture means a vision of revelation as a poetic, literary, and participatory act that leads directly into literary theology. This approach sees the Word of God as an aesthetic happening that must be read, inhabited, and lived to be understood. If the biblical text, like all great literature, calls the reader beyond mere analysis into moral and imaginative transformation, then theology must reflect this narrative depth. Reading Scripture rightly requires more than comprehension; it demands that one steps into its poetic unfolding, letting it destabilize assumptions and reshape desires. The Word is never merely a text—it is an event, a happening, a world-breaking and world-remaking reality.

Cone draws parallels between the crucifixion of Jesus and the lynching of Black individuals, suggesting that both events reveal the ultimate expression of suffering and injustice. He writes, "The cross and the lynching tree are the two most emotionally charged symbols of the African American experience."[114] This assertion highlights how the Black literary imagination is deeply rooted in the historical traumas of slavery

113. Balthasar, *Glory of the Lord*, 124.

114. Cone, *Cross and the Lynching Tree*, 3.

and lynching, which serve as a backdrop for the narratives that emerge from this community. Cone's work emphasizes that literature is a means of confronting these painful histories, allowing for a collective processing of trauma and a reclamation of identity.

Moreover, Cone's exploration of the Black literary imagination informs a theological framework that emphasizes the significance of hope and redemption. He contends that literature has the power to envision alternative futures and to inspire collective action. Cone states, "The Black literary imagination is a source of hope, a way of envisioning a world where justice prevails."[115] This notion of hope is crucial in understanding how Black writers navigate the complexities of their realities while simultaneously aspiring for a better future. Their work does not escape the weight of suffering. However, it transforms it into a vision of liberation—a vision sustained not only by individual resolve but also by shared memory and communal imagination.

Cone also engages with the concept of community in the Black literary imagination, emphasizing that hope is never merely personal—it is forged in the context of collective struggle. For Cone, Black literature does not present isolated expressions of faith or pain but arises from a deeply communal experience where memory, resistance, and survival are cultivated together.

He posits that literature is a communal space where shared experiences and collective memories find room. This communal aspect is essential for fostering a sense of belonging and identity among Black individuals. This emphasis on community underscores the relational nature of the Black literary imagination, where individual narratives contribute to a larger tapestry of collective identity.

Morrison and Cone advocate for the transformative power of narrative to envision alternative futures. Morrison's exploration of hope and redemption is evident in her characters' journeys toward self-discovery and empowerment. She asserts that literature can inspire change and challenge dominant narratives. Cone echoes this sentiment, arguing that the Black literary and theological traditions serve as sources of hope and resistance against systemic injustice. This shared belief in the power of narrative to effect change underscores the interconnectedness of Morrison's literary imagination and Cone's theological insights.

115. Cone, *Cross and the Lynching Tree*, 93.

The connection between Toni Morrison and James Cone lies in their shared commitment to exploring the complexities of the African American experience through the lenses of suffering, community, and hope. Both figures utilize their respective mediums to articulate the enduring impact of historical trauma while advocating for resilience and justice. Their works serve as powerful testaments to the importance of storytelling in confronting oppression and envisioning a more equitable future.

A Literary Theology: Critique of Ideology

With this theologically nuanced emphasis on literary theology, one should ask how it might impact reading Scripture. Though the Scripture was a tool for abolitionists and the Black community, many white supremacist readings of the biblical text led to violence and death. In short, lynchings of Black people were justified through Scripture. Is it wishful thinking, then, that an aesthetic, literary imagination could offer a compelling alternative to the harsh interpretations of much more popular readings of white supremacists? I argue that rather than wishful thinking, the Black literary imagination, in the face of such realities, visualizes the beautiful triune Lord in which Scripture participates and is obscured by white supremacy. Cone, Morrison, and others in the Black community articulate a sense of style more faithful to the living triune Lord and, by using Scripture, illustrate how it participates in the economy of salvation.

I argue that literary theology enables a critique of Christian nationalism by emphasizing the beauty of the triune Lord. The literary imagination just outlined illustrates how figures use the experience of marginalized communities to articulate a literary narrative to express their suffering. However, Cone performs a crucial next step. The imagination that he cultivates, along with Morrison, places the cross next to the suffering of this marginalized community. This binding leads to rereading the biblical themes and teasing out a new life. The cross gives a new perspective on God's life with the world. God will, through the cross, find identification with the crucified, the lynched, and the marginalized, standing in solidarity with those whom history has cast aside. This divine identification is not merely an act of empathy but a radical inversion of worldly power, where the suffering God upends the logic of dominance and exclusion. In this reversal, the cross does more than expose injustice—it redefines the foundation of moral order.

For Cone, ideology is not merely a set of false ideas but a distortion of truth that excludes the biblical story from shaping reality. He argues that:

> Ideology in the *total* sense represents that form of thinking whose intellectual grid excludes a priori the truth of the biblical story. This is characteristic of people who do not think in categories intrinsic to the story of divine liberation. They think in categories contradicting the social a priori of biblical revelation and its form as a story. Truth is often interpreted in legalistic and philosophical categories.[116]

In this sense, ideology does not simply misinterpret Scripture—it fundamentally displaces the biblical narrative, substituting a secular logic of control, acceleration, and technique in place of the disruptive Word of God. This insight is crucial for resisting fundamentalist Christian nationalism, which falsely claims to uphold biblical authority while subjecting Scripture to ideological frameworks that betray its liberative content. Cone's critique of ideology exposes how FCN manipulates Scripture to serve the interests of nationalism, racial supremacy, and cultural hegemony, stripping it of its aesthetic, prophetic, and literary depth.

At the heart of Cone's resistance to ideology is the recovery of the biblical story as a primal narrative—a story that does not conform to static doctrinal systems or nationalist mythologies but instead unfolds as a disruptive, world-shattering revelation. The primal narrative of Scripture is not an abstract set of principles but a dynamic movement of divine liberation—a drama in which God speaks, acts, and enters history on behalf of the oppressed. FCN replaces this unfolding narrative with a rigid, systematic theology prioritizing law and order over divine disruption. It substitutes national identity for covenant, obedience to the state for prophetic resistance, and doctrinal purity for transformative love. By contrast, Cone insists that the Word of God cannot be contained within static formulas—it is a poetic happening, a divine speech act that shatters false structures, overturns human hierarchies, and reorders the world according to God's justice.

Cone's emphasis on literary imagination provides a necessary counterpoint to the ideological capture of Scripture. If ideology reduces

116. Cone, *God of the Oppressed*, 86. Emphasis original.

biblical narrative to legalistic and philosophical categories, then literary theology resists this reduction by preserving the story's complexity, depth, and poetic force. A literary reading of Scripture resists acceleration and technique, slowing down the text to let its imagery, metaphors, and aesthetic weight shape the reader rather than assimilate them into ideological talking points. This is why Cone engages Du Bois, Morrison, and Baldwin, seeing in their literary vision a form of theological resistance—a refusal to let black suffering be narrated through the ideological categories of the dominant order. Just as Du Bois's literary imagination resists the racialized logic of modernity, so too must theology resist the instrumentalization of Scripture in service of power.

FCN functions through technological mediation, where biblical meaning is flattened into sound bites, weaponized in political discourse, and repurposed as a tool for national identity formation. The literary imagination disrupts this mechanism, restoring the biblical story's narrative depth, aesthetic force, and revelatory unpredictability. The Bible, Cone insists, is not a set of moral axioms but a divine drama in which the reader participates. Ideology seeks to make the text a dead artifact, a museum piece wielded for social control; literary theology restores it as a living Word that continues to speak, confront, and transform.

At the core of Cone's vision is the insistence that the Word of God is not reducible to the text of Scripture. The Bible is a witness to the Word, but the Word itself is God's living, active speech, breaking into history in ways that ideological frameworks cannot control. In this sense, the cross is the ultimate disruption of ideological stability, revealing the ugliness of power, the violence of human systems, and the radical inversion of values required to enter God's reign. Engaging Cone alongside Hans Urs von Balthasar helps illuminate this aesthetic dimension: true beauty is not found in harmonizing the status quo but in the rupture that unveils the world's contradictions. The glory of the cross is precisely in its rejection of worldly aesthetics—it is not an image of dominance but of divine solidarity with the crucified peoples of history.

Thus, the primal narrative, literary imagination, and the living Word of God converge in Cone's theology as an aesthetic, disruptive force. Against the acceleration, secularity, and technological mediation of FCN, Cone offers a slow, poetic, and participatory engagement with Scripture and history—one that refuses to let the Bible be co-opted by nationalistic ideology and instead insists that it remains a radical witness to divine liberation, transvaluation, and beauty.

Literary theology's insistence on the aesthetic and literary dimensions of theology is not incidental but central to Cone's vision, for it is through the disruptive, paradoxical beauty of the cross that the gospel performs its deepest transformation. The cross is the indicative site where human values are overturned, the ideological scripts of power and oppression are unmasked, and divine justice emerges not through domination but through suffering love. The indicative of the gospel is the most profound transvaluation of values, according to Cone, which subverts the order of morality, dismantling systems of oppression and reconfiguring the meaning of justice, righteousness, and power.[117] The cross unmasks that human mimetic desire leads to the death of innocence. Like the lynching tree, it exposes immoral systems of values and the codes that support such structures of power. In short, it is the touchstone by which one can see whether one's ethical commitments connect to the life-empowering message of the gospel. However, this transvaluation of values also saves humanity from what Cone describes as false pieties.[118] The cross is not an abstract symbol of disembodied sentimentality but rather one that guides judgments about the world and other people.[119] As Karl Barth describes this cross, "Christian ethics is the fruit that grows from this tree."[120] Combining the insights of Cone and Barth, one sees that the ethics of the cross are an ethics of failure in comparison to the ethics of the world. Barth and Cone note that God interacts with the world through the perceived failure of the cross. "Good," as Barth argues, "in the Christian sense, is that behavior and action of people which corresponds to the behavior and action of God in this history."[121] Ethics must correspond to *this* encounter of God with history, namely as a willing risk of failure according to metrics of success in a world of powers. Ethics is a paradoxical encounter with the world, according to God's folly (1 Cor 1:25).

The cross possesses this social function in history, but it arises from the deeper, cosmological dynamic of the cross. To glimpse this cosmological aspect, I turn to the apocalyptic Paul as an interpreter of the cross. As his readers note, Paul offers the most theologically rich yet paradoxical descriptions of the cross, crucifixion, and the crucified.

117. Cone, *Cross and the Lynching Tree*, 157.

118. Cone, *Cross and the Lynching Tree*, 161.

119. Cone, *Cross and the Lynching Tree*, 161.

120. Barth, "Christian Ethics," 3.

121. Barth, "Christian Ethics," 3.

Consider particularly Paul's statement in Galatians 6:14, "May I never boast of anything except the cross of our Lord Jesus Christ, by which the world has been crucified to me, and I to the world" (NRSV). Paul here echoes a mystery found earlier in Galatians 2:19–20, "I have been crucified with Christ; and it is no longer I who live, but it is Christ who lives in me. And the life I now live in the flesh I live by faith in the Son of God" (NRSV). In both accounts, Paul identifies with the crucified Lord and proclaims a particular kind of death disclosed through the cross—a death that appears as foolishness to those who are perishing (1 Cor 1:26). The identification of the perishing comes with a larger apocalyptic theme, namely that the world is passing away as the new creation arrives (1 Cor 7:31). This arrival is a true advent, as theologian Christopher Morse argues, "that is not accounted for as an extrapolation from any available residue of what has gone before."[122] The cross is not merely a past event, but rather, it is the kingdom's inauguration, which continually confronts the believer with good news. Paul's language is rich here because it lacks the conventional wisdom of the present evil age (Gal 1:4) and rather brings to an end the wisdom and the entire cosmological structure that undergirds that wisdom. Returning to Galatians 6:14, Paul, then, must appeal to the end of one world and the beginning of another through the former's death that gives birth to the latter. As J. Louis Martyn understands, this arises from the Galatian understanding that the cosmos rests upon a fundamental pair of opposites, such as good and evil, circumcised and uncircumcised.[123] To crucify the cosmos is to bring an end to this ordering of the world according to this antinomy. In this way the cross inaugurates the new creation through a new ordering according to this age and the age coming to pass. In this new age, the old divisions do not account for their former weight, for Paul states that, for example, law observance or non-law observance amounts to anything (cf. Gal 5:6 and 1 Cor 7:19).[124] The antinomy that now divides the present age and the age to come is such a division, and antinomy, but the new age does not operate according to the former divisions. The death of the old world, then, comes through a death of its "fundamental structures . . . [and] that those fundamental structures of the cosmos were certain

122. Morse, *Difference Heaven Makes*, 46.

123. Martyn, "Apocalyptic Antinomies."

124. Martyn, *Theological Issues*, 115.

identifiable pairs of opposites."[125] Rather than the harsh antinomy of the law, the new creation rests upon an indicative of grace. As such, the wisdom of this age would see the cross as folly because it not only denies but puts the structure that undergirds it to death. In short, the cross defames and decenters the wisdom of the age.

Cone uses Black poets and artists as a model in his transvaluation of values and provides a new account of aesthetics for a disruptive account of beauty. As a theologian, Hans Urs von Balthasar writes, "The 'glory' of Christian transfiguration is in no way less resplendent than the transfiguring glory of worldly beauty, but the fact is that the glory of Christ unites splendor and radiance with solid reality, as we see pre-eminently in the Resurrection and its anticipation through faith in the Christian Life."[126] Balthasar offers keen insight into the aesthetic quality of Cone's theology of the cross. Balthasar echoes Cone's theology that the cross is disruptive and transvalues all values. The cross images the unbearable, ugly nature of the world. Its judgment is on those who try to destroy luminously beautiful creatures held in the love of God. Cone's theology of the cross serves as a medium to display the harsh nature of the sin in the world that destroys and excludes even God. Cone extends even this part of the world's fallenness into the very life of God. As Balthasar writes, the cross "embraces the most abysmal ugliness of sin and hell by virtue of the condescension of divine life, which has brought even sin and hell into that divine art for which there is no human analog."[127] The cross embraces "everything else which a worldly aesthetics (even of a realistic kind) discards as no longer bearable."[128] The cross requires the location of beauty inside the crucifixion as a challenge and destruction of false dichotomies of lynching. Only *this* kind of transvaluation truly destroys the structures of social exclusion and its supporting buttresses so that a new kind of moral community can emerge.

PART V. SCRIPTURE BEYOND FCN

Suppose Cone's theology of the cross exposes and transvalues worldly aesthetics. In that case, the next challenge is ensuring that Scripture is

125. Martyn, *Theological Issues*, 118.
126. Balthasar, *Glory of the Lord*, 124.
127. Balthasar, *Glory of the Lord*, 124.
128. Balthasar, *Glory of the Lord*, 124.

not trapped within the ideological structures that the cross dismantles. Fundamentalist Christian nationalism, like all ideological distortions of faith, attempts to make Scripture a tool for power rather than a witness to divine truth. It does so by flattening the Bible into a literalist, static text, where doctrine functions as propaganda rather than as an invitation to encounter God. This ideological capture of faith is deeply connected to what Charles Taylor calls the secular age, marked by acceleration, technological mediation, and the loss of transcendent depth. In such a context, the Bible is not read but wielded, its richness replaced by simplistic slogans that conform to nationalistic or moralistic agendas. Literary theology, however, resists this reduction, keeping Scripture open to mystery, complexity, and transformative beauty.

FCN thrives on a hermeneutic of control—a reading of Scripture that seeks to domesticate divine revelation into rigid doctrinal systems, nationalistic mythologies, and moralistic purity codes. In this framework, the Bible ceases to be a literary and theological drama and instead becomes a fixed set of ideological imperatives used to define boundaries of inclusion and exclusion. This reduction strips Scripture of its aesthetic depth, where its paradoxes, tensions, and unsettling demands are flattened into simplistic absolutes. It mirrors what Taylor describes as the condition of secular modernity, in which faith is no longer an open horizon of discovery but a system of certainties that must be defended against perceived threats. The need to control the text is driven by the anxieties of acceleration and technological mediation, where theological discourse is increasingly shaped by mass consumption, digital rhetoric, and the instant validation of ideological claims.

In this context, Scripture is no longer approached with patience or reverence but with the urgency of political utility. It is used to justify law-and-order politics, national identity, and cultural hegemony, reinforcing the idea that faith is primarily about securing social order rather than opening oneself to the disruptive presence of God. The Bible, once a text that breaks open human assumptions and reconfigures reality, is now treated as an artifact of absolute knowledge, wielded to silence dissent and foreclose alternative readings. This tendency is particularly evident in Christian nationalism's use of Romans 13:1–7, which is often cited to demand submission to governmental authority—except when that authority is perceived as threatening Christian cultural dominance. Such an approach reveals that the Bible is not being read for transformation but deployed as a weapon for cultural control.

A literary theology resists this ideological capture by refusing to let the text become a site of simplistic resolution. It insists that Scripture, in all its complexity, must remain open to God's ongoing revelation, inviting the reader not into certainty but into a process of discovery, transformation, and moral imagination. Suppose fundamentalism approaches the Bible as a closed system. In that case, literary theology approaches it as an unfolding drama, where meaning is always reconstituted through the interplay of history, experience, and divine encounter. This way of reading echoes the poetic happening Cone describes, where theology is not a mere repetition of doctrinal formulas but an aesthetic, historical, and ethical engagement with the living Word of God.

By resisting the secular logic of acceleration, literary theology reintroduces slowness and contemplation into the act of reading. The Bible is no longer a tool of power but a disruptive witness, calling the reader into an encounter that challenges rather than confirms their assumptions. It preserves the mystery of the text rather than reducing it to an ideological certainty, ensuring that interpretation remains an act of faithful listening rather than a quest for dominance.

FCN is deeply modern in its structure—it thrives on acceleration and technique in the immanent frame, reducing faith to instant certainty and propagandistic, mass dissemination of ideology. It does not cultivate patience in reading but instead seeks immediate validation of pre-existing beliefs. The digital age exacerbates this tendency, as theological discourse is increasingly shaped by memes, social media rhetoric, and algorithmic confirmation bias, which reward provocation over contemplation. In this framework, the Bible ceases to be a text that shapes the reader and instead becomes an ideological weapon, justifying political power and social hierarchy. Literary theology, by contrast, insists that Scripture cannot be consumed in haste or read as a proof-text for nationalistic or moralistic purposes. Instead, it demands slow, careful engagement that allows the biblical text to break open human assumptions rather than reinforce them. It insists that the Bible is not an artifact of a past age to be defended but a literary and theological drama to be entered into and inhabited.

Cone's vision of disruptive beauty in the cross insists that true theology cannot be co-opted into neat ideological categories. A literary theology follows this insight by insisting that Scripture cannot be reduced to a nationalistic or moralistic agenda—it is always larger, more disruptive, and more beautiful than any ideological containment. Fundamentalist

Christian nationalism seeks to narrow the interpretive field, creating a rigid boundary between *true believers* and enemies of the faith. It turns theology into propaganda, where belief is measured not by faithfulness to the mystery of God but by adherence to a political or cultural order.

A literary theology resists propaganda by refusing to allow doctrine to become static, absolute, or lifeless. Instead, it insists that theological truth must always be encountered anew, wrestled with, and seen afresh in every generation. This requires an openness to the poetic nature of Scripture, where meaning is not simply stated but evoked, revealed, and deepened over time. If fundamentalism flattens doctrine into a set of fixed positions, literary theology understands doctrine as an aesthetic event—an unfolding, participatory engagement with the divine mystery that can never be exhausted.

Thus, just as Cone's theology of the cross demands a transvaluation of worldly values, literary theology demands a transvaluation of how we engage Scripture itself. It refuses to let the Bible be reduced to a nationalist manifesto or a rigid moral code, instead embracing it as a witness to the infinite love, justice, and beauty of God—a love that is always disruptive, is always beyond our control, and always calls the reader into deeper transformation.

CONCLUSION

This chapter presents the Word of God as a living, relational reality that resists static or ideological interpretations, instead functioning as a dynamic, disruptive force that continually speaks in new and transformative ways. The theological insights of Barth, Webster, and Brueggemann emphasize the interplay of revelation, Scripture, and the Spirit, grounding the Word's coherence in God's ongoing engagement with humanity rather than in abstract principles. Morrison, Cone, and Du Bois further enrich this vision, demonstrating how the literary imagination exposes systemic injustices and unveils divine beauty in unexpected places. Cone and Du Bois, drawing on Girard's scapegoat theory, reveal Christ's identification with the lynched body as a challenge to violent power structures. At the same time, David Bentley Hart and Iris Murdoch argue that true beauty disrupts false certainties and compels a deeper vision of reality. Jenson and Frei extend these insights by presenting Scripture as an unfolding divine drama that demands participation.

Together, these perspectives reveal Scripture not as a fixed doctrine but as an ever-unfolding divine act that calls for engagement, confrontation, and transformation. Rather than affirming existing beliefs, the Word radically reorients readers, shaping and reshaping their vision of God, themselves, and the world.

4

The Two Gileads

"You can believe in Gilead or you could believe in God, but not both."[1]

Becka, an Aunt

INTRODUCTION: SCRIPTURE, NARRATIVE, AND THE RHYTHMS OF GRACE

If the previous chapter explored the Word of God as a living drama that resists ideological captivity and continually disrupts human expectations, then this chapter moves deeper into how Scripture shapes and is shaped by the communities that interpret it. Building upon the insights of Barth, Brueggemann, Cone, Morrison, and O'Connor, this chapter examines the tension between Scripture as a liberating narrative of grace and Scripture as a weapon of control. Nowhere is this contrast more vividly explored in literature than in the two Gileads—the dystopian Republic of Gilead from Margaret Atwood's *The Handmaid's Tale* and *The Testaments* and the small-town Gilead, Iowa, from Marilynne Robinson's Gilead quadrilogy. These opposing visions are powerful reflections on how Scripture constructs meaning, defines community, and shapes the moral imagination.

1. Atwood, *Testaments*, 304.

Atwood's Gilead presents a stark warning about the dangers of Scripture when co-opted by authoritarianism, fundamentalism, and Christian nationalism. It exposes the way biblical language, when divorced from grace and justice, can become a tool for oppression, exclusion, and control. Her dystopia is not merely a cautionary tale but an unsettling mirror, revealing how Scripture, when weaponized, reinforces systemic violence rather than liberating those on its margins. In contrast, Robinson's Gilead is where Scripture unfolds as a living, relational reality—fragile yet luminous, shaped by human vulnerability and divine presence. Rather than a rigid system of control, Robinson's vision of faith is marked by mystery, generosity, and the rhythms of grace. Her novels explore what it means to live within a scriptural imagination that does not demand certainty but instead invites patience, attentiveness, and love.

This chapter draws upon the theological themes of the primal narrative—creation, covenant, exile, redemption—to frame these two Gileads as competing hermeneutics of Scripture and community. Just as Barth and Brueggemann remind us that the Word of God is not a static text but a disruptive, unfolding story, these literary Gileads illustrate the stakes of biblical interpretation: one leads to exclusion and violence; the other to grace and human dignity.

Furthermore, this chapter engages with literary theology and imagination as essential tools for resisting the logic of fundamentalism and Christian nationalism. As *The Handmaid's Tale* and *The Testaments* expose, fundamentalist readings of Scripture collapse the biblical drama into rigid ideology, stripping it of its capacity to surprise, convict, and transform. In contrast, *Gilead*, *Home*, *Lila*, and *Jack* offer a different theological vision—one in which faith is not about control but about living into the unpredictable, redemptive movement of grace.

Alongside these literary and theological reflections, this chapter also considers the role of hermeneutics and the reader's responsibility. How we approach Scripture determines whether it functions as a weapon of exclusion or a source of renewal. What does it mean to read the Bible with an awareness of historical trauma, systemic exclusion, and the need for communal healing? How can the literary imagination expand our understanding of Scripture's redemptive possibilities rather than reducing it to ideology?

By examining these narratives together, this chapter challenges us to recognize that Scripture is not inherently liberating or oppressive—the act of interpretation, shaped by community and ethical responsibility, determines how it is wielded. It invites us to resist ideological distortions of the Word and instead embrace the open-ended, surprising rhythms of grace that call us beyond certainty and control into God's ever-unfolding redemptive purposes.

The Necessity of Hermeneutics: An Augustinian Account

James Cone's literary theology of the cross confronts the distortions of power, history, and interpretation that have allowed Christian theology to justify oppression rather than expose and resist it. By centering the crucified Christ, the lynched Jesus, and the voices of the oppressed, Cone reclaims theology as an act of truth-telling and liberation, insisting that the Word of God is a poetic happening that breaks open false ideologies and calls readers into new ways of being. However, reading Scripture must be transformed if theology is literary and revelation is narrative, poetic, and disruptive. A theological vision like Cone's necessitates a hermeneutic that resists fundamentalism, ideology, and the idolatrous reduction of Scripture to a static text. If revelation occurs within history, language, and suffering, then how one reads and interprets becomes a deeply theological act.

This is where Augustine's hermeneutic becomes vital. The dangers Cone identifies—the weaponization of Scripture in support of white supremacy, nationalism, and exclusionary politics—are deeply connected to how the Bible is read and misread. Fundamentalism, in particular, treats the Bible as a self-contained, literalistic authority divorced from history and the ethical demand of love. Augustine, however, offers a radically different approach. His semiotic and theological reading of Scripture in *De Doctrina Christiana* insists that the Bible is a sign (signum) that points beyond itself to the reality of God (res). This distinction is crucial: to read Scripture rightly is not to treat it as a rigid system of law but to approach it as a witness that must be interpreted through the lens of divine love (*caritas*).

If Cone's theology of the cross demands a hermeneutic that resists the ideological capture of Scripture, then Augustine provides a framework for doing so. By insisting that all interpretation must lead to greater love of God and neighbor, Augustine refuses to let Scripture become a tool for exclusion, nationalism, or moral legalism. His emphasis on figural reading ensures that texts that appear to justify violence or injustice must be reinterpreted in light of Christ's love. Just as Cone insists that Christian theology must reject any reading of the cross that supports oppression, Augustine demands that Scripture be read in a way that fosters justice, humility, and love. This Augustinian hermeneutic, informed by modern thinkers such as Hans-Georg Gadamer and Paul Ricoeur, provides the literary, theological, and ethical foundation to resist fundamentalism and Christian nationalism.

Thus, Cone's theology leads necessarily to Augustine's hermeneutic of *caritas*—a way of reading that prevents biblical interpretation from becoming an idol, a weapon, or a justification for power. If the Word of God is a poetic happening, then reading itself must be an ethical, spiritual, and transformative event—one that does not bind the text to rigid literalism but instead opens the reader to God's love, justice, and ongoing revelation.

Bible as Sign: A Late Modern, Augustinian Hermeneutic

Resisting fundamentalism and Christian nationalism presents significant challenges to a faithful and ethical application of Scripture. Both tendencies often reduce the Bible to a static, literalistic text that serves ideological or political purposes rather than inviting contemplation of the divine mystery and love for one's neighbor. An Augustinian hermeneutic, informed by the insights of Hans-Georg Gadamer, Paul Ricoeur, and Iris Murdoch, provides a robust framework for resisting these distortions. These late-modern figures help contextualize Augustine's approach. By emphasizing the transcendent nature of God, the ethical imperative of loving one's neighbor, and the transformative power of interpretation, this approach offers a compelling method to apply Scripture to ethical issues.

In *De Doctrina Christiana* (English: *On Christian Teaching*), Augustine develops a hermeneutical framework that distinguishes between things (*res*) and signs (*signa*). For Augustine, the Bible is a sign pointing beyond itself to the ultimate thing: God. He writes, "All teaching is teaching of either things or signs, but things are learned through signs."[2] The Bible, therefore, serves as a sign that leads the reader to contemplate the divine nature. Scripture's purpose is not merely intellectual; it aims to cultivate the love of God and neighbor, the twin commands that summarize

2. Augustine, *On Christian Teaching*, 8.

the ethical vision of the Christian life. Augustine's hermeneutic insists that Scripture is not an end but a means to the ultimate good, countering the fundamentalist error of treating the Bible as an object of veneration rather than a vehicle for divine truth.

For Augustine, charity (*caritas*) serves as the central rule of interpretation. He asserts that any reading of Scripture must lead to greater love. He writes, "Whoever, therefore, thinks that he understands the divine Scriptures, or any part of them, so that it does not build the double love of God and neighbor, does not understand it at all."[3] Here, Augustine establishes a criterion that resists distortions of Scripture used for exclusion, division, or power. Furthermore, Augustine proposes that both literal *and* figurative readings of Scripture can aid one's understanding of it. Literal readings, while important, do not always capture the fullness of divine truth. Figurative readings, however, invite contemplation of deeper spiritual realities. Augustine urges readers to seek the meaning that aligns with the love of God and neighbor. When the literal interpretation cannot, on its own, reveal the truth of neighbor love, then Augustine argues that the Lord intends a figural one. This insistence on humility before the transcendent nature of God guards against the idolatry of equating human interpretations with divine truth. By acknowledging the limits of human understanding, Augustine provides a hermeneutic that fosters reverence and openness rather than rigidity.

This humility in interpretation is not an end but is directed toward a greater purpose: the cultivation of love. For Augustine, the love of God and neighbor (*caritas*) is hermeneutics's goal and central guiding principle. He insists that any interpretation of Scripture must cultivate a deeper love for God and neighbor; if it fails, the interpretation is fundamentally flawed. These hermeneutics shape both the broader ethical and theological implications of biblical interpretation. As an interpretive criterion, *caritas* directs readers to evaluate their understanding of Scripture not primarily by intellectual rigor or doctrinal precision, but by how it fosters love and spiritual growth. Any interpretation that leads to pride, division, or harm falls short in Augustine's vision. Therefore, interpreters must approach Scripture with humility and charity, recognizing their limitations and engaging the text and others with generosity and openness. This approach deepens individual understanding and strengthens communal love, turning the interpretive process into a mutual act of edification.

3. Augustine, *On Christian Teaching*, 27.

Augustine's focus on *caritas* also informs his balance between literal and figurative readings of Scripture. While he acknowledges that some passages require figurative interpretation to reveal deeper theological truths, the rule of love ensures that such readings align with the ethical imperative to love God and neighbor. This balance prevents excessive allegorization while avoiding rigid literalism, allowing Scripture to retain its transformative power. Augustine's emphasis on *caritas* carries significant implications for resisting the misuse of Scripture. By prioritizing love over legalism or political agendas, his framework challenges interpretations that justify exclusion, oppression, or violence, such as those found in Christian nationalism or fundamentalism. It also reorients hermeneutics as a profoundly ethical practice, ensuring that the interpretive process transforms individuals into more virtuous and compassionate people while inspiring communities to pursue justice, mercy, and solidarity with the marginalized.

By anchoring hermeneutics in *caritas*, Augustine also underscores the unity of Scripture, where the command to love ties its diverse parts into a cohesive whole. Like the primal narrative, this thread brings our understanding to a practical and unified whole. Any interpretation that does not align with the crucified and resurrected abolitionist God, or fails to build up a love of this God and the neighbors for whom this God died, must be judged theologically deficient (Rom 14:15). Whether interpreting laws, parables, or prophetic texts, *caritas* reveals the interconnectedness of God's redemptive work and the overarching narrative of divine love. This holistic approach deepens theological reflection, ensuring that interpretations remain centered on the heart of the Christian faith. Moreover, *caritas* fosters openness to the infinite mystery of God, reminding readers that Scripture ultimately points beyond itself to divine transcendence. One must love God *beyond* the text, not the text as God. This orientation cultivates a sense of wonder and humility, as interpreters recognize that their understanding is always partial and contingent on God's grace. Augustine transforms the interpretive process into an act of worship and ethical engagement by making *caritas* the foundation of hermeneutics. This framework safeguards against the misuse of Scripture, enriches theological understanding, and fosters interpretations reflecting divine love's beauty, justice, and transformative power.

Figural or Literal: An Augustinian Division

A figural or allegorical reading of Scripture becomes necessary when the literal sense alone cannot fully illuminate the divine truth the text seeks to convey, particularly when it fails to cultivate *caritas*—the love of God and neighbor. Augustine's hermeneutic insists that Scripture's purpose is not merely to communicate historical facts or rigid laws but to shape the soul, guiding the reader toward divine love. This is especially crucial when confronting passages that, if taken literally, seem to endorse violence, exclusion, or an incomplete vision of God's justice. When a literal reading contradicts the overarching redemptive movement of Scripture, a figural reading becomes essential for discerning the deeper spiritual and ethical realities at work. Augustine argues that God, as the ultimate author of Scripture, intends for readers to seek meanings that align with divine love, even when they require moving beyond the surface of the text.

This is particularly evident in how figural interpretation functions within the primal narrative—the overarching scriptural drama of creation, fall, redemption, and consummation. Much like how the primal narrative unifies the biblical text into a coherent witness to divine love, figural reading allows disparate texts to be understood as about Christ, fulfilling Scripture's deepest meaning. Paul's reading of the Hebrew Scriptures, for instance, exemplifies this approach: he interprets Hagar and Sarah (Gal 4:21–31), the Exodus (1 Cor 10:1–4), and circumcision (Rom 2:28–29) through the lens of Christ, demonstrating that Scripture's significance unfolds in ways that surpass its immediate historical context. This interpretive move is not an arbitrary imposition but a theological necessity, ensuring that Scripture remains consistent with its ultimate goal—revealing God's redemptive love.

Furthermore, figural readings are essential in cases where a literalist approach risks reinforcing ideologies of oppression rather than fostering divine justice. For instance, rigid interpretations of biblical laws concerning slavery, gender roles, or divine violence have historically been used to justify systems of domination and exclusion. However, when read through a figural lens, these texts take on new meaning, which places them within the arc of God's liberating work. The abolitionist reading of Scripture, for example, sees the exodus as not merely an ancient historical event but as an ongoing revelation of God's commitment to the oppressed. Similarly, prophetic denunciations of injustice are not simply moral critiques of ancient societies but a figural call to every generation to embody God's justice in their own time.

Augustine's insistence on *caritas* as the guiding principle of interpretation ensures that figural readings do not devolve into arbitrary speculation but remain tethered to the ethical and theological heart of Scripture. Augustine's hermeneutic is particularly relevant when engaging problematic texts that, if read with a rigid literalism, could be used to justify violence, exclusion, or injustice. Augustine's approach challenges interpreters to ask: Does this reading lead to greater love of God and neighbor, or does it produce harm? If the latter, then a figural reading is not only permissible but necessary. In this way, figural interpretation serves as a safeguard against ideological distortions of Scripture, ensuring that biblical interpretation remains a means of grace rather than a tool for coercion.

Moreover, Augustine's vision of figural reading resists the fundamentalist temptation to venerate the text rather than the God to whom it points. He reminds us that Scripture is a sign (*signum*), not the ultimate thing (*res*); its purpose is to lead readers into the mystery of divine love. For Augustine, the Bible is not an object to be enjoyed (*frui*) but a sign that points beyond itself to God. He makes a crucial distinction between things to be used (*uti*) and things to be enjoyed (*frui*). Only God is to be enjoyed as the ultimate good, while everything else—including Scripture—functions as a means to that end. The Bible is not an end but a divinely given instrument for leading believers toward the love of God and neighbor. If one fixates on the text without recognizing its referential function, one risks idolatry—mistaking the sign for the reality it signifies.

This perspective safeguards against fundamentalism, which often treats Scripture as an end rather than a means, leading to a rigid, literalist approach that fails to account for its deeper theological meaning. By insisting that Scripture must be used properly rather than venerated, Augustine provides a hermeneutical framework that resists the dangers of bibliolatry—the worship of the Bible itself rather than the God to whom it points. A fundamentalist reading assumes that the text, in its literal sense, fully, statically contains divine truth. However, Augustine's semiotic approach emphasizes that the true meaning of Scripture is dynamic, unfolding as the reader is led deeper into love and communion with God.

Moreover, Augustine's emphasis on love as the guiding principle of biblical interpretation reinforces this protection against fundamentalism. If Scripture is a sign whose proper function is to direct us toward love, then any interpretation that leads to hatred, division, or injustice is a misreading. A literal reading can distort the text's purpose, whereas Augustine's approach demands that interpretation be governed by the aim of fostering love of God and neighbor. This allows for a richer, more spiritually fruitful engagement with Scripture—one that is flexible and responsive to the movement of the Spirit rather than bound by a rigid literalism. In this way, Augustine preserves the authority of Scripture and ensures that it remains a living sign, leading the faithful into deeper participation in God's truth rather than a dead letter subject to misuse. This distinction prevents the idolatry of rigid literalism, which risks treating Scripture as a static law code rather than a living witness to God's unfolding grace.

In sum, figural interpretation is not an optional method but a theological necessity when the literal sense of Scripture fails to reveal the love of God and neighbor. It allows Scripture to remain coherent, liberating, and ethically transformative, ensuring that biblical interpretation is not a weapon of exclusion but a means of divine grace. By anchoring interpretation in *caritas*, the crucified and resurrected Christ, and the primal narrative, Augustine offers an intellectually sound and spiritually vital hermeneutic, calling interpreters into deeper humility, justice, and love.

Origen and Allegorical Readings: An Augustinian Case Study

If Augustine's hermeneutic insists that *caritas* must guide all scriptural interpretation, then Origen's allegorical exegesis of Scripture provides a vital precedent for this vision, demonstrating how figural reading is not only permissible but necessary for discerning the gospel's deepest truths. While Augustine frames biblical interpretation as a moral and theological practice ordered toward love, Origen embodies this principle by showing how the Scriptures, particularly the Song of Songs, function as a living proclamation of the divine-human relationship. For Origen, figural reading is not merely an intellectual exercise; it is a way of encountering Christ in the text and being drawn more deeply into the mystery of divine love.

Origen's allegorical method emerges from a conviction that Scripture speaks in multiple registers, accommodating both the spiritually mature and those who require more elementary instruction. The literal sense of a passage may provide moral or historical insight. However, the deeper, spiritual meaning—the figural unfolding of Christ and the gospel—truly nourishes the soul. For Origen, any allegorical reading must be propelled by the gospel, namely the proclamation that Jesus is Lord. This emphasis on figural reading is particularly crucial for texts like the Song of Songs, where the immediate, literal sense does not fully disclose its theological significance. While on the surface the Song appears to be a poetic exchange between lovers, Origen—like Augustine after him—sees the unfolding mystery of divine love, where human desire and longing serve as images of God's pursuit of the soul.

Thus Origen understands Scripture's aesthetic quality and how beauty informs interpretation. For Origen, as theologian J. Louis Martyn writes, "the fundamental arrow in the link joining scripture and gospel points from the gospel story to the scripture and not from scripture to the gospel story."[4] As such, Origen articulates a very important feature of the early church's reading of Scripture. It is not merely that the Bible contains the Word of God or the Gospel as an object to be possessed by it, but rather the gospel gives the Bible and any interpretation of their life.

Origen believed that some interpretations of Scripture were unworthy of God because they took the texts literally or simplistically in ways that attributed human imperfections, irrationality, or morally objectionable characteristics to God. He argued that God, as perfectly good and wise, cannot be the subject of narratives depicting actions or emotions inconsistent with divine perfection. Therefore, Origen insisted that Scripture often contained deeper spiritual meanings beneath the literal or surface level. Proper interpretation, for Origen, required an allegorical or spiritual reading that elevates the meaning of Scripture to something consistent with God's perfect nature rather than diminishing God through overly literalistic or anthropomorphic readings. Origen puts it best when he writes,

> If the usefulness . . . and the beauty of the narrative were evident from the outset throughout, we would not have believed that any other meaning could be understood in the Scriptures besides the obvious, [so instead] the Word of God has arranged that certain *stumbling blocks,* as it were, *obstacles and impossibilities* be inserted into the midst of the Law and the narrative, in order that we may not be drawn away completely by the sheer attractiveness of the language and so we either completely reject

4. Martyn, *Theological Issues*, 216.

> the teaching, learning nothing worthy of God, or, not moving away from the letter, we learning nothing more divine.[5]

Origen's statement here emphasizes his conviction that the presence of difficult or problematic passages (e.g., stumbling blocks) in Scripture serves a deliberate pedagogical purpose designed by the Word of God. If the biblical narrative and laws were immediately clear, coherent, and appealing on a literal level alone, readers would be tempted to remain satisfied with superficial interpretations. Consequently, they would never venture into deeper spiritual readings that reflect God's true nature and character.

According to Origen, these stumbling blocks function as signals alerting readers that something beyond the literal meaning must be sought. Therefore, literal interpretations that ascribe irrationality, contradictions, moral imperfections, or impossibilities to God are deliberately placed in Scripture to encourage the interpreter to move past the literal sense. The obstacles prevent readers from dismissing the texts entirely (because the literal meaning seems unworthy of a divine origin) or accepting them at face value without further contemplation (thus missing their deeper spiritual truths). In other words, Origen suggests that God has intentionally arranged Scripture so that these textual difficulties compel readers toward a deeper, allegorical, and spiritual interpretation that is genuinely worthy of God. This interpretive strategy aligns closely with Origen's insistence that proper scriptural interpretation must always elevate the meaning of Scripture to reflect the perfection and transcendence of the divine nature.

A clear example of Origen's interpretive principle here and, thus, the need for allegorical interpretation comes from Gregory of Nyssa and the slaughter of the innocent in the Passover in Egypt. Gregory has this to say:

> It does not seem good to me to pass this interpretation by without further contemplation. How would a concept worthy of God be preserved in describing what happened if one looked only at the history? The Egyptians act unjustly, and in his place is punished his newborn child, who in his infancy cannot discern what is good and what is not. His life has no experience of evil, for infancy is not capable of passion. He does not know to distinguish between his right hand and his left . . . where is justice? Where is piety? Where is holiness? . . . Therefore, as we look for the true spiritual meaning, seeking to determine whether

5. Origen, *On First Principles*, 261. Emphasis original.

> the events took place typologically, we should be prepared to believe that the lawgiver has taught through the things said. The teaching is this: when through virtue one comes to grips with any evil, he must completely destroy the first beginnings of evil.[6]

Gregory of Nyssa offers an interpretation of the exodus Passover that perfectly illustrates Origen's broader point about scriptural interpretation. If one were to read the Passover narrative strictly at the literal, historical level, significant ethical and theological problems would arise. Specifically, the literal story depicts God punishing innocent Egyptian infants—children who were morally incapable of understanding, let alone committing, evil actions. Gregory explicitly highlights this ethical difficulty: "Where is justice? Where is piety? Where is holiness?" At face value, the narrative would portray God as unjust or cruel, something utterly incompatible with the divine nature. Gregory argues that precisely because such literal readings create these ethical and rational impossibilities—these "stumbling blocks"—they point readers beyond the literal to a deeper, spiritual meaning intended by God. Thus, Gregory interprets this troubling story typologically. The innocent Egyptian infants symbolize the "first beginnings of evil"—initial sinful impulses, inclinations, or harmful passions within the human soul. In other words, the story allegorically teaches the importance of rooting out even the smallest beginnings of sin before they mature into greater spiritual harm. This symbolic interpretation transforms what appears ethically problematic on the literal level into a powerful spiritual lesson emphasizing vigilance against sin. It underscores Gregory's central interpretive principle: that passages seemingly unworthy of God at a literal level must be read spiritually, morally, and symbolically to reflect divine perfection, holiness, and justice.

The theological readings of Origen, Gregory of Nyssa, and Augustine offer a profound vision of Scripture as an aesthetic and transformative encounter that refuses to be confined to literalism or simplistic moralism. Their shared insistence on figural interpretation is not a move away from the text's integrity but a deeper engagement with its true vocation: to disclose God's beauty, justice, and mystery. For these theologians, Scripture is not a flat moral code but a poetic and dramatic proclamation—what James Cone might call a "poetic happening"—that draws the soul toward divine love and eschatological union. In this sense, the biblical text does not merely transmit doctrine but evokes participation,

6. Gregory of Nyssa, *Life of Moses*, 56–57.

shaping the reader's desire and imagination through the rhythm and resonance of the Word of God.

This theological vision resonates with the primal narrative—the story that binds together the disparate voices of Scripture through the central drama of creation, fall, redemption, and consummation. Origen's interpretation of the Song of Songs—as divine speech in dramatic, erotic, and eschatological form—reveals the heart of the primal narrative as an invitation into intimate union with God. This is no abstract philosophy; it is a theo-drama, a movement of love so powerful it is "strong as death" (Song 8:6). Such imagery is not accidental—it is the deliberate poetic language of Scripture itself, where the Word of God speaks not only in propositions but in parables, poetry, and passion. The literary imagination here is not decorative but revelatory. It unveils the mystery of divine love that burns through judgment, redeems the broken, and reorients history.

In this way, aesthetics is not a marginal concern but central to biblical interpretation. The figural reading of difficult or seemingly opaque texts is necessary to preserve theological coherence and to encounter the beauty of God's redemptive economy. When Gregory of Nyssa interprets the slaughter of the Egyptian infants as an allegory for the defeat of spiritual evil rather than divine cruelty, he is not spiritualizing the text to make it more palatable—he is locating the beauty of God in the narrative arc of liberation, the same arc that begins with exodus and culminates in the resurrection. The Word of God is not static; it is dynamic, enfleshed, and spoken into history, yet always exceeding the bounds of any cultural or linguistic frame. As Barth, Jenson, and Cone insist, this Word must be heard anew in every generation—often from the underside of history.

The literary imagination, shaped by love and guided by the Spirit, becomes the interpretive bridge between the text and the reader's world. Origen's reading of the Song of Songs insists that poetic desire is theologically necessary—it allows Scripture to form not just knowledge but longing. This longing is the heartbeat of the primal narrative, the gravitational pull toward the God who raises the dead and frees the enslaved. Like the bride who proclaims herself "black and beautiful," the church is invited to hear the echoes of divine affirmation in the margins of Scripture. Moreover, like the poetic cadence of Black preaching and literature that Cone celebrates, this reading is both aesthetic and political: it reveals a divine economy that overturns human hierarchies and names the crucified as beloved.

Ultimately, the figural reading of Scripture—especially in texts like the Song of Songs—is not a retreat into abstraction but a recovery of

Scripture's power as proclamation. It insists that the Word of God is not exhausted by the witness to past revelation but speaks through it, calling forth a new world. This is the deep logic of the primal narrative: a drama of divine love that begins in liberation, finds its climax in the cross, and opens outward toward the eschatological horizon. The literary imagination does not distract from theological truth within this narrative—it delivers it. The Song of the bride and bridegroom is about human desire and the fire of divine love that reshapes the soul and the world. In this, the aesthetic, the imaginative, and the theological are one.

The Horizons of Love: Gadamer on Augustinian Hermeneutics

Though Augustine offers a rich and powerful account of hermeneutics, bringing his work into conversation with late-modern works on hermeneutics provides a nuance to Augustine by interpreting contemporary modern audiences. To begin, Hans-Georg Gadamer provides heralded hermeneutics, as articulated in *Truth and Method*, that complements Augustine by emphasizing the dialogical and historical nature of understanding. Gadamer's concept of the *fusion of horizons* highlights the interplay between the text's historical context and the interpreter's contemporary context.[7] The text is not isolated but interacts dynamically with the reader's presuppositions and historical location. By reclaiming prejudice (*Vorurteil*) as the necessary starting point for understanding, Gadamer critiques the Enlightenment tradition, whose prejudice was against prejudice itself.[8] However, prejudice is exactly the starting point for understanding. It challenges the notion that there is a single, ahistorical *correct* reading of ancient texts like Scripture, thus resisting fundamentalism's claims to possess the definitive interpretation. Interpretation, thus, is not about correct information; combining Augustine and Gadamer, the only correct interpretations are those that encourage the love of God and neighbor.

The ability to create space for multiple interpretations and interpreters encourages greater dialogue and openness in interpretation, which guards against the rigidity of Christian nationalism and its tendency to weaponize Scripture for political ends. Interpretation, for Gadamer, is

7. Gadamer, *Truth and Method*, 270–71.

8. Gadamer, *Truth and Method*, 270.

not about mastery but transformation, which fits well with Augustine's emphasis. The reader must allow the text to question and confront their assumptions. Gadamer would argue that understanding is not a matter of method at all. Rather, it is itself an event.[9] The event of understanding occurs as the reader's horizon merges with the text's horizon, leading to a new, *shared* perspective. Gadamer's insistence that understanding always involves *application* ensures that documents like Scripture remain a living world capable of addressing ethical issues in every generation. This dynamic approach allows Scripture to speak prophetically to contemporary concerns without being reduced to an ideological tool. At all times, the horizon fuses at the site where interpretation requires the greatest illustration of neighbor love and love of God.

De-Demonizing Love: Ricoeur on Augustinian Hermeneutics with Käsemann

Another late-modern figure who complements Augustine's approach is Paul Ricoeur, who bridges the gap between critique and faith, offering a balanced approach to interpretation. Ricouer offers a hermeneutics of suspicion that targets ideologies that distort Scripture, while his hermeneutics of retrieval seeks to recover its transformative meaning. Ricoeur engages with figures such as Marx, Freud, and Nietzsche to teach interpreters to unmask how power, ideology, or unconscious biases distort biblical interpretation. For Ricoeur, what we call hermeneutics is the exercise of suspicion, but this suspicion is balanced by a conviction *that meaning can be restored.*[10] He writes, "The problem of interpretation is not exhausted by the hermeneutics of suspicion. The function of symbols gives rise to another hermeneutics, a hermeneutics of restoration."[11] This approach is particularly vital for exposing how Christian nationalism uses Scripture to justify exclusion, violence, and domination.

Ricoeur's hermeneutics of suspicion finds an important companion in his hermeneutics of retrieval, which forms a key aspect of his broader interpretive philosophy. The balance between critical engagement and the recovery of meaning is important to the hermeneutics of retrieval. Building on his hermeneutics of suspicion, which seeks to unmask the

9. Gadamer, *Truth and Method*, 490, 499.

10. See Ricoeur, *Freud and Philosophy*, 27–32; Ricoeur, *Conflict of Interpretations*, 349.

11. Ricoeur, *Freud and Philosophy*, 28.

ideologies, biases, and distortions within texts, Ricoeur's hermeneutics of retrieval focuses on reclaiming the transformative potential and deeper truths embedded in those same texts. For Ricoeur, interpretation is not merely about exposing power dynamics or deconstructing meaning but also about restoring the capacity of a text to speak to readers in ways that inspire reflection, transformation, and ethical action. Interpretation is not the projection of the reader's subjectivity but the mediation of meaning through the dialectic of explanation and understanding.[12] This dual process reflects Ricoeur's conviction that suspicion and faith are complementary in the interpretive task: critique prevents naive or ideological readings, while retrieval ensures the interpreter does not lose sight of the constructive and redemptive possibilities within a text. In other words, the hermeneutics of suspicion clears the way for the primal narrative, while retrieval allows it to speak.

Central to Ricoeur's hermeneutics of retrieval is his concept of textual autonomy. Once written, a text becomes detached from its author's intent and original context, opening it to a surplus of meaning. He writes, "the text's career escapes the finite horizon of its author. What the text means now matters more than what the author meant."[13] Ricoeur does not, in a backward way, advocate for inerrancy or plenary inspiration. Rather, textual autonomy allows texts, especially sacred or narrative ones, to generate interpretations that resonate across historical and cultural boundaries. For Ricoeur, retrieval involves engaging this *surplus of meaning*, drawing out insights that speak to contemporary concerns without reducing the text to a singular or rigid interpretation from a specific point in time. Narrative plays a vital role in this process, as stories create imaginative worlds, inviting readers to new perspectives. Through metaphor and symbolism, texts offer possibilities for reconfiguring reality, fostering moral imagination, and inspiring action. Ricoeur's hermeneutics of retrieval thus bridges the gap between critique and hope, enabling interpreters to uncover deeper truths that remain relevant and transformative for modern audiences.

The implications of Ricoeur's hermeneutics of retrieval for biblical interpretation are profound. By treating Scripture as a living and dynamic text, Ricoeur's framework resists fundamentalist tendencies to fix meaning in rigid, literal terms, as well as overly skeptical approaches that dismiss its

12. Ricoeur, *Interpretation Theory*, 30.

13. Ricoeur, *Interpretation Theory*, 30.

theological value, denying this surplus. Instead, retrieval encourages a creative engagement with Scripture, where its metaphors and narratives are explored for their ability to shape identity, reimagine community, and foster justice. In this sense, Ricoeur's hermeneutics of retrieval complements Augustine's emphasis on the love of God and neighbor, as both approaches prioritize interpretation's transformative and ethical dimensions. Through retrieval, Scripture is freed to speak anew, continually offering its surplus of meaning to inspire individuals and communities toward deeper, mutual understanding of the biblical text and faithful action.

In addition to Augustine's hermeneutic of love, Ricoeur's concept of textual autonomy aligns with Augustine's view that the Bible is a sign pointing beyond itself. Once written, a text becomes autonomous and detached from the author's intent, opening up the surplus of meaning.[14] This autonomy resists any reduction of Scripture to a single, rigid interpretation and opens a plurality similar to that envisioned by Gadamer. Additionally, Ricoeur's exploration of metaphor and narrative highlights the creative process of meaning-making in Scripture. Metaphors, for Ricoeur, generate new ways of understanding the world, while narratives invite readers into a transformative engagement with the text. This creative and contemplative process directly counters fundamentalism's preference for propositional truths and literal readings.[15]

Metaphor-making, coupled with the surplus of meaning, allows for contemporary interpretations of the text that seek to express love toward the neighbor. Thus, one can deploy interpretations of Scripture toward contemporary ends and express love in ways not tied to specific elements of the author's worldview. This modern hermeneutic contemporizes Augustine's work to include a surplus of meaning open to literal and figural interpretations.

Before turning from Ricouer's surplus of meaning and hermeneutic of suspicion and retrieval, one must also wrestle with the apocalyptic dimension of his hermeneutic. How biblical authority operates in FCN is by granting absolute authority to one interpretation, namely the one that secures privilege for an in-group or a narrow set of beliefs. Ricoeur provides the language to open up interpretation in a broader way. Furthermore, his hermeneutics move against ideological capture of interpretation. One must place these rigid interpretations inside a larger language

14. Ricoeur, *Interpretation Theory*, 30.

15. Ricoeur, *Interpretation Theory*, 56–57.

of idolatry as they serve not as a connection to the transcendent Lord but to the worship of a people, party, and book. To this end, Ernst Käsemann profoundly develops not only a metaphor for contemporary hermeneutics but also a suspicion that extends beyond the text to the demonic ideologies that often haunt readings of the text. Käsemann connects the concept of fallen apocalyptic powers with the systemic evils of racism, colonialism, and global oppression, arguing that these are manifestations of cosmic forces that enslave the earth. Käsemann's theology views the world as a battlefield between God and the demonic forces of sin and death, with humanity and creation caught in the struggle. He emphasizes that apocalyptic theology must address these powers in their historical and social expressions, challenging the systems that perpetuate inequality, exploitation, and dehumanization.

Käsemann identifies the persistence of racism and white supremacy as modern embodiments of the demonic powers described in the New Testament. He critiques the complicity of the German evangelical church and Western theology in supporting systems of racial and economic oppression. For Käsemann, racism and colonialism are not merely moral failings but the outworking of cosmic forces that distort human relationships and structures. He writes that "the Christian life is never a private affair" and that discipleship requires confronting these powers wherever they manifest.[16]

Käsemann's demythologizing project extends to the global realities of colonialism and neocolonialism, which he describes as a continuation of imperialism under the guise of a free market economy. He states, "The first commandment is also directed against the dance around the golden calf in the capitalistic economy, against its defense through an armament that scorns God and the earth."[17] This system, he argues, creates a global divide where a minority accumulates wealth at the expense of the majority, relegating vast populations to poverty and despair.[18]

Käsemann's experiences with the Confessing Church's resistance to Nazism and his later engagement with global liberation movements deeply shaped his understanding of the powers. Käsemann's theology of resistance emphasizes that true discipleship demands opposition to these idols and solidarity with the oppressed. He highlights the importance of

16. Käsemann, *On Being a Disciple*, 131.

17. Käsemann, *On Being a Disciple*, 192.

18. Käsemann, *On Being a Disciple*, 201.

liberation as central to the gospel, stating that the first commandment's call for freedom is concretized in the struggle against systemic injustice.[19]

Käsemann's encounter with liberation theology and participation in the ecumenical movement further deepened his critique of Western Christianity. He identified the global liberation movements of the Third World as contemporary expressions of the apocalyptic struggle against demonic powers. Käsemann argued that the church must align itself with these movements, recognizing the presence of Christ among the crucified peoples of the earth. He warned that Western theology often reinforces oppressive systems by failing to address their structural and spiritual dimensions.

In connecting fallen apocalyptic powers with racism, colonialism, and global oppression, Käsemann challenges Christians to see these systems as manifestations of the powers Christ has defeated. As such, an apocalyptic theology calls for active resistance and solidarity with the oppressed, insisting that the gospel demands material liberation, not accommodation to the status quo. He bravely calls out contemporary idols disguised in modern progress (economy, colonialism, and political power). These must not only be demythologized, but must be de-demonized. He writes, "demythologizing, evangelically conceived and rooted, denotes ridding humanity and the earth of the demonic."[20] These are the demons classically understood and the ones that hide in plain sight. This approach integrates biblical exegesis, political critique, and a profound commitment to justice, making Käsemann's theology a powerful framework for addressing contemporary inequality and systemic sin.

PART II. THE FIRST GILEAD: THE REPUBLIC OF GILEAD

Margaret Atwood's *The Handmaid's Tale* and its sequel, *The Testaments*, provide profound explorations of power, oppression, and resistance within the dystopian theocracy of the Republic of Gilead. Atwood's depiction of Gilead offers a cautionary lens for examining how Scripture and ideology can be weaponized to enforce hierarchy, deny personhood, and perpetuate systemic oppression. Yet, within the oppressive structures

19. Käsemann, *On Being a Disciple*, 192.

20. Käsemann, *On Being a Disciple*, 200.

of Gilead, seeds of resistance emerge, particularly through the voices of women who navigate the ambiguities of complicity and defiance.

This section engages with Atwood's portrayal of Gilead to reflect on the dangers of distorting the primal narrative—God's redemptive story of resurrection and liberation—into a tool of power, exclusion, and coercion. Offred, Aunt Lydia, Agnes, and Daisy's stories provide rich narratives illuminating the primal narrative's power to inspire resistance and reimagine community, even in the most dehumanizing contexts. By weaving together biblical themes, personal testimony, and historical memory, Atwood's works challenge readers to confront the fragility of human rights and the enduring possibility of grace and liberation.

The Handmaid's Tale

The Handmaid's Tale is a dystopian novel set within a near-future version of the United States, now transformed into the totalitarian theocracy of Gilead. In this society, a fundamentalist religious regime has overthrown the US government, establishing a rigidly controlled social structure based on extreme patriarchal values and biblical interpretations. Due to widespread environmental pollution and a resulting fertility crisis, the state places a heavy emphasis on controlling women's bodies and their reproductive roles. The story follows the life of a woman named Offred, one of the "Handmaids" forced into reproductive servitude by the Gileadean regime.

The narrative unfolds through Offred's first-person account, interspersed with flashbacks that reveal her life before Gilead. Before the regime's rise to power, she was a woman with a family, a job, and personal freedoms. She was married to a man named Luke, with whom she had a daughter. However, in the wake of a violent coup, the new government strips women of all rights, freezes their bank accounts, and forces them into designated roles, stripping them of their individuality and autonomy. Offred is separated from her family, and Luke and her daughter's fates remain unknown throughout the story.

In Gilead, women are divided into rigid classes, each identified by distinct uniforms and roles. The primary roles for women include Wives, the esteemed but childless wives of the Commanders; Marthas, domestic servants who handle cooking and cleaning; Aunts, women responsible for indoctrinating and controlling other women; and Handmaids, who are fertile women assigned to Commanders' households to bear children on behalf of the Wives. Handmaids like Offred are dressed in red and subjected to a life of strict surveillance, submission, and ritualized sexual servitude under the pretense of "biblical" tradition.[21]

As a Handmaid, Offred lives in the household of a high-ranking Commander and his Wife, Serena Joy.[22] Each month, during a ritual called the "Ceremony," Offred is forced to engage in sexual intercourse with the Commander. At the same time, Serena Joy is present, all under the guise of fulfilling her biblical duty to produce a child.[23] The Ceremony is emotionally traumatic for Offred, and she copes by suppressing her emotions, retreating into her thoughts, and holding onto memories of her past.

Throughout her life in Gilead, Offred encounters both sympathizers and enforcers of the regime's theocratic rules. The Aunts, led by Aunt Lydia, are women who reinforce Gilead's Christian nationalist ideology, teaching Handmaids that bearing children is their sole biblical purpose. Aunt Lydia emphasizes "biblical" obedience, modesty, and submission, using fear and punishment to maintain control. However, Offred also meets other women who quietly resist. Ofglen, another Handmaid, is secretly involved in an underground resistance movement called Mayday, which works to undermine the Gileadean regime and smuggle women out of the country. Although Offred is initially reluctant to join, her interactions with Ofglen and others awaken a cautious hope for escape and resistance.

After Offred becomes more deeply involved in a relationship with a guard named Nick and begins having secret meetings with the Commander—ostensibly to play Scrabble and read forbidden texts—she grows increasingly anxious about her precarious position. Offred's desire to survive and find some semblance of freedom clashes with her fear of punishment. The tension culminates when Serena Joy discovers Offred's secret outings with the Commander, putting Offred's life in immediate danger. Just as it seems she may face severe punishment, a black van with the emblem of the Eyes (Gilead's secret police) arrives to take her away.[24]

The novel's ambiguous ending leaves Offred's fate uncertain. As she is escorted into the van, Nick whispers that the people taking her are

21. Atwood, *Handmaid's Tale*, 16.

22. Atwood, *Handmaid's Tale*, 93–95.

23. Atwood, *Handmaid's Tale*, 88.

24. Atwood, *Handmaid's Tale*, 294–95.

part of Mayday and that she may be escaping to freedom rather than imprisonment. However, Offred is unsure whether she can trust Nick or whether he is simply leading her to her doom. Her final thoughts convey hope and despair as she contemplates the uncertainty of her future: "And so I step up, into the darkness within; or else the light."[25]

The Testaments

Atwood's *The Testaments* is the sequel to *The Handmaid's Tale*, set approximately fifteen years after the first novel's events. While *The Handmaid's Tale* leaves readers in suspense about the fate of Gilead and the future of its protagonist, Offred, *The Testaments* provides new insights into the inner workings of Gilead and follows the journeys of three narrators: Aunt Lydia, Agnes Jemima, and Daisy (later known as Jade). Through these interconnected perspectives, *The Testaments* deepens the world introduced in *The Handmaid's Tale*, offering a multi-voiced narrative that illuminates the inner workings and eventual unraveling of the oppressive theocratic regime of Gilead. Atwood explores themes of resistance, complicity, and the slow, often hidden, emergence of subversive hope within control systems.

In a very poignant part of the novel, Agnes and her friend Becka discuss what they learn in their study of Scripture. Aunts were among the few women in Gilead allowed to read. Becka began her training earlier than Agnes, and she retells when her superior, Aunt Estée, taught about the passage from Judges 19, recounts the horrific story of a Levite and his concubine, in which the woman is brutally raped and killed by a mob in the town of Gibeah, prompting the Levite to dismember her body and send the parts throughout Israel, igniting a national crisis and civil war. As Aunt Estée recounts, the concubine is brave because she "was sorry for having been disobedient, so she sacrificed herself rather than allowing her owner to be raped by the wicked Benjamites."[26] However, when Becka entered her reading time, she found this interpretation false. "The girl," as Becka found, "was simply shoved out the door and raped to death, then cut up like a cow by a man who'd treated her like a purchased animal when she'd been alive."[27] This experience led Becka to question the "truth-

25. Atwood, *Handmaid's Tale*, 295.

26. Atwood, *Testaments*, 303.

27. Atwood, *Testaments*, 303.

fulness of Gilead's theology" under the weight of these "contradictions."[28] Becka describes it well: "God isn't what they say . . . you could believe in Gilead or you could believe in God, but not both."[29] Agnes responds that she "wasn't sure she could choose."[30] This conversation highlights the profound fissures in the foundation of FCN. With no formal training or help, Becka reads these texts and sees their profound critique of Gilead. Becka's reading is a lived, embodied critique of the foundations of Christian nationalism. Her literal reading unmasks the gap between the ideological nature of Christian nationalism in Gilead. Much like Offred, Becka shows a different way and interpretation of the Christian faith.

Excurses: The Handmaid's Tale Television Series

One of the unique contributions of the TV adaptation of *The Handmaid's Tale* is its deeper exploration of Gilead's religious hypocrisy, particularly through dialogue between characters like Offred and Ofglen.[31] While Margaret Atwood's novel presents the theocratic regime's brutality through Offred's internal reflections, the series expands these moments by allowing characters to openly discuss Gilead's contradictions. A striking example is the conversation between Offred and Ofglen as they walk past an area known only as the Wall, where the bodies of executed traitors hang as a warning. Among them is a priest, a victim of Gilead's religious purges. In the novel, this moment is a quiet but chilling observation. At the same time, the series enhances its impact through Ofglen's commentary, making clear that even religious figures who do not conform to the regime's ideology are marked for death. This exchange underscores Gilead's fundamental paradox: although it claims to be a Christian society, it destroys those who represent alternative expressions of faith.

The show further emphasizes this tension in a pivotal scene where Ofglen and Offred witness the destruction of a historic cathedral. In the book, Gilead's erasure of history is a background detail. However, in the series, it becomes a focal point of dialogue, reinforcing the regime's effort to rewrite the past and eliminate religious diversity, even other Christian religions that do not fit the narrow interpretation of the state. Ofglen's

28. Atwood, *The Testaments*, 303.
29. Atwood, *The Testaments*, 304.
30. Atwood, *The Testaments*, 304.
31. *Handmaid's Tale* TV series, created by Bruce Miller.

reaction—filled with quiet horror and resistance—contrasts with Offred's conditioned silence, illustrating how Gilead's citizens navigate their awareness of oppression in different ways. Through these expanded conversations, the show highlights how Gilead's religious rhetoric is hollow, using faith as a tool for control rather than a path to divine truth.

The Performance of Christian Nationalism and Fundamentalism: Scripture and Nation

A deeper analysis of the Republic of Gilead within the context of FCN reveals the complex ways these ideologies manipulate Scripture, merge with authoritarianism, and rely on propaganda to reinforce a theocratic vision of society. In Gilead, Scripture is reinterpreted, fragmented, and wielded as a tool of ideological control, creating a social order where fundamentalist doctrine governs every aspect of life. This fictional society embodies and intensifies many of the themes outlined in our earlier chapters, particularly regarding manipulating Scripture, using ideology and technique, and aligning with secular power structures to maintain dominance.

In Gilead, Scripture is not merely a sacred text but a carefully controlled instrument that justifies the social hierarchy and brutal enforcement of religious law. Gilead's fundamentalism hinges on an inerrant interpretation of Scripture, distorted to support patriarchal dominance and oppress marginalized groups, particularly women. The Bible's authority in its (assumed) literal meaning has absolute authority. Select verses are taken out of context to maintain control, while access to the full Bible is restricted, making it available only to male leaders like the Commanders. This selective use of Scripture reflects the "deep story" within Christian nationalism, where Scripture is the ultimate authority that legitimizes a specific social order and defines American identity. In the Republic of Gilead, this translates into a system where women are forcibly categorized—Handmaids for reproduction, Marthas for domestic labor, and Wives as the respectable spouses of Commanders—all based on distorted biblical mandates that reinforce male power.

Atwood's Gilead thus becomes a fictional extension of the fundamentalist approach that seeks not an authentic understanding of Scripture but rather an interpretation designed to justify preexisting hierarchies. The terror and brilliance of Atwood's story is that everything in her work is possible. Puritan Christian nationalism, with its fundamentalist vision, is a historical reality, and the Republic of Gilead is only an extension of that. The Handmaids, for example, are subjected to ritualized sexual exploitation framed as a biblically sanctioned ceremony, justified by twisted references to stories like that of Rachel and Leah. Since the text is the highest authority, it is justified and proper. Though this feels like a leap to most individuals, it nonetheless illustrates how fundamentalist interpretations of Scripture *can be used* toward these ends. We need only recall Shelia and Sessions from the Introduction to see just how a fundamentalist approach to the Bible and a nationalist ideology can lead to such distortions. When the absolute authority of the text mobilizes to fit nationalism, dangerous things occur. Such manipulation illustrates how Christian nationalist movements can weaponize religious texts to provide moral cover for actions and policies that would otherwise be ethically indefensible.

The Paradox of Secularity in the Republic of Gilead's Christian Nationalism

A striking aspect of the Republic's structure is its paradoxical secularity. While Gilead claims to be based on biblical principles, its mechanisms of influence—military enforcement, bureaucratic organization, and psychological manipulation—are secular. It is secular not in the sense of secular one or two, but in the sense of secular three. It attempts to rule contested space with little appeal to transcendence. Christian nationalism is secular in its immanent goals. Its methods create a system that outwardly claims divine authority but inwardly depends on immanent power structures to secure a space *for* God. Gilead, despite its religious rhetoric, operates more as a political machine than a genuinely spiritual community, its leaders leveraging both religion and secular power for control.

Atwood's portrayal highlights the potential for authoritarian systems to use religion as a veneer for oppression, masking a fundamentally secular pursuit of power. When the Bible becomes a technology used to gain this space, you see how easily the rhetoric works. In the television adaptation, one sees this in two distinct ways. First, we witness a construction group tearing down a cathedral in a scene featuring Offred and Ofglen (a fellow Handmaid). In addition, the pair pass a priest hanging from a wall with other traitors to the Republic. Other forms of the Christian faith that do not perpetuate Gilead are false because they lack the conclusions that make such support possible. The Republic of Gilead is secular in that priests and pastors of Christian churches become clear threats. Second, we see the sexual promiscuity of the Commanders. The Commanders' indulgence in forbidden activities, such as patronizing a secret brothel, shows that Gilead's elite view religion not as a moral framework that they must follow but as a convenient justification for their dominance. This reinforces the critique of Christian nationalism in the United States in its tolerance of wildly immoral figures. Thus, fundamentalism and Christian nationalism operate as secular ideologies, prioritizing political power as religious piety.

The Role of Accelerated Techniques in the Maintenance of Gilead

The technological and bureaucratic methods that Gilead employs to enforce its religious laws illustrate the technique central to fundamentalist and nationalist systems. Gilead maintains control through advanced surveillance, strict punishment for dissent, and systematic indoctrination. These techniques create a society where the demands of the state entirely subsume individual autonomy. The best interpretation of the Bible is the one that secures obedience. One sees this in misquoting Scripture in Gilead, such as "blessed are the silent."[32] The Bible is a technology that secures obedience, and the only interpretation to be considered is the one that performs this function. Thus, interpretation is the performance of a technique.

This reliance on technique reflects secularity, which sustains Christian nationalism. Atwood shows that Gilead's religious veneer is a tool of power rather than a genuine pursuit of piety. The Aunts' role in indoctrinating women into accepting their oppression, for instance, represents how technique—whether through propaganda, punishment, or isolation—becomes the primary means of sustaining a society built on ideological control.

Ultimately, Atwood's Gilead is an exaggerated, fictional embodiment of the ideologies outlined in the first two chapters, particularly the dangers of combining fundamentalist doctrine with nationalist fervor. Through selective Scripture, rigid social roles, and the paradoxical use of secular methods, Gilead becomes a cautionary tale about the dangers of

32. Atwood, *Handmaid's Tale*, 89.

religious fundamentalism in a nationalist guise. Scripture, manipulated to justify oppression, becomes Gilead's ideological backbone, while the regime's use of modern techniques reinforces its grip on power. This exploration of fundamentalism highlights the potential consequences of a society that subordinates individual freedoms to an authoritarian religious vision, demonstrating the complex interplay of faith, ideology, and power.

The Scapegoat Mechanism and the Primal Narrative

In *The Handmaid's Tale* and *The Testaments*, Margaret Atwood vividly illustrates René Girard's concept of the scapegoat mechanism through women's experiences under the oppressive rule of the Republic of Gilead. Girard's theory suggests that societies under strain or conflict often channel their tensions by selecting a scapegoat—typically a marginalized person or vulnerable group—onto whom they project blame and aggression. In Gilead, women serve as these scapegoats, absorbing societal anxieties, embodying blamed desires, and ultimately bearing the violence of a regime that seeks to preserve order through their subjugation and sacrifice.

In *The Handmaid's Tale*, the establishment of Gilead is a response to a fertility crisis and a society struggling with pollution, moral decay, and dwindling birth rates. Girardian theory would interpret this as a mimetic crisis—a social and existential tension that demands release. Gilead's leaders channel this anxiety by scapegoating women, especially fertile women, making them responsible for both the solution and perceived "corruption" of the crisis. To control and purify society, the regime places an intense focus on women's bodies, creating strict hierarchies and roles like Handmaids, Wives, Marthas, and Aunts. In the role of Handmaids, women are ritually exploited in a ceremony that echoes Girard's scapegoat mechanism. They are seen not as individuals but as vessels for procreation, reducing them to objects while society places on them the burden of restoring God's order. Like Girard's scapegoats, they are blamed and ritually "sacrificed" to resolve societal tensions, stripped of rights and autonomy to appease Gilead's ideological vision of purity and divine favor.

Offred, the protagonist of *The Handmaid's Tale*, endures this scapegoating firsthand. She represents both the dehumanized object of societal fears and the projection of society's collective guilt. The monthly ceremony she undergoes is depicted as a "biblically" sanctioned ritual. This process mirrors the violence inherent in Girard's scapegoat mechanism: she is forcibly sacrificed to stabilize the fragile power structure of Gilead. The myth constructed around her role—embodying the biblical mandate for fertility and submission—is a story that obscures the cruelty and manipulation of this system. The narratives surrounding the Handmaids sanctify the violence they endure, convincing the society of its necessity and suppressing the inherent injustice. These myths allow Gilead's leaders to rationalize their exploitation of women, presenting it as an act of divine obedience, much as Girard explains that societies obscure their violence behind the veneer of sacred narratives.

Yet, like the Gospels, Atwood's narrative shows the innocence of these victims and performs a truly transcendent reading of the Bible. No example exceeds the excellence of Offred's deployment of Scripture and rereading the entire system as incorrect. In her abuse, Offred articulates the primal narrative, and she reveals that she is innocent in contrast with her abusers, who possess all the right techniques and codes. We see this most clearly in Offred's version of Matthew 6:9–13 (i.e., the Lord's Prayer). This prayer is apophatic and gestures beyond the Republic of Gilead through negation toward the Living God. At the beginning of the prayer, Offred prays to God in heaven to know God's true name.[33] The God in whose name the Republic of Gilead carries out its business is not the God to whom Jesus teaches his disciples to pray. Offred negates Gilead's God in favor of the living God by insisting that "what's going on out there is [not] what You meant."[34] The prayer represents one seeking survival and meaning beyond the life given to her by the Republic of Gilead. This prayer is an atheistic ritual to the God of Gilead, and instead, it seeks the living God who sees Offred and the Handmaids. This performative gesture transforms Offred by giving her hope not in Gilead but in God. God is beyond, living, and inverts the order of meaning in the Republic of Gilead.

Transitioning Gileads

The theological and ideological concerns of Atwood's Republic of Gilead stand in stark contrast to those of Marilynne Robinson's Gilead, yet both

33. Atwood, *Handmaid's Tale*, 194.
34. Atwood, *Handmaid's Tale*, 194.

works engage deeply with questions of faith, suffering, and the moral shape of history. Atwood's Republic of Gilead presents a dystopian world where religious fundamentalism has been weaponized to justify systemic oppression, with Scripture twisted to serve the aims of power rather than truth. In contrast, Robinson's Gilead offers a vision of faith as a source of grace, memory, and reconciliation, centering on the quiet reflections of Reverend John Ames as he contemplates his life, legacy, and the mystery of divine providence. Where Atwood's Republic of Gilead warns against the dangers of theological distortion, Robinson's Gilead explores the redemptive potential of faith when rooted in humility and love.

Despite these differences, both works wrestle with the enduring question of how religious narratives shape human lives, whether as instruments of oppression or as sources of deep moral and spiritual insight. Atwood's dystopian Republic of Gilead demonstrates the dangers of rigid dogma, where theocratic rule erases individuality and justifies cruelty in the name of order. Robinson's Gilead, on the other hand, presents an intimate, deeply personal account of faith lived out in the complexities of everyday existence, where doubt and grace coexist. Moving from Atwood's stark critique to Robinson's luminous meditation, we transition from a world where faith is a mechanism of control to one where it becomes a source of contemplation, kindness, and human connection.

PART III. THE SECOND GILEAD: GILEAD, IOWA

The Gilead quadrilogy by Marilynne Robinson offers a profound exploration of grace, redemption, and human imperfection through its interwoven narratives and deeply theological reflections. Comprised of *Gilead*, *Home*, *Lila*, and *Jack*, the series centers on the small, fictional town of Gilead, Iowa, and the lives of its inhabitants, particularly its pastors and their families. These novels delve into themes of faith, forgiveness, and the search for meaning, creating a tapestry of human relationships that reflect personal struggles and divine grace. Through rich, introspective prose, Robinson crafts a world where characters confront their failures, grapple with existential questions, and find moments of redemption and connection in the face of suffering.

This section examines how Robinson's work engages theological and narrative themes, framing Gilead as a modern reflection of the primal narrative. The series presents a nuanced portrayal of a flawed yet grace-filled community by focusing on the complex lives of figures like Reverend John Ames, Lila Ames, and Jack Boughton. These narratives highlight the interplay of human frailty and divine action, emphasizing inclusion, transformation, and the eschatological hope that binds all creation. Through the lens of Robinson's work, we can explore how the Gilead novels embody a vision of faith and community that resonates with the primal narrative's call to disrupt, renew, and embrace the forgotten.

The first novel, *Gilead*, unfolds as a letter from Reverend John Ames to his young son, offering reflections on mortality, faith, and legacy. As Ames recounts his spiritual lineage—his grandfather a radical abolitionist and his father a pacifist—he grapples with his role in that tradition, particularly in his response to the return of Jack Boughton, the estranged son of his best friend. Ames's struggle to extend forgiveness to Jack forces him to confront the limits of his grace and deepens the novel's exploration of Christian love and reconciliation.

The second and third novels, *Home* and *Lila*, expand this world from new perspectives, layering the original narrative with emotional and theological nuance. *Home* follows Glory Boughton and her attempts to care for her aging father as Jack returns home, burdened by guilt and estrangement. Through Glory's eyes, Robinson tenderly unpacks familial disappointment, religious hope, and the enduring ache for belonging. Lila's story shifts to the marginalized woman who becomes Ames's wife, tracing her journey from abandonment and poverty to unexpected love and spiritual curiosity. Lila's mistrust of institutions and her halting embrace of faith offers a powerful counterpoint to Ames's inherited piety, making her story a meditation on the fragility and possibility of human connection.

Jack, the fourth novel, plunges deeper into the life of its most enigmatic character, tracing his existential struggle in postwar St. Louis and his forbidden love for Della Miles, a Black schoolteacher. Their interracial relationship, marked by tenderness and peril, defies the norms of both their religious upbringings and a racially segregated society. Through Jack's tormented introspection and Della's quiet strength, Robinson explores the redemptive possibilities of grace and love in a world of exclusion. Across the series, Robinson's prose—at once lyrical and theological—reveals a literary imagination shaped by a primal narrative of fall and redemption, where the Word of God animates ordinary lives and beauty emerges through the cracks of suffering and grace.

Analysis of the Gilead Quadrilogy

The Gilead quadrilogy is a deeply reflective exploration of faith, grace, and redemption, with each novel offering a distinct but interwoven narrative that builds on the others. The novels are infused with theological insights, particularly focusing on the concept of grace—a recurring theme in each character's journey. John Ames's gentle, reflective spirituality contrasts with Jack's existential struggles. At the same time, Lila's journey from alienation to acceptance and Glory's quiet strength offer other facets of the human response to suffering and the desire for connection.

Robinson's prose style, marked by its lyrical beauty and contemplative tone, underscores the series' themes, inviting readers to engage with the complexity of each character's inner life and moral struggles. The quadrilogy portrays Gilead not as a utopia but as a deeply human community where faith and doubt coexist and love and redemption are hard-won. Through these interconnected stories, Robinson creates a rich tapestry of characters whose lives are marked by flaws and failures and an enduring search for meaning, connection, and grace. Together, *Gilead*, *Home*, *Lila*, and *Jack* offer a profound meditation on the possibilities of redemption and the enduring impact of human kindness and forgiveness in a world often marked by suffering and loss.

Excursus: Beloved and Racism in Gilead, Iowa

Before turning away from *Gilead*, it is important to acknowledge a weakness in Marilynne Robinson's otherwise grace-filled depiction of the town—its unaddressed legacy of racism. While the tension of race exists within the narrative, particularly through Jack and Della's relationship and the ideological divide between Ames's grandfather and father, it remains at the margins rather than being fully confronted. Jack struggles against racism, but the novel focuses primarily on his personal battles rather than the broader social realities of racial injustice. To contrast and complement *Gilead*, I turn to Toni Morrison's *Beloved*, which amplifies Robinson's themes of grace, redemption, and community while addressing the historical trauma that *Gilead* largely overlooks.

As noted earlier, *Beloved* is a haunting examination of slavery's enduring psychological scars, following Sethe, an escaped enslaved woman grappling with guilt, grief, and a fractured sense of self. The ghostly presence of her deceased daughter, Beloved, symbolizes unresolved trauma, disrupting Sethe's attempts at healing and underscoring how the past refuses to be forgotten. Through a nonlinear, fragmented narrative, Morrison explores how slavery's wounds extend across generations, isolating individuals and shaping their identities. While *Gilead* and its companion novels focus on introspective spiritual struggles within a predominantly white, Midwestern setting, Morrison's novel insists on reckoning with historical trauma as an essential part of grace and redemption. The communal exorcism in *Beloved*—where Black women unite to free Sethe from Beloved's consuming power—offers a collective vision of healing rather than solely personal. This climactic moment disrupts the myth of individual salvation by showing that liberation from trauma, particularly the generational trauma of slavery, must be undertaken in community. The women's gathering is not only an act of spiritual resistance but also an embodied protest against the isolating effects of white supremacy and systemic violence. In coming together, they reclaim agency and dignity, challenging the dehumanization that slavery imposed on their bodies and spirits. Morrison thus reframes healing as a communal, liturgical act—one that draws upon the shared strength and memory of Black women to confront a history that white America has refused to acknowledge. Exorcism becomes an act of political and theological imagination, pushing back against the racism that seeks to erase Black suffering and love from the national narrative.[35] In contrast, *Gilead* remains largely private in its moral reckonings, leaving race an underdeveloped theme. Placing these two works in conversation, *Beloved* serves as a necessary counterpoint, demonstrating that any theological vision of grace and redemption in America must fully account for race, history, and the communal nature of healing.

Lila and the Figural Gospel

Though this Gilead shares a name with its larger, nationalistic brother, it nonetheless offers a compelling alternative account of Scripture and community exceeding the Republic of Gilead. It is not a utopia. Estrangement, racism, and vice all exist in its borders. In this town, one finds a variety of strange characters such as John Ames, the aging preacher writing letters to his infant son; Jack Boughton, the estranged son of a minister filled with questions and doubts; and Lila, a drifter living on the outskirts

35. Morrison, *Beloved*, 282–311.

of Gilead, but who finds her way to the center of the town's life. These characters and many others gather in their imperfections and provide a different Christian life. The emphasis on imperfection already signals a difference between the two Gileads. Robinson's small town lacks the crushing order of their nationalistic sibling and, thus, the technique of perfection of a republic. The town of Gilead, Iowa, showcases people who look *imperfectly* outside and beyond the community and are not fundamentally concerned with the perfect performance of an interpretation. The town aches with what only can be called a thirst for transcendent reality that will inform their lives. The Reverend John Ames, the narrator of the first novel, attempts to describe this indescribable reality when he states, "I mean a reality embracing this one but exceeding it."[36] The people of Gilead are haunted by the holiness that exceeds and embraces them, and this hidden character motivates a strange grace that brings them together.

No single person represents Gilead, Iowa, better than the character Lila. When Lila arrives in Gilead, she quickly lands on the radar of a town minister and main character of the first novel in the *Gilead* series, John Ames. Lila resists the charity and kindness of Ames and his community, instead preferring to find work for herself. However, the consistent care and concern by Ames and his church ultimately win Lila over to an uneasy relationship. She has a Bible and starts to write the books word for word. This way of engaging with the text maps the beginning of her engagement with the one beyond it. The pages of her Bible become a conduit to the transcendent that helps her make sense of the kindness she cannot explain and initiate her inner transformation.

After interacting with Ames and his local church, Lila meets a young boy squatting in the shack near her.[37] The boy, a runaway, claims he killed his father after a heated fight. The boy confesses to Lila that he has not slept due to the cold weather, so she offers the boy clothes, food, and shelter in town. This activity resembles the charity offered to Lila upon her arrival in Gilead, and the boy, like Lila, refuses. However, the grace of God is obvious in her because she wishes to do well by him.

Lila's longing to do right by this boy is tethered to the memory of Doll, the fierce and tender woman who once cradled her in a world of rootless wanderers. The rough hands of those who cared for her—outcasts,

36. Robinson, *Gilead*, 142.

37. Robinson, *Lila*, 145–55.

drifters, the disreputable, and the kind—shaped in her a quiet, instinctive charity, a way of reading Scripture with the mind and the heart. Through providence or something like it, Lila sees how God has stitched together the people of her past into a living tapestry that makes faith possible and luminous. As she lingers over the words of Scripture, she begins to see more clearly: the home Ames longs for her to enter, the heaven he so often preaches, is already peopled with those who have shaped her, their love and their burdens stretching beyond time into eternity itself. She thinks, "In that eternity of [Ames's], where everybody will be happy, how could he feel the lack of her, the loss of her? She had to think about that . . . It must be always be true that there are the stragglers, people somebody couldn't bear to be without, no matter what they'd been up to in this life."[38] The reality of eternity presses on Lila and her past community as she extends this desire for her to a wholly other cloud of witnesses. These characters made Lila who she is. These are the people who "no one [else] would miss . . .who just lived and died as well as they could manage."[39] Lila reads Scripture with an eschatological vision that refuses exclusion, drawing into its embrace those others might overlook. Her reading resonates with Augustine's hermeneutic, where love—rooted in God and neighbor—forms our identity and eternal belonging. For Lila, the love that shaped her in this life cannot be severed from the life to come; the faces and hands that taught her grace are inscribed into eternity itself. Scripture, like a lantern, reveals this enduring love. In that revelation, Lila finds the deepest meaning of God's goodness—a goodness inseparable from the love that binds us to one another, both now and forever.[40]

In *Gilead*, Marilynne Robinson crafts a world where grace lingers in the cracks of human frailty, where the past weaves itself into eternity. The town is a quiet witness to the primal story—a tale of exile and return, of covenant and belonging, where God's redemptive presence unfolds not in grand proclamations but in the hush of ordinary lives. Lila, a wanderer drawn into the slow rhythm of grace, reads Scripture with a heart shaped by the forgotten and the forsaken. She carries within her the memory of Doll's care, the kindness of outcasts, the rough tenderness of those the world would discard. In them, she finds the echoes of a love that is neither conditional nor neat but stubborn, enduring—a love that cannot be confined to this life alone. To Lila, eternity must hold them all, for love

38. Robinson, *Lila*, 258.

39. Robinson, *Lila*, 258.

40. Robinson, *Lila*, 258.

cannot forget its own. In this way, her reading of Scripture becomes an act of inclusion, a vision of a God whose goodness is measured not by exclusion but by embracing the stragglers of history.

John Ames, too, speaks of a reality that both holds this world and exceeds it, a grace that spills over the limits of human understanding. In the quiet cadence of his sermons and the longing of his prayers, he names a God who disrupts, remakes, remembers, and restores. This is the rhythm of the primal narrative, the story that pulses through the lives of Gilead's imperfect saints—through Ames, through Lila, through the flawed yet faithful community that carries both sin and redemption in its bones.

In *Gilead*, holiness is hidden in the ordinary, and salvation unfolds in the slow work of love. The town's vision of community stands in quiet defiance against the rigid, nationalistic order of its dystopian namesake. Here, grace is not transactional but abiding; not reserved for the worthy, but given to those who never expected it. This is the beauty of the primal story—that God's redemption is not for the perfect, but for the broken, the wandering, the ones who have long since lost their way.

To read the Gilead quadrilogy is to be drawn into a world where the gospel does not erase imperfection but transfigures it, where love does not forget but carries its beloved into eternity. The town becomes a parable, a witness to the truth that God's mercy is not bound by time, that grace makes space for the lost, and that even the smallest lives are gathered into the vastness of redemption.

PART IV. BETWEEN TWO GILEADS: THE AESTHETICS OF GOD VS. THE AESTHETICS OF NATIONALISM

The stark contrast between Margaret Atwood's dystopian Republic of Gilead and Marilynne Robinson's small-town Gilead, Iowa, reveals not merely two competing social orders but two fundamentally different ways of reading Scripture, community, and beauty. Both worlds wrestle with questions of moral order, constraint, and redemption. However, where Atwood's Gilead distorts Scripture into an instrument of technocratic control, Robinson's Gilead presents an alternative—a fragile but redemptive space where grace is lived rather than imposed. The beauty of Gilead, Iowa, is not incidental but disruptive, unsettling the rigid moral order of the Republic and offering a counter-witness to its perversion of divine revelation. To read the primal narrative through these two Gileads is to confront the dangers of ideology while recovering the redemptive potential of embodied, communal life in a fallen world.

In the Republic of Gilead, Scripture is severed from its relational and transformative nature, reduced to a weapon wielded in service of hierarchy and oppression. This echoes the critiques of fundamentalism, and Christian nationalism explored in our previous chapters—visions of faith that prize control over mystery and rigid perfection over dynamic grace. By contrast, Robinson's Gilead enacts the primal narrative in its rhythms of disruption and renewal, a story not of ideological purity but of lives knit together in humility, suffering, and love. Ames, Lila, and their community embody an Augustinian hermeneutic of love. Scripture is not a static legal code but a lived reality that draws human hearts into deeper communion with God and neighbor.

Reverend Ames's reflection on a reality embracing this one but exceeding it gestures toward the divine drama unfolding within and beyond human understanding—a drama in which Lila, the wanderer, becomes an unexpected participant. Her story mirrors the primal themes of exile and return, of being called into a community that precedes her yet makes space for her. The hospitality extended to Lila—hesitant, imperfect, but real—reflects the nature of the church as a narrative-shaped community. In this, Robinson's Gilead offers an Augustinian corrective to the Republic: true order is not imposed through coercion but discovered in the humble, shared life of those who seek God together.

Yet Robinson's vision, for all its depth, requires the corrective of Toni Morrison's *Beloved*, lest it remain inattentive to the racialized wounds and exclusions that have shaped American Christianity. Like James Cone, Morrison insists that the primal narrative must be read from below—from the perspective of the crucified and enslaved. Cone's Christ is not the distant arbiter of moral order but the lynched Son of God, whose resurrection turns the world upside down, reordering love and justice in its wake. As Jon Sobrino reminds us, this reordering demands more than passive sympathy; it calls for the active work of "taking the crucified down from their crosses."[41] In *Beloved*'s final act of communal exorcism, Morrison expands Robinson's vision of community, pressing readers to

41. Sobrino, *No Salvation Outside the Poor*, 8.

reckon with the weight of collective memory, the necessity of lament, and the unfinished work of redemption.

Between these two Gileads, and with Morrison's prophetic voice in the background, a fuller vision of the primal narrative emerges. Scripture, as both text and lived reality, must resist the temptations of ideological enclosure and perfectionist control. The Republic of Gilead warns against the idolatry of order divorced from love. At the same time, Gilead, Iowa, gestures toward the possibilities of grace lived in the tensions of an imperfect community. Morrison's *Beloved* ensures that this grace is neither cheap nor amnesiac—it must reckon with history, exclusion, and suffering that lingers.

To read the primal narrative toward Gilead, Iowa, is to embrace a vision of God's story that is expansive, inclusive, and deeply attuned to the wounds and wonders of human life. It is to adopt an Augustinian hermeneutic of love—one that resists the will to control, seeking instead the redemptive presence of the God who is always beyond yet always with us. Between these two Gileads, we are confronted with the challenge of living faithfully in a fractured world: to hold fast to the rhythms of grace that disrupt, restore, and continually draw us into the hope of God's redemptive purposes.

CONCLUSION

At the heart of this chapter lies the tension between two Gileads—Atwood's dystopian Republic and Robinson's small-town vision—each offering a radically different reading of Scripture and human community. The Republic of Gilead distorts Scripture into a rigid mechanism of authoritarian control, enforcing hierarchy and exclusion in a way that mirrors the dangers of Christian nationalism and fundamentalism. In contrast, Robinson's Gilead, Iowa, embodies a scriptural hermeneutic of grace, relationality, and imperfection, echoing an Augustinian approach that reads Scripture as a dynamic, redemptive story, drawing humanity deeper into the love of God and neighbor.

However, Robinson's vision alone is not sufficient. Morrison's *Beloved* compels us to reckon with history's wounds, reminding us that grace cannot be detached from justice nor redemption from the communal work of remembering and healing. The primal narrative—God's redemptive movement in history—demands not only hospitality and humility but also a confrontation with the systems of oppression that Scripture has too often been weaponized to sustain. To read Scripture rightly is to resist enclosure within ideology, to refuse the perfectionist impulse that suppresses human complexity, and to embrace instead the unfolding, disruptive rhythms of divine love.

This vision of Scripture as a living, redemptive narrative challenges the way Christian nationalists and fundamentalists often invoke texts like Romans 13 to justify obedience to oppressive structures. If Scripture is not a static legal code but a divine drama of liberation, how should we interpret passages used to sanctify power? A figural reading of Romans 13—attuned to the crucified and risen Christ—offers an alternative to authoritarian misuses of Scripture. Rather than enshrining submission to empire, Romans 13 must be read within the broader biblical arc of exodus, exile, and redemption, where divine authority is revealed not in coercive rule but in Christ's suffering, liberating love. The next chapter turns to this contested text, reexamining its role in the theological imagination and proposing a figural hermeneutic that reorients our understanding of power, justice, and Christian witness in the world.

5

A Balm in Gilead

Romans 13:1–7 and Christian Political Theology

"There is a balm in Gilead that makes her people whole."

Harry Thacker Burleigh

INTRODUCTION

The debate over Romans 13:1–7 has long occupied a central place in Christian theology, shaping how believers engage with political authority, justice, and divine sovereignty. From the early church's precarious existence under Roman rule to the theological disputes of the Reformation, and from the rise of totalitarian regimes in the twentieth century to the political maneuvers of American evangelicalism today, this passage has been invoked both to justify submission to governing powers and to legitimize resistance when those powers defy divine justice. The history of Romans 13's interpretation reveals the fluidity of its application and the theological stakes involved in how Scripture is read, lived, and weaponized.

Building upon the themes of the previous chapter, this final chapter contends that interpretations of Romans 13 have often been shaped by the same fundamentalist and nationalist impulses that distort Scripture into an instrument of control. With its rigid ideological use of Scripture, the Republic of Gilead illustrates the dangers of reading Romans 13 as an unconditional mandate for obedience—an approach frequently employed by Christian nationalists to sanctify political power. In contrast, a figural reading of Romans 13, rooted in an Augustinian hermeneutic of love, resists the reduction of Scripture to a mere political tool and instead situates it within the broader biblical drama of redemption.

A figural interpretation reorients Romans 13 within the cruciform logic of Christ's reign, where divine authority is not synonymous with the earthly empire. However, it is revealed in the crucified and risen Lord. Christ's reign is from this boundary, and the reading of Romans 13:1–7 will occur *there*. This reading challenges authoritarian distortions, calling Christians not to passive submission but to active participation in God's redemptive work—especially among the marginalized and oppressed. If, as Morrison's *Beloved* reminds us, true grace demands a reckoning with history, then reading Romans 13 rightly requires attending to how it has been used to justify oppression and how it might instead call the church to the liberating justice of God.

This chapter, therefore, undertakes both a historical and theological reassessment of Romans 13, tracing its use across key historical moments while offering a constructive alternative to its misuse by Christian nationalists and fundamentalists. By recovering a figural, Christ-centered reading of the text, this chapter seeks to reclaim Romans 13 as a passage not of uncritical allegiance but of discerning faithfulness—one that resists the idolization of power and instead calls the church to embody the love, justice, and mercy of God in the world.

ROMANS 13:1–7 IN HISTORICAL PERSPECTIVE

Romans 13:1–7 has been one of the most contested biblical passages in Christian thought, shaping debates on authority, obedience, and power limits. Paul's instruction to "be subject to the governing authorities" has been interpreted differently across centuries, reflecting shifting political, theological, and social contexts. From the early church's struggles under Roman persecution to medieval theories of dual authority and Reformation-era debates on resistance to modern discussions on civil disobedience, the passage has been invoked to justify both submission to rulers and the right to oppose tyranny. This study traces the evolving interpretation of Romans 13, examining how theologians, popes, canon lawyers, and political thinkers have understood its implications for the relationship between church and state. By exploring these historical developments, we gain deeper insight into the enduring tensions between divine sovereignty, human governance, and the moral obligations of Christians in political life.

The Early Church and Romans 13:1–7: Key Theologians' Perspectives

The early church's interpretation of Romans 13:1–7 reflected a careful balance between respecting civil authority as divinely instituted and maintaining ultimate allegiance to God. While Paul's depiction of rulers as "servants of God" established a framework for civic responsibility, early theologians consistently emphasized that such authority was conditional on justice. Clement of Rome, Justin Martyr, and Irenaeus affirmed civil order but warned against blind obedience, recognizing that rulers must align with divine law to remain legitimate. Tertullian and Origen clarified this tension, distinguishing between civic engagement and unwavering devotion to God. At the same time, Cyprian and Lactantius insisted that submission to rulers was valid only if they upheld justice and did not compel Christians to betray their faith.

This interpretation shaped the lived experience of early Christians, many of whom faced persecution for refusing to compromise their ultimate loyalty to Christ. While governing structures are a part of God's providential order, their legitimacy was never absolute. When rulers acted unjustly—oppressing the vulnerable, demanding idolatrous allegiance, or wielding power in ways that contradicted divine justice—early Christians maintained that such authorities forfeited their moral standing. Rather than placing their trust in earthly rulers, they anchored their hope in the eternal reign of Christ, which instilled a radical courage to resist injustice through nonviolent defiance, refusal to participate in state-sponsored idolatry, and a willingness to suffer for their faith.

Augustine: The High Mark of Christendom

As Christianity transitioned from a persecuted minority to an imperial religion, these early convictions took on new complexity. Augustine of

Hippo (354–430 CE) provided one of the most enduring interpretations of Romans 13:1–7, blending the early church's resistance to injustice with the realities of a Christian empire. He affirmed that earthly governments, though flawed, were part of God's providential order, necessary for restraining sin and maintaining peace. However, he insisted that civil authority is only legitimate if it aligns with divine justice. For Augustine, obedience to the government was a Christian duty. However, he upheld the biblical principle that when rulers enacted unjust laws, Christians must resist, as seen in the defiance of the Hebrew midwives (Exod 1) and the apostles (Acts 5:29).

Augustine saw peace and order as essential for the church's mission, describing the earthly city's stability as a "tranquility of order" that allowed Christians to worship freely. However, he remained clear that all earthly kingdoms are temporary, yielding to Christ's eternal reign. His reading of Romans 13 provided a theological framework that urged Christians to respect civil authority without equating it with the kingdom of God. This perspective continues to shape Christian engagement with political power today.

The High Middle Ages and Romans 13:1–7: Key Figures and Perspectives

Augustine's interpretation of Romans 13:1–7 laid the foundation for medieval debates on the relationship between church and state. His distinction between the City of God and the City of Man helped shape Christian thought on civil authority, affirming its divine purpose while insisting on its subordination to divine justice. As medieval society grew more complex, theologians such as John of Salisbury and Thomas Aquinas expanded on Augustine's insights, refining the role of governance, the limits of obedience, and the legitimacy of resistance.

In the High Middle Ages (eleventh–thirteenth centuries), the growing power struggle between the church and secular rulers led to renewed engagement with Romans 13. John of Salisbury (1115–1180) argued that rulers were servants of God, but their legitimacy depended on governing justly. Tyrannical rulers, he claimed, could be resisted or even overthrown. Thomas Aquinas (1225–1274) built upon this distinction, integrating Aristotelian natural law to assert that authority is just only when it serves the common good. For Aquinas, rulers who enacted unjust laws forfeited their moral legitimacy, and Christians were not bound to obey laws that contradicted divine or natural law. His synthesis provided one of the most enduring frameworks for balancing civic obedience with the moral imperative to resist injustice.

At the same time, papal authority expanded, developing the "two swords doctrine," which distinguished spiritual and temporal power. Popes such as Innocent III and Boniface VIII used Romans 13 to argue for the church's supremacy over secular rulers. At the same time, canon lawyers like Gratian provided legal frameworks for defining the limits of both church and state authority. These debates shaped the legal and theological tensions defining medieval Christendom as popes and monarchs vied for ultimate authority.

By the High Middle Ages, Romans 13:1–7 had evolved from a pragmatic call for submission in the early church to a sophisticated theological foundation for political legitimacy, justice, and resistance. Figures like John of Salisbury and Aquinas emphasized that rulers derived their power from God only insofar as they governed justly. At the same time, the rise of papal supremacy reinterpreted civil authority as subordinate to the church. These developments reflected the ongoing tension between theological ideals and political realities, shaping Christian engagement with governance for centuries.

The Reformation Period and Romans 13:1–7: Major Interpretations

The Reformation (sixteenth–seventeenth centuries) brought new urgency to the interpretation of Romans 13:1–7, as reformers wrestled with questions of religious reform, political authority, and the growing power of nation-states. Figures such as Martin Luther, John Calvin, and Ulrich Zwingli upheld the idea that God ordained civil rulers to maintain order and justice. However, they differed on the limits of obedience and the right to resist tyranny.

Luther affirmed submission to secular rulers as part of God's providence but insisted that obedience ended where rulers commanded what was contrary to God's law. Luther's two kingdoms' doctrine distinguished between spiritual and civil authority, allowing religious autonomy while maintaining social stability. Calvin built on this by stressing that rulers themselves were accountable to God, and he introduced the idea of lawful resistance through the doctrine of the lesser magistrates, which argued that lower officials could oppose tyrannical rulers. Zwingli, in contrast, saw the church and state as partners in upholding God's law and integrating civic and religious authority in his vision of a godly society.

The Radical Reformation took a different approach. Anabaptists, led by figures like Menno Simons, rejected state power and military involvement, interpreting Romans 13 as affirming civil authority while calling Christians separate from worldly politics. Their commitment to nonviolence and religious autonomy led to persecution from both Catholic and Protestant rulers. Meanwhile, English Puritans and Scottish Covenanters applied Calvin's resistance theory in their struggles against monarchy, using Romans 13 to justify rebellion against rulers who violated God's justice—ideas that later influenced the English Civil War.

By the late Reformation, Romans 13:1–7 had been interpreted across a spectrum ranging from absolute obedience to conditional resistance. Luther and Calvin emphasized submission to lawful authority, but Calvin's framework allowed for resistance when rulers became unjust. Zwingli fused church and state, while Anabaptists rejected state entanglement altogether. These interpretations reflected a fundamental tension in Christian political thought—how to reconcile obedience to civil authority with the demands of divine justice—a debate that continues to shape discussions on faith and governance today.

The Long Nineteenth Century and Romans 13:1–7: Interpretation and Application

The long nineteenth century (1789–1914 CE) saw dramatic shifts in the interpretation of Romans 13:1–7, as political revolutions, the rise of nationalism, industrialization, and colonial expansion reshaped Christian engagement with civil authority. This period saw competing readings of the passage, with traditionalists invoking it to defend monarchy and hierarchical authority. At the same time, liberals, abolitionists, and revolutionaries used it to justify democratic governance and resistance to injustice. The passage became a theological battleground, reflecting the deepening struggle between obedience to the state and moral resistance to oppression.

Traditionalists, particularly within Catholicism, upheld Romans 13 as a defense of monarchies and hierarchical rule. Popes Gregory XVI and Pius IX condemned liberalism and revolution, warning that disobedience to rulers led to social chaos and spiritual decline. Documents like the *Syllabus of Errors* (1864) reinforced a conservative interpretation, opposing secularism and emphasizing obedience to divinely ordained rulers. Conversely, liberal theologians and democratic reformers argued that true authority rested on the people's will, not a divine right, reframing Romans 13 as a call to uphold just governance rather than submission to oppressive regimes. Protestant leaders like Charles Finney in the US emphasized that rulers were accountable to divine justice, not merely institutional power.

Romans 13 also became a contested text in the fight against slavery. Pro-slavery advocates cited it to justify compliance with the law, arguing that Christians should not resist government policies upholding slavery. Abolitionists like Frederick Douglass and William Lloyd Garrison countered that Romans 13 must be read in light of God's higher moral law, which demands justice and freedom. This debate extended to other social justice movements, including women's suffrage, labor rights, and anti-colonial resistance, as reformers reinterpreted Paul's words to support civil disobedience against unjust laws.

Meanwhile, the rise of socialism and revolutionary movements in the late nineteenth century introduced radical interpretations of Romans 13. Figures like Leo Tolstoy rejected state authority, arguing that true Christian obedience meant resisting coercion and violence. Others, particularly Christian socialists, saw the passage as a call for systemic change rather than passive submission. These tensions reflected the broader struggle over whether Romans 13 upheld the status quo or legitimized resistance to unjust power.

Romans 13:1–7 in Twentieth-Century Europe and North America: A Contextual Overview

The twentieth century brought a crisis in the interpretation of Romans 13:1–7, particularly in the face of totalitarian regimes such as Nazi Germany. The passage became a battleground for theological and ethical reflection, as it was used to justify submission to oppressive rule and call for faithful resistance. The Nazi regime invoked Romans 13 to demand obedience, claiming that Hitler's government was divinely ordained and, therefore, not to be opposed. Many within the Deutsche Christen (German Christian) movement accepted this interpretation, aligning Christianity with the state's nationalist and racist ideology. However, the Confessing

Church, led by figures such as Karl Barth and Dietrich Bonhoeffer, resisted this reading, arguing that submission to governing authorities could never override allegiance to Christ and the demands of divine justice. Barth's Barmen Declaration (1934) rejected state control over the church, and Bonhoeffer ultimately participated in active resistance, demonstrating that the passage could not be used to sanction injustice.

The atrocities of World War II and the Holocaust forced a profound reassessment of Romans 13 in Christian theology. The complicity of some church leaders in Nazi rule highlighted the dangers of uncritical submission to civil authority, prompting theologians to explore the balance between obedience and moral resistance. The postwar period saw a renewed emphasis on the broader biblical narrative, particularly themes of justice, liberation, and the lordship of Christ, which reoriented interpretations of Romans 13 toward a theology of discernment rather than blind obedience. Figures such as Emil Brunner and Reinhold Niebuhr argued that Christian engagement with the state must be guided by ethical responsibility, resisting any authority contradicting God's moral law. This period cemented Romans 13 as a text requiring contextual interpretation, shaping discussions on civil rights, social justice, and the church's role in opposing unjust regimes.

In the twenty-first century, Romans 13 continues to shape political and religious discourse, particularly in American evangelicalism and Christian nationalism. The passage has been invoked to justify both submission to authority and resistance to perceived threats to religious and national identity. In the post-9/11 era, Romans 13 was cited to support government actions on national security, military intervention, and law-and-order policies. Figures associated with the Religious Right and the Moral Majority—such as Jerry Falwell Sr. and James Dobson—emphasized obedience to government if it aligned with conservative morality. However, as cultural shifts progressed, many evangelicals interpreted Romans 13 conditionally, arguing that resistance was justified if the government acted against Christian values. This was particularly evident in opposition to abortion rights, LGBTQ+ protections, and pluralistic democratic governance.

Romans 13 took on renewed significance during the Trump presidency in Christian nationalist circles. Many evangelicals framed Trump as a divinely appointed leader, citing Romans 13 to defend his legitimacy and policies, including controversial stances on immigration and religious liberty. In 2018, Attorney General Jeff Sessions explicitly cited Romans 13 to justify the administration's family separation policy at the US-Mexico border, a move that sparked widespread criticism from religious leaders across ideological lines. More recently, Christian nationalist movements have used Romans 13 to advocate for an America governed by biblical law, supporting initiatives that weaken the separation of church and state.

As Christian nationalism and progressive Christian activism continue to shape public discourse, Romans 13 remains a text of tension and transformation, challenging believers to wrestle with the demands of faith, justice, and political allegiance in an ever-changing world.

PART II. AN APOCALYPTIC PROLEGOMENA TO A FIGURAL READING OF ROMANS 13:1–7

The exploration of Romans 13:1–7 has been a focal point for theologians grappling with the relationship between divine sovereignty, human authority, and the presence of oppressive powers in the world. This section delves into the interpretations and critiques of prominent interpreters of Romans 13 for the sake of an apocalyptic interpretation. Each offers a unique perspective on how Christians should understand and respond to governing authorities, especially in contexts marked by injustice, oppression, and the manifestation of what Paul refers to as the powers or principalities.

For the figural reading I will develop, I will state and unpack several images that will set the stage for the figural interpretation of Romans 13:1–7. Following the lead of both Augustine and Origen, figural readings must proceed from the guiding logic of the gospel proclamation: Jesus is Lord. Yet this proclamation is not abstract or metaphysical—it is embedded in the historical drama of the primal narrative, which tells of the life, crucifixion, resurrection, and ascension of Jesus of Nazareth. The statement "Jesus is Lord" is unintelligible apart from this narrative of divine disruption, solidarity, and renewal.

Developing concrete, imaginative images to interpret Romans 13 figurally in light of that narrative becomes necessary. This need arises not only from the hermeneutical tradition of the church, as seen in Augustine's emphasis on *caritas* and Origen's poetic theology of desire, but also from the aesthetic and political urgency we find in James Cone's literary theology. Cone teaches us that Scripture must not be flattened into abstraction or ideology—it must be read through the cries of the oppressed, through the literary imagination that sees the lynching tree as the clearest image of the crucified Christ in America. Cone's use of poetry, story, and symbol challenges us to take seriously the aesthetic dimensions of theological meaning: beauty, horror, irony, and rupture.

Augustine, too, urges us to move beyond the surface of the text toward the deeper truth that cultivates a love of God and neighbor. For Cone and Augustine, interpretation is not the static act of decoding meaning—it is the spiritual and ethical performance of truth. Therefore, we must construct images that can bear the theological weight of figural reading—images that arise from the primal narrative and speak with poetic depth to our present political and ecclesial moment. These images are not decorative but necessary; they allow the figural meaning of Romans 13 to unfold in a way that resists ideological capture and draws us deeper into the drama of God's justice, mercy, and sovereignty. In performing my literary theology in the Spirit of Cone and Augustine, these images will act as imaginative scaffolding, inviting readers to interpret and to inhabit the gospel claim that Jesus, and not Caesar, is Lord. The images will follow as the Lordless Powers, Non-Power and Presence, and Jesus before Pilate. I will begin by reclaiming a lost element of Paul's context that sets his apocalyptic theology within the colonial context of the ancient world. The proclamation that Jesus is Lord comes under this condition. Only here do the images make sense, and does our understanding of Romans 13:1–7 occur.

Paul's Forgotten Context: Colonialism

Neil Elliott advocates re-examining Paul's writings, emphasizing their potential to critique rather than reinforce oppressive systems. Though he cites many advances in Pauline studies that lead him to this conclusion, his exploration of the apostle's context and apocalyptic approach grants him this insight. Elliot identifies two major influences that led him to his rejection of oppressive fortunes: first, Paul's Pharisaic past in his colonial context and, second, the converting reality of the cross.

As a Pharisee, Paul believed in his responsibility to preserve the Jewish people and their national identity. In this world, Pharisees practiced realism to preserve themselves from destruction.[1] Elliot notes that the Pharisees were on the side of law and order.[2] Furthermore, the Pharisees, much like later Puritan figures, understood governance through an

1. Elliott, *Liberating Paul*, 161.
2. Elliott, *Liberating Paul*, 161.

apocalyptic lens, interpreting political life as the outworking of heavenly forces.[3] The Pharisees could be patient and remain outside political resistance or the path of the zealots.

The apolitical posture of the apocalyptic theology at work in this understanding served the remnant of Israel now under Roman rule. As Elliot writes, "The belief that God has given absolute powers into the hands of the conqueror is particularly appealing to the survivors, who must explain to themselves why others have suffered and died around them."[4] Yet even still others, due to this apocalyptic perspective, believed that the powers of Rome and conquers acted against God's will and God's people. Paul must be understood in this way of thinking. Paul's conversion occurs in deep connection to the crucifixion. This event must live in its apocalyptic context at the turning of the ages. Elliot writes,

> Paul heard in the proclamation of the crucified Messiah an apocalyptic announcement *and a direct challenge to Rome.* If one crucified by Rome had been vindicated by God—vindicated *by being raised from the dead already*—then the "time given to Rome" was at an end, the "time of the kingdom of the Most High" was at hand. The proclamation of the crucified was a declaration that the changing of the ages was at hand.[5]

As Elliot continues, Paul would not immediately convert after hearing this message. Paul and all in Judea still witnessed the authority of Pilate and Caesar. Furthermore, Paul continued, even in light of this revelation, to protect the larger Jewish community from a small number of Christ-followers whose actions placed their Jewish siblings at risk.[6]

Paul need not be envisioned as a vindictive character who relished violence and death.[7] This realist approach unseats and supplants Paul's apocalyptic sensitivities. The turning of the ages must reflect this realism or be discarded. However, the vision of the resurrected Christ claims Paul and challenges his realism. When Christ speaks to Paul, "Why do you persecute me?" (Acts 9:4, NRSVue), Paul must confront a radical truth, namely, "that God had raised Jesus from the dead."[8] Furthermore,

3. Elliott, *Liberating Paul,* 163.
4. Elliott, *Liberating Paul,* 168.
5. Elliott, *Liberating Paul,* 170. Emphasis original.
6. Elliott, *Liberating Paul,* 170–171.
7. Elliott, *Liberating Paul,* 170.
8. Elliott, *Liberating Paul,* 171.

through this vision, Paul must confront his participation in what Elliot terms sacred violence.[9] In short, the vision of the resurrected Christ revealed (*apocalypse*) to Paul his crucifixion of Christ, who was sacrificed to Roman violence as a means to save others *from* Roman violence.[10] The crucifixion alone did not warrant this change in Paul, but the resurrection of the crucified Lord did. Thus, Paul began the proclamation of a different power at work. If Christ is indeed raised, then "the Law of life, had invaded the realm of Death with an unconquerable power."[11] The powers and principalities, as such, are on notice that their schemes in this world are indeed passing away.[12]

This transformation in Paul shifts the realism in Paul's thought. To be sure, the revelation of the crucified and resurrected Lord was and is profoundly unrealistic according to the metric of the balance of powers through terror and violence.[13] Paul still believed in the mission of Israel, which was to achieve God's righteousness in the world. However, he changed his methods from a realism that balanced and relied on these powers. Instead, Paul worked among the gentiles to proclaim Israel's Messiah and open Israel's story and promise to them. This message that proclaimed a new power in the world extends well past Paul's life and into the present in all those who work against the powers. As Elliot concludes, Paul's

> "conversion" changed not his goal but the strategy that he would now adopt to reach the goal; the apocalypse of the crucified Messiah convinced Paul that God did not work through the balance of terror through which successive empires enacted their will . . . By the grace of God, men and women nevertheless continue to live out the power of the resurrection even within the realm of Death, decked out in the splendor of the current world power and to defy the thunderous threats of Death, trusting themselves to a God who gives life to the dead. Those men and women are Paul's true legacy today.[14]

Paul then accepts a new realism that appears unrealistic to the realism of the balance of powers and terror. Instead, Paul shifts his realism to account for a different kingdom, and his actions reflect that shift.

9. Elliott, *Liberating Paul*, 172.
10. Elliott, *Liberating Paul*, 172.
11. Elliott, *Liberating Paul*, 172.
12. Elliott, *Liberating Paul*, 173.
13. Elliott, *Liberating Paul*, 180.
14. Elliott, *Liberating Paul*, 179–80.

There is no greater example of this shift than the new communities organized under Paul's proclamation of the apocalypse. Elliott emphasizes that Paul's assemblies (*ekklesia*) intended to embody the countercultural body of Christ, rejecting imperial distinctions like those between enslaved people and free citizens.[15] According to Elliott, Paul's theology of mutuality and solidarity with the weak stands in stark contrast to the hierarchical structures of the Roman Empire and contemporary deployments of this passage in service of empire.

Elliott's insightful reading of Paul aligns remarkably with Gadamer's hermeneutical position, whereby interpretive engagement with historical texts brings about new, transformative insights. Gadamer emphasizes that understanding arises from the dialogue between the text's horizon and the interpreter's contemporary context. Elliott's examination of Paul similarly engages with both the apostle's Pharisaic and colonial past and the transforming reality of the cross, bringing forth a renewed understanding that critiques oppressive systems rather than reinforcing them.

In Elliott's approach, Paul's Pharisaic realism initially prioritizes survival and national preservation under oppressive powers, reflecting the historical horizon of Jewish life under Roman rule. However, Paul's encounter with the resurrected Christ represents a radical shift—a fusion of horizons between his inherited realism and the revelatory, apocalyptic reality of Christ's resurrection. This encounter dismantles Paul's former adherence to a realism sustained by imperial terror, replacing it with a revolutionary realism grounded in divine power overcoming death.

A powerful interpretation is made possible when one utilizes contemporary hermeneutics to bring his work into the present. Gadamer's fusion of horizons elucidates how Elliott's reading transcends traditional interpretations, allowing contemporary readers to see Paul not as reinforcing hierarchical oppression but as prophetically resisting it through communities embodying solidarity and mutuality. Thus, Elliott's interpretation exemplifies Gadamer's theory: the dialogue between Paul's historical context and our contemporary horizon reveals a liberating and countercultural vision, inviting readers to participate anew in Paul's legacy of confronting oppressive structures with the transformative power of the resurrection.

In conclusion, Elliott calls for the church to embrace Paul's radical legacy by aligning itself with the poor and oppressed, challenging

15. Elliott, "Liberating Paul," 4.

imperial ideologies, and embodying the body of Christ in the world. He asserts that when read through the lens of liberation, Paul's writings offer profound resources for resisting injustice and envisioning a more just and equitable world. The interpretive shift articulated by Elliott, wherein Paul's letters become resources for resisting injustice, sets the stage for exploring how theology engages deeply with the complexities of power, judgment, and redemption. While Elliott emphasizes Pauline theology's practical, liberation-oriented implications, Karl Barth's theological framework provides an essential complementary lens, highlighting the ultimate divine judgment enacted in Jesus Christ, which judges and relativizes all earthly powers.

Image #1: The Lordless Powers and Romans 13:1–7

Interpreting Romans 13:1–7 through allegorical lenses provides a powerful method for exploring complex theological dynamics between divine sovereignty and earthly authority. By drawing upon vivid imagery from the Gospels, we can illuminate Paul's nuanced message and deepen our understanding of how human authority functions under divine rule. Karl Barth's treatment of this passage invites precisely this kind of imaginative exploration as he navigates the tension between the origin of authority in God's providence and its frequent moral ambiguity in human hands. This approach allows us to probe the subtleties of Barth's dialectical theology, particularly his insistence that while all power originates from God, human institutions remain subject to judgment and critique. Thus, by intertwining Gospel imagery with Barth's interpretation, we gain fresh perspectives on Romans 13, uncovering deeper truths about the lordless powers operating in our world.

Barth's interpretation of Romans 13:1–7 is a nuanced and dialectical exploration of the relationship between divine sovereignty and human authority. He begins by affirming the fundamental theological principle that all powers and authorities derive their existence from God. He writes, "Every power is from God. There is no authority except from God."[16] This statement grounds Barth's interpretation in recognition of divine providence, emphasizing that human governance is not autonomous but subject to God's ultimate will. However, Barth immediately complicates this affirmation by distinguishing between divine ordination and divine

16. Barth, *Epistle to the Romans*, 482.

endorsement. While God establishes authority, it is not inherently righteous or judgment-free.

Barth critiques any simplistic or uncritical allegiance to human authority. He warns against conflating obedience to the state with obedience to God, stating that "authority is not the bearer of its own legitimacy."[17] For Barth, human rulers and institutions operate under the mysterious purposes of God's governance, but they remain fallible and subject to divine scrutiny. This theological framework resists the temptation to sanctify political power or view it as an extension of divine will without qualification. Barth is clear that human authority exists within the tension of God's judgment and grace, and its legitimacy must always be evaluated in light of God's justice.

Barth's interpretation also addresses the ethical implications of the believer's relationship to authority. He acknowledges Paul's call to "be subject to governing authorities" (Rom 13:1) but emphasizes that this subjection is not equivalent to passive compliance. Barth writes, "Resistance to authority becomes resistance to God's ordinance only insofar as it contradicts God's justice."[18] This statement introduces a critical element of discernment: Christians are called to obey governing authorities only to the extent that such obedience aligns with God's commands. Barth underscores that the believer's ultimate allegiance is to God, not to the state. When human authority deviates from divine justice, resistance may become a necessary expression of faithfulness to God.

Moreover, Barth resists ideological distortions of the passage, critiquing both conservative and revolutionary interpretations. He rejects the conservative tendency to justify absolute submission to authority, noting that such a stance can lead to complicity in injustice. At the same time, he critiques revolutionary attitudes that glorify rebellion as inherently virtuous. He states, "The Christian is neither to glorify the state nor to idolize revolution but to remain steadfast in allegiance to God, who alone is righteous."[19] Barth insists that both attitudes fail to grasp the theological complexity of Romans 13:1–7, which situates human authority within the context of divine sovereignty and judgment.

Barth's treatment of Romans 13:1–7 also highlights the provisional nature of human governance. He views all political systems and rulers as temporary and subordinate to God's eschatological purposes. This

17. Barth, *Epistle to the Romans*, 483.

18. Barth, *Epistle to the Romans*, 484.

19. Barth, *Epistle to the Romans*, 484.

eschatological dimension reframes the believer's engagement with authority, reminding Christians that human governments are not ultimate. Barth writes, "The state has no future. It exists only in the shadow of the coming Kingdom of God."[20] This perspective challenges believers to consider their loyalty to earthly powers lightly and focus instead on their participation in God's redemptive work.

Barth's interpretation of Romans 13:1–7 offers a profound and nuanced theological framework for understanding the relationship between divine sovereignty and human authority. Barth calls Christians to a posture of theological humility and ethical discernment by affirming the God-ordained nature of authority while critically engaging its limitations. His emphasis on the provisional and contingent nature of human power and his insistence on ultimate allegiance to God provide a robust framework for navigating the complexities of political engagement.

Though Barth's *Römerbrief* deals directly with Romans 13:1–7, he nonetheless takes up the concept of the lordless powers, which resonates deeply with his exegesis of Romans. Barth provides a theological and nuanced framework for understanding forces within creation that rebel against God's sovereignty. Though created and originally ordered under God, these powers have rejected their rightful place within divine lordship and seek to assert their autonomy. They manifest in various domains of life—social, political, economic, cultural, and even religious—subverting God's intentions for creation and exploiting human vulnerabilities.

Barth begins by affirming that the powers are part of God's good creation, endowed with specific purposes within the divine order. However, through their rebellion, these powers distort their roles and strive to function as ultimate authorities, seeking to rival God's sovereignty. They are lordless not because they are truly independent but because they reject the authority of Christ and attempt to establish themselves as self-sufficient. As Barth states, "Their rebellion does not remove them from God's control, but it constitutes a disorder that disrupts the harmony of creation."[21] The lordless powers are not merely abstract or metaphysical entities; they manifest tangibly in human institutions, ideologies, and systems. Barth identifies these powers as operating in realms such as government, economics, culture, and even religion, where they can become entrenched as idols. When governments act as the ultimate arbiters of

20. Barth, *Epistle to the Romans*, 486.

21. Barth, *Christian Life*, 211.

justice, economic systems prioritize profit over human dignity, or religious institutions prioritize their power over the faithful witness to the gospel, the lordless powers are at work.

Barth is particularly concerned with how the lordless powers exploit human frailty. These powers prey on fear, ambition, and pride, leading individuals and communities into complicity with their rebellion. Barth emphasizes that human beings are both victims and agents of these powers. While the powers manipulate and oppress, humanity's sinful inclinations—greed, desire for control, and selfishness—provide fertile ground for their influence. Barth describes this symbiotic relationship as a "dark partnership" where the powers thrive on human cooperation, perpetuating cycles of domination and alienation.

Despite their rebellion, the lordless powers remain within the orbit of God's sovereignty. Barth insists that their existence and activity are not autonomous; God permitted them within the divine economy, though always under judgment. Barth writes, "The powers are only lordless in their pretensions. God's providence restrains them, and their rebellion is absurd in the face of Christ's victory."[22] This paradox underscores Barth's insistence that these powers, despite their devastating effects, do not stand outside God's ultimate control.

Barth situates the lordless powers within the eschatological tension of the already and the not yet. In Christ's life, death, and resurrection, the ultimate defeat of the powers has been secured. Barth proclaims, "As the One who suffered and conquered on the cross, He has destroyed it once and for all and in all its forms. But this means that in the world reconciled by God in Jesus Christ there is no secular sphere abandoned by Him or withdrawn from His control, even where from the human standpoint it seems to approximate most dangerously to the pure and absolute form of utter godlessness."[23] However, the final eradication of their influence awaits the consummation of God's kingdom.

This eschatological perspective provides a critical lens for understanding the powers' ongoing activity. Barth explains that their rebellion persists between Christ's victory and its full realization. Therefore, the Christian response to the powers is not one of passive waiting but of active resistance grounded in the assurance of Christ's triumph.

22. Barth, *Christian Life*, 213.

23. Barth, *Church Dogmatics*, IV.3, Study Edition 27, 118.

Barth identifies several defining characteristics of the lordless powers that reveal their rebellious and corrupt nature. We have already discussed how these powers reject their rightful place under God's lordship, striving for autonomy and dominance. This rejection leads to the second characteristic: the distortion of goodness. The powers corrupt what God has created for good, twisting human institutions, systems, and relationships into instruments of oppression and exploitation, thereby subverting their original purposes. Third, the powers exhibit idolatrous pretensions, demanding ultimate allegiance and positioning themselves as substitutes for God. This idolatry is evident in political ideologies, economic systems, and cultural movements that claim absolute authority or demand unconditional loyalty, thereby supplanting the worship of God. Fourth, the powers exploit human sinfulness, preying on weaknesses such as fear, greed, and pride to perpetuate their influence. Barth describes this dynamic as a vicious cycle in which humanity enables the powers, and the powers, in turn, enslave humanity, deepening the disorder they cause. Finally, despite their rebellion, the powers remain subject to divine judgment. They are not autonomous but exist within the scope of God's sovereignty. Their rebellion is futile, as their idolatry and distortion are exposed in the light of Christ's victory, which condemns and overthrows their pretensions. Together, these characteristics reveal the pervasive and destructive influence of the lordless powers while underscoring their ultimate subjection to God's authority and redemptive purposes.

Barth's theology of the lordless powers has profound implications for Christian thought and practice. It challenges believers to recognize the pervasive influence of these powers in their lives and communities, calling them to resist complicity with systems of oppression and idolatry. He writes, "Christian resistance is an act of hope, grounded in the knowledge that the powers' dominion is temporary and their defeat is assured."[24] Resistance, for Barth, is not an act of human strength but a faithful witness to the redemptive work of Christ, who has already disarmed the powers through the cross (Col 2:15).

In sum, Barth's definition of the lordless powers encompasses their rebellious nature, their distortion of God's creation, and their parasitic relationship with human sinfulness. Yet, Barth's theology remains deeply hopeful, affirming that these powers, though disruptive and dangerous, cannot thwart God's ultimate purposes. The Christian's task is to live in the

24. Barth, *Christian Life*, 228.

tension of this already-defeated but not-yet-eradicated rebellion, bearing witness to the lordship of Christ and the coming kingdom of God.

Image #2: Exorcism

This theological posture of resistance and hope—of living amid the ruins of powers already judged—sets the stage for reimagining how we read texts like Romans 13:1–7. Suppose the lordless powers described by Barth are both cosmic and concrete, entangling themselves with institutions and ideologies. In that case, discerning their influence requires a theological imagination capable of both diagnosis and liberation. It is here that the image of exorcism becomes vital. To read Romans 13 rightly, we must move beyond surface-level obedience and attend to the deeper apocalyptic drama in which Paul is immersed—a drama where the real conflict is not between citizens and civil authority but between the reign of God and the enslaving powers of sin and death. Beverly Roberts Gaventa's apocalyptic reading of Romans invites us into precisely this kind of interpretive framework, one in which the submission Paul envisions is not capitulation to the empire but a form of discernment shaped by the cosmic lordship of Christ.

Interpreting Romans 13:1–7 through an apocalyptic theological lens, as biblical scholar Beverly Roberts Gaventa consistently advocates, positions these verses within the expansive cosmic narrative of the Letter to the Romans—particularly the invasive and transformative action of God in Jesus Christ. Gaventa's commentary on Romans emphasizes that these seven verses "rank among the most difficult in a letter that overflows with interpretive challenges."[25] She argues that Paul's vision situates earthly powers as secondary and ultimately provisional within the broader framework of God's redemptive activity, set against cosmic powers such as sin and death.

Gaventa asserts that Paul's theology in Romans is fundamentally apocalyptic, portraying the gospel as God's power intruding into a world dominated by hostile cosmic forces. She states explicitly that "the gospel is nothing less than God's reclaiming of a cosmos held captive by Sin and Death."[26] This larger divine drama portrays human structures, including governing authorities, as subordinate entities. Gaventa explains

25. Gaventa, *Romans*, 355.

26. Gaventa, *Romans*, 13.

that Paul characterizes these authorities as "servants of God" (Rom 13:4), highlighting their derivative authority and signaling their ultimate accountability to God's purposes.[27] Far from being absolute or inherently righteous, human authority is thereby relativized, existing only insofar as God permits it within the present age.

Gaventa further deepens this insight by linking Romans 13 to her analysis of Paul's treatment of Pharaoh in Romans 9. She underlines that Paul's portrayal of authority figures reflects their instrumental and subordinate position within God's cosmic plan. Gaventa notes that Paul's depiction of Pharaoh reveals a divine strategy in which even the most oppositional rulers ultimately serve to magnify God's redemptive power and purpose.[28] This illustrates Paul's broader theological approach, viewing human authority through the lens of divine sovereignty and eschatological fulfillment rather than immediate moral rectitude.

Gaventa cautions readers against isolating Romans 13:1–7 from its broader ethical and theological context, notably the preceding chapter's emphasis on transformative love, humility, and non-retaliation (Rom 12:9–21). For Gaventa, Christian submission is thus contextualized as a faithful witness within the cosmic struggle against sin and death under the sovereign lordship of Christ. She argues that Paul's ethical teachings in Romans consistently reflect the now-time inaugurated by the death and resurrection of Christ, a time characterized by "apocalyptic urgency."[29] Further clarifying Paul's understanding of earthly authority, Gaventa points to the inherent delusion and misunderstanding associated with human power when detached from its divine accountability.[30] Echoing her analysis of Paul's portrayal of sin as a deceptive cosmic power, she suggests that human authorities often mistakenly perceive themselves as ultimate, failing to recognize their instrumental and temporary roles within God's cosmic plan.[31] Drawing parallels with Simone Weil's conception of "force," Gaventa argues that Paul views human authority similarly—as a deluded form of power ultimately incapable of achieving its finality. She insightfully notes that this type of force "imagines that

27. Gaventa, *Romans*, 355–57.

28. Gaventa, "Reading Romans 13 with Simone Weil," 15; Gaventa, *Romans*, 362–63.

29. Gaventa, *Romans*, 369.

30. Gaventa, *Romans*, 360–61.

31. Gaventa, *Romans*, 363.

each conflict will be the controlling event" but remains unaware of its subordinate role within God's redemptive purposes.[32]

Gaventa underscores the eschatological tension in Romans. Governing authorities are provisional precisely because the fullness of God's kingdom has not yet arrived. The tension between already and not yet frames Paul's call to submission as simultaneously practical and subversive. By submitting, Christians witness their allegiance to a greater, coming kingdom that relativizes and ultimately judges all earthly regimes. Gaventa highlights that this allegiance renders human submission inherently provisional and reflective of a deeper commitment to the reality of God's coming reign.[33]

Finally, Gaventa emphasizes that Paul's refusal to categorically "other" human authorities aligns with his larger rhetorical strategy throughout Romans, where Paul consistently undermines rigid distinctions between "insiders" and "outsiders."[34] This rhetorical approach reflects Paul's conviction that God's redemptive purpose encompasses all humanity, even authorities who might seem oppositional or hostile.

Thus, according to Gaventa, Romans 13:1–7 becomes comprehensible and meaningful only when read in the apocalyptic framework that defines Paul's theological imagination. Human authority is provisional, instrumental, and always subject to divine evaluation. Christians' submission, therefore, is a complex ethical stance grounded in eschatological hope and an unwavering commitment to God's ultimate sovereignty and redemptive victory in Christ.

Gaventa's apocalyptic lens reveals that Paul's exhortation to submit to governing authorities in Romans 13 must be interpreted within a larger cosmic battle, where the true conflict is between God's redemptive reign and the enslaving dominion of sin and death. Gaventa's framing aligns closely with Ernst Käsemann's conviction that theology must function as a kind of exorcism—an ongoing act of resistance against the demonic powers that pervade systems and structures and theological imagination. Käsemann locates the exorcising work inside of the modern project of demythologization.[35] For Käsemann, such work is not mere abstraction but an urgent ethical and theological imperative that arises directly from the first commandment: to fear, love, and trust God above all things.

32. Gaventa, "Reading Romans 13 with Simone Weil," 15.

33. Gaventa, *Romans*, 360.

34. Gaventa, "Reading Romans 13 with Simone Weil," 18; Gaventa, *Romans*, 368–69.

35. Käsemann, *On Being a Disciple*, 200.

In this light, submission to earthly authorities cannot be an unquestioning obedience to whatever powers happen to govern. Instead, it must be a discerned and disciplined recognition of these authorities' provisional role within God's broader redemptive economy—and a readiness to resist when they become idolatrous or demonic. Käsemann's emphasis on superstition as "everything that does not allow us most deeply and without compromise to fear, love, and trust God" exposes the theological error of treating state power as ultimate or sacrosanct. When political authority demands ultimate loyalty, it ceases to be merely human. It takes on the character of a "lordless power"—a false god that must be exorcised through theological clarity and prophetic resistance.

For Gaventa, this task is not optional but constitutive of Christian witness. In her apocalyptic reading, Paul is not legitimating the empire but subverting it by reframing all authority under the Lordship of Christ. Just as Käsemann sees demythologizing as the necessary clearing away of idolatrous distortions to make room for genuine trust in God, Gaventa sees the apocalyptic unveiling of God's justice as an act of theological exorcism—displacing the pretensions of worldly rule and exposing its limitations. Romans 13 becomes not a divine endorsement of the empire but a summons to recognize that no authority stands above God's.

This exorcistic stance also means Christians must remain vigilant against the subtle ways in which worldly powers disguise themselves as divine will. As Käsemann's insight suggests, superstition is not confined to primitive beliefs but includes the ideological absolutizing of anything that eclipses God. In our context, this includes nationalism, capitalism, whiteness, or even distorted uses of Scripture itself—each of which must be resisted when they attempt to claim what belongs to God alone. Gaventa's apocalyptic Paul demands that Christians see the present order through the lens of the cross and resurrection, which unmasks the false promises of power and unveils a new creation breaking into the old.

Thus, to interpret Romans 13 faithfully is to enter the struggle that Käsemann names: a battle against the demonic, against everything that violates the first commandment. It is a call to theological discernment that resists superstition in its most sophisticated forms. Instead, it aligns Christian ethics with the radical gospel proclamation that Jesus—and not Caesar—is Lord.

Image #3: The Presence of the Kingdom and Non-Power

Exploring the evocative imagery of exorcism offers profound insight into how spiritual and theological symbols can critique oppressive power structures often embraced by FCN. Exorcism, as depicted in the Gospels, symbolizes liberation from oppressive and destructive spiritual forces, vividly illustrating the struggle against powers that seek domination and control. This powerful metaphor invites reflection on how authority functions like an invasive spiritual force that must be actively resisted and cast out, especially when corrupted. Transitioning from this imagery of exorcism to the liberation theology articulated by Jacques Ellul, we encounter a contrasting vision of divine power—"non-power"—rooted in humility, presence, and sacrificial love. Ellul's theology presents an alternative model of authority that embodies God's presence through Christ's self-giving vulnerability, profoundly critiquing oppressive power structures and aligning deeply with the transformative action symbolized in the Gospels' language of exorcism.

In Ellul's theology, presence is a profound and multifaceted concept that underscores the Christian calling to embody the divine presence in the world. For Ellul, the incarnation of Jesus Christ reveals God's presence, where God enters human history in a concrete and transformative way. This act of self-revelation is the ultimate expression of divine love and a disruption of human categories of power, control, and understanding. As Ellul writes,

> Christians need to immerse themselves in social and political problems so that they can act in the world, not in the hope of making it a paradise, but only rendering it tolerable. Not of attenuating the opposition between this world and the kingdom of God, but only the opposition between this world's disorder and the order of preservation that God wants for it. Not of making the kingdom of God come, but so that the Gospel may be proclaimed, that all people may hear *truly* the good news of salvation and resurrection.[36]

This presence is personal and sacrificial, showing a God who stands in solidarity with human brokenness rather than remaining distant or indifferent.

For Christians, presence is both a gift and a task. Ellul emphasizes that believers must reflect the presence of God in their own lives, particularly

36. Ellul, *Presence in the Modern World*, 29.

by engaging with the world's suffering, alienation, and injustice. This calling is rooted in the model of Christ, who demonstrated that true presence involves humility, vulnerability, and a willingness to serve others. Ellul critiques modern technological and bureaucratic systems, which he believes alienate and dehumanize individuals, replacing authentic relationships with impersonal efficiency. In contrast, the Christian calling is to counteract these forces by being present with others deeply, relationally, and incarnationally. This involves prioritizing human connection, compassion, and community over the abstract logic of systems.

Ellul's theology of presence also has an eschatological dimension, pointing toward the ultimate fulfillment of God's kingdom. He believes that while God's presence in the world is real and transformative, it remains incomplete until the eschaton, when God will fully restore creation. Until then, Christians are called to live as signs of this coming kingdom, embodying hope and reconciliation in the face of a fractured world. Ellul writes, "Hope is the relation with God of the person liberated by God."[37] This presence is not about achieving earthly success or imposing a vision of the kingdom through human effort but about living faithfully in the tension between the present reality and the future promise of God's ultimate reign.

Ellul also highlights the paradoxical nature of presence, as it involves both action and restraint. For him, being present in the world does not mean succumbing to activism or a frantic pursuit of change; rather, it requires a quiet, steadfast commitment to truth, love, and humility. This perspective challenges Christians to resist the idolatry of busyness and instead focus on embodying the character of Christ in their daily lives. Ellul's concept of presence is thus deeply countercultural. It rejects the idols of efficiency, power, and control that dominate modern society, calling instead for a way of life that reflects the humility and love of God. This presence is active, as it involves engaging with the world's pain and injustice, but it is also contemplative, rooted in the assurance of God's ultimate sovereignty.

Ellul's idea of non-power becomes especially nuanced when considering those who already lack conventional power or are marginalized within society. Ellul carefully distinguishes voluntary "non-power," an intentional Christian stance of faithful obedience to Christ's example, from involuntary "powerlessness," imposed by oppressive social and political

37. Ellul, *Hope in Time of Abandonment*, 239.

systems.[38] The difference, for Ellul, lies in choice. When one possesses the freedom to choose, one must choose non-power. Ellul writes, "If I am materially stronger than the one who slaps me, and if I give him my left check, that is non-power; if I am materially less strong, that is powerlessness, and I need not find glory in not having fought."[39] In this way, Ellul affirms that non-power is only meaningful when it arises from agency rather than imposed vulnerability, preserving the dignity of those who resist domination not because they must but because they are free to follow a different way.

The distinction between powerlessness and non-power becomes even clearer when Ellul articulates the essence of non-power in one of his most striking definitions: "Non-power means being able and not being willing to do it. It is choosing not to exercise domination, efficiency attesting that the dimension of power and success does not have the final word of our human condition."[40] Ellul offers a profound lens to understand Christian ethics and resistance to Christian nationalism. Non-power challenges the assumption that power must always exert itself when one possesses it. Instead, it is a voluntary renunciation of domination—a deliberate choice not to wield authority over others when one can do so. Far from weakness, this restraint reflects a deep wisdom that mirrors the example of Christ, who, though possessing divine authority, chose the path of crucifixion. The crucifixion is a refusal to exercise domination or efficiency, which attests that power and success do not have the final word of our human condition. In contrast, the gospel calls humanity to a different kind of flourishing rooted in love and solidarity rather than success and control.

This ethic of non-power directly challenges Christian nationalism, which seeks to fuse Christian identity with political dominance. Christian nationalism attempts to baptize coercion in the name of Christ, advancing a vision of faith that is deeply incompatible with the gospel. Non-power, in this context, becomes a radical act of resistance. It refuses to play by the rules of worldly power. Instead, it testifies to a different kind of kingdom that does not grow through conquest or cultural control but through faithfulness, humility, and witness. By rejecting domination, the church becomes a living sign of the kingdom of God, whose power is made perfect in weakness. In this way, choosing non-power means

38. Ellul, *Theology and Technique*, 245.
39. Ellul, *Theology and Technique*, 245
40. Ellul, *Theology and Technique*, 242.

resisting the idolatries of nationalism, bearing witness to Christ crucified, and embodying the hope of a world made new not by force but by love.

Non-power only makes sense when read within Ellul's broader account of ethics, particularly his critique of means and ends. In secular ethical frameworks shaped by technological society, ends such as efficiency and control dictate the means by which they are pursued. Ellul objects,

> In reality, what justified the means today is whatever succeeds. Whatever is effective, whatever possesses in itself an "efficiency," is justified. By applying means, a result is produced. This result is judged by these simplistic criteria of "more": larger, faster, more precise, and so on. Simply by applying this criterion, the means is declared good. What succeeds is good, what fails is bad.[41]

One can hear echoes of Ellul in Rosa and Fromm in this account of means and ends. The push for efficiency is the push for control and power. The means, thus, are self-justifying because they work well. This is the way of the modern world and, as such, FCN. Ellul will still argue that the church is God's means in the world and the presence of the kingdom. One must be present to the world and see it in its technological capture. Thus, they must embody the gospel. Non-power in this light speaks to the refusal of Christians to take power in the way that FCN does. It must not control, dominate, or oppress. Instead, it seeks only to do what has been done in Christ. He writes, "[Christian ethics] is not an ethic of conquest, but of obedience. It has no goal, only a starting point. It does not have an objective, only a reason."[42] Thus, Christian ethics is "good for nothing."[43] These actions are not self-justifying but only justified eschatologically, making all ethics provisional and subject to revision and completely inefficient.[44] This is so that Christians may embody a realism that can be present to the world in its technological lusts and capture and model the presence of the kingdom.

Ellul highlighted that in the Christian narrative, the incarnation of Christ serves as both the means and the realization of God's kingdom. This unity implies that Christ's presence signifies the kingdom's arrival, illustrating that the process and the outcome are intertwined. Therefore,

41. Ellul, *Presence in the Modern World*, 45.

42. Ellul, *To Will & To Do*, 2:88.

43. Ellul, *To Will & To Do*, 2:88.

44. Ellul, *To Will & To Do*, 2:89.

Christian actions should reflect this harmony, where the pursuit of objectives like justice and peace is conducted through just and peaceful means, embodying the very essence of the desired end.

In sum, to resist Christian nationalism is to engage in a kind of spiritual exorcism—a casting out of the false gods of domination, coercion, and control that have cloaked themselves in religious language. As in the Gospel narratives, where exorcism confronts and disarms oppressive spiritual forces, the church is called to unmask and reject every attempt to wed faith with supremacy. However, this resistance is not waged with the weapons of the world. It is not a matter of overpowering or outmaneuvering but of embodying a deeper truth—the non-power of Christ.

Ellul's theology offers the church a profoundly countercultural imagination. At the heart of this vision is the paradox of *non-power*—the decision, even when capable, not to dominate. It is the strength of presence over spectacle, humility over triumph, love over efficiency. In a world seduced by the allure of power and measurable success, non-power bears witness to the God revealed in Christ crucified—the one who enters human history not with force but with flesh, not to conquer but to redeem. Non-power is not passivity; it is active fidelity. It refuses to mirror the logic of the empire and instead enacts the slow, relational work of incarnation. In Ellul's words, it is choosing not to exercise domination because domination itself is a betrayal of the kingdom's character.

This ethic finds its sharpest edge in Ellul's conviction that Christian means must embody eschatological ends. Unlike secular ideologies that justify any method so long as the outcome appears righteous, the church witnesses through integrity—a unity between what it does and what it proclaims. In this, presence becomes both method and message: to be with others in suffering, to work for justice with justice, and to pursue peace peacefully. The church resists Christian nationalism not by fighting for control but by *refusing to seek control*—becoming a living contradiction to the spirit of domination.

In the end, Ellul offers not merely a critique of corrupted religion but a vision of a faithful church: exorcising idols through presence, rejecting coercion through non-power, and transforming the world not by winning it but by loving it as Christ has loved us. This is the church that bears witness to the kingdom—not as empire restored but as grace incarnate.

Image #4: Jesus Before Pilate or the Judge Judged in Our Place

Following Ellul, Christians are called to resist and subvert oppressive societal structures through acts of humble presence rather than authoritarian control. The evocative power of imagery further enriches this theological conversation. Images, particularly those drawn from the Gospels, vividly illustrate these theological concepts, making abstract ideas tangible and deeply impactful. Such images invite us to reimagine divine authority, not as exercising coercive power but as a profound act of humility and self-sacrifice, epitomized in Christ's submission to earthly judgment.

Karl Barth's theology profoundly underscores the paradoxical reality that Jesus Christ, the divine Judge, allowed himself to be judged by earthly authorities, exemplified poignantly in the trial before Pilate in John 18:28–40. This encounter, where Christ faces the judgment of Pilate, epitomizes Barth's theological assertion that the Judge became the judged for humanity's reconciliation with God, and that is where the Word of God speaks today.

Barth begins with the foundational conviction that Jesus Christ is the ultimate Judge, the embodiment of divine righteousness, whose judgment upholds order and peace while exposing human sinfulness. In Barth's interpretation, the divine Judge takes our place by undergoing the judgment humanity deserves, demonstrating God's profound commitment to human salvation.[45] This act is not an abdication of Christ's authority but the ultimate expression of divine sovereignty.[46]

In John 18:28–40, the irony of Christ's trial lies in the inversion of roles: Pilate, a Roman governor representing earthly authority, presides over the judgment of Christ, the true and divine Judge. Pilate's interrogation centers on the question of kingship: "Are you the King of the Jews?" (John 18:33). Jesus's response, "My kingdom is not of this world," reveals the contrast between earthly and divine authority. Barth interprets this exchange as a testament to Christ's willing self-subjection to human judgment, which unveils the true nature of his kingdom—a kingdom characterized by grace and reconciliation rather than coercion and power.

The episode with Pilate reflects humanity's misguided claim to autonomy and judgment. As Barth notes, the essence of sin lies in humanity's attempt to be its judge, rejecting divine sovereignty and establishing

45. Barth, *Church Dogmatics* Vol. IV.1, Study Edition 21, 213–17.

46. Barth, *Church Dogmatics* Vol. IV.1, Study Edition 21, 216–17.

itself as the measure of all things.[47] By submitting to Pilate's judgment, Jesus confronts and overturns this sinful tendency, exposing the fragility and corruption of human justice systems. Barth's interpretation of this moment emphasizes Christ's radical humility, who "did not float over the human situation like a being of a completely different kind but entered into it as a man with men."[48] In allowing himself to be judged by Pilate, Christ identifies fully with humanity's broken condition, bearing the consequences of sin while remaining the Judge who offers grace.

James Cone's Important Critique of Barth's Political Theology

James Cone offers a critique of Barth that provides a necessary corrective by situating this theological insight within the concrete realities of oppression and systemic injustice. Cone challenges Barth's lack of engagement with specific historical injustices, such as racism and colonialism, arguing that the Judge must also stand in solidarity with the marginalized. For Cone, the trial before Pilate resonates profoundly with the experiences of oppressed peoples judged unjustly by systems of power.

Cone's emphasis on the political dimension of theology deepens Barth's insight by highlighting how Christ's judgment on human sin also includes a critique of oppressive systems. Pilate represents not only individual sin but also the structural injustices of the empire. Barth's theology, when read alongside Cone's, challenges Christians to see Jesus's trial as a judgment on the entire system of domination that perpetuates violence and exclusion.

Barth and Cone's perspectives affirm that Jesus, as the Judge judged, reveals the depth of God's grace and the extent of his solidarity with humanity. In John 18, Christ does not resist Pilate's authority but transforms the nature of judgment by enduring it. Barth's emphasis on the paradox of the Judge judged illuminates the universal scope of this act, while Cone's critique ensures that this universalism does not overlook the particularities of human suffering and injustice.

This dual lens challenges believers to recognize both the cosmic and political dimensions of Christ's trial. The Judge judged is a theological truth and a call to embody Christ's humility and solidarity with those judged unfairly by worldly powers. Barth and Cone invite Christians to

47. Barth, *Church Dogmatics* Vol. IV.1, Study Edition 21, 217.

48. Barth, *Church Dogmatics* Vol. IV.1, Study Edition 21, 209.

live in the tension of a faith that proclaims ultimate reconciliation while actively resisting the systemic injustices that Christ's judgment exposes.

It is important to note the possibilities made possible by Barth's exegesis while also acknowledging his limitations. For Barth, God's sovereignty over the powers and principalities shapes our understanding. Barth can even reflect on the powers' lordlessness, but he will ultimately provide a reason for their justification. The powers can, as Paul states in Romans, "rulers are not a terror to good conduct but to bad." (13:3) Therefore, Barth will defend the authority of the powers to execute "divine wrath" on "evildoers" (13:4). While this interpretation cannot be ignored, one should note that it does create a *necessary* other that can be the subject of civil punishment under divine authority. This makes resistance to unjust systems of government largely impossible. Thus, a nuance and critique of Barth and any interpretation of Romans 13:1–7 perpetuates this possibility.

To this end, I return to James Cone's theology, which critiques Barth for neglecting the concrete realities of oppression and racial injustice. For Cone, Barth's theology, while rejecting anthropocentrism and aligning with God's grace, does not sufficiently engage with the historical realities of racism and economic exploitation. In Cone's view, Barth's theology lacks this contextual immediacy.[49] While Barth's theology critiques human ideologies and powers, Cone argues that it does not sufficiently empower communities to resist oppression actively.

For example, Barth's exegesis of Romans 13:1–7 reflects his understanding of the provisional nature of earthly powers under God's sovereignty. Thus, submission to governing authorities is conditional and always subject to God's overarching judgment. To be clear, Barth does not read Romans 13 as a theological endorsement of tyranny but as a call to see all earthly authority as subordinate to God's will. Rather, he interprets Romans 13:1–7 through a Christocentric framework, asserting that all human authorities are under the lordship of Christ. However, his focus on divine sovereignty often leads to a lack of specific engagement with the implications of unjust systems.

While affirming God's transcendence and sovereignty, Cone also critiques Barth's theology for its abstract universalism, which fails to address the concrete historical realities of oppression.[50] Cone challenges

49. Cone, *God of the Oppressed*, 107–9.

50. Cone, *God of the Oppressed*, 116, 120.

any theology, Barthian or otherwise, that would approach Romans 13:1–7 and underplay how this passage has been historically misused to justify slavery, colonialism, and systemic racism. Cone argues that theology must speak to the lived experiences of the oppressed, addressing their specific conditions rather than relying solely on abstract principles. Barth's interpretation of Romans 13, which relativizes human authorities under God's ultimate rule, does not go far enough in empowering communities to resist systems of oppression actively. Cone asserts that theology must engage these realities to be relevant, providing both a critique of injustice and a framework for liberation.

Barth's theology, including his reading of Romans 13, provides a framework for critiquing human authority under God's sovereignty. However, Cone challenges Barth to move beyond critique to active solidarity with the oppressed. Cone's critique urges theologians, including Barth, to reinterpret Romans 13:1–7 in ways that prioritize the liberation of the marginalized over abstract theological principles. By focusing on the lived realities of oppression, Cone reframes the theological task as one that demands direct engagement with injustice, making theology an instrument of liberation rather than mere interpretation. Barth's emphasis on the sovereignty of God and the ultimate lordship of Christ is a crucial foundation. However, Cone demands that this foundation be built upon an active, political, and liberating praxis that aligns theology with the needs and struggles of the oppressed.

PART III. INTERPRETING ROMANS 13:1–7

Romans 13:1–7 has long been a contested text, frequently invoked to justify submission to governing authorities. Moreover, as history has shown, such interpretations have often been co-opted to serve nationalist and fundamentalist agendas, reinforcing systems of injustice rather than resisting them. This section seeks to challenge these distortions by drawing upon apocalyptic Christology and allegorical interpretation, providing a liberating reading of Romans 13:1–7. Building upon the literary imagination developed in previous chapters, this reading resists fundamentalist and Christian nationalist sympathies by reframing Paul's discussion of authority through the lens of the crucified and risen Christ.

An apocalyptic Christology recognizes Christ as the victim of the governing powers, exposing their rebellion against God. As Karl Barth argues, these powers—whether political, religious, or social—are anti-God when they align against Christ. In his crucifixion, Christ does not model passive submission to power but unveils its corruption, marking the beginning of its end. This perspective compels a reinterpretation of Romans 13, not as an endorsement of earthly rulers but as an invitation to see the world through the lens of the cross. Just as the primal narrative reveals a God who liberates Israel from Egypt, so too does the resurrection of the crucified Lord disrupt human claims to authority, redefining the nature of power and justice.

Engaging literary imagination and theological critique, we propose a reading of Romans 13:1–7 that is deeply attuned to the realities of systemic power. Drawing from allegory and figures such as Morrison, Cone, and Du Bois, it highlights how marginalized communities navigate authority—resisting and surviving within oppressive structures. Just as parents in marginalized contexts teach their children to understand power critically, Paul's exhortation to the early church must be read as a strategic and prophetic acknowledgment of dangerous realities rather than a call to uncritical obedience. Through this lens, Romans 13 becomes not a tool for submission to unjust rule but a summons to discern, resist, and ultimately participate in the in-breaking reign of Christ, where the powers of this world are held accountable to divine justice.

A Balm in Gilead: Apocalyptic Christ, Literary Imagination, and Allegory

The exegesis and history of interpreting Romans 13:1–7 and the above theological periscope are necessary for a new interpretation in light of Christian nationalism and fundamentalism. Considering these claims, Romans 13:1–7 justifies certain rules or authority. However, it will often play into the hands of nationalist or Puritan sympathies to perpetuate injustices and secure power. Therefore, the literary imagination built in chapters 3 and 4 must now focus its periscope on interpreting Romans 13:1–7 to resist fundamentalist and Christian nationalist sympathies developed in chapters 1 and 2.

Only an apocalyptic Christology and allegorical interpretation can account for a liberating vision of Romans 13:1–7. Christ is a victim of the lordless powers. As Barth illustrates, these powers are anti-God, as seen in the treatment of Christ. He is the crucified victim who is the Judge judged in our place, which is salvation for both victim and oppressor. This Christology will highlight the place to think about Romans 13:1–7.

Jesus was subject to the governing authorities through crucifixion (Phil 2:6–8). Jesus's submission is not a model for human conduct but rather an invitation to think of the radical disruption occurring here. The Word of God (John 1:1) is the second person of the triune Lord in human form (John 1:14). This one was with the criminals crucified (Luke 23:32). Are the governing authorities here a terror to good conduct (Rom 13:3)? What happens in Christ's crucifixion is the co-opting of the religious and political authorities organized against God. They are in active rebellion against God, namely the forces of the present, evil age (Gal 1:4). The powers of sin and death are aligned and remain in this pattern from Adam onward (Rom 5:12–14).

Yet, this is where Christians should boast (Gal 6:14). The primal narrative is that the Lord and Savior Jesus Christ was raised from his crucified death. This is in continuity with the God who raised Israel out of Egypt. Was Egypt only a terror to bad conduct? The primal narrative illustrates that God identifies with those whom the powers crucify and enslave. The boasting of Christianity constitutes the confidence of the Christian. It reframes the whole cosmos, which is crucified to me and I to the cosmos (Gal 6:14).

The crucified Lord is a different realism than the one proposed by Christian nationalism. It reflects more of Paul's declaration in 1 Corinthians,

> Yet among the mature, we speak wisdom, though it is not a wisdom of this age or of the rulers of this age, who are being destroyed. But we speak God's wisdom, a hidden mystery, which God decreed before the ages for our glory and which none of the rulers of this age understood, for if they had, they would not have crucified the Lord of glory. (2:6–8, NRSVue)

Here, Christ opposes the powers and even foretells their destruction. Christ's authority exists in this place of submission to the powers not in order to affirm them unconditionally but to bring them to an end (1 Cor 15:25–28). As Paul writes in Galatians, "May I never boast of anything except the cross of our Lord Jesus Christ, by which the world has been crucified to me and I to the world" (6:14, NRSVue). One can see the powers and their imminent defeat through the crucified Christ. It is *in* this vision that the presence that believers enact the presence of the kingdom.

The bifocal vision allows us to see the powers for what they are. Thus, they can embody a different way of being in the world than the fallen powers.

Apocalyptic Christology proposes a different kind of activity than the one performed by FCN. It does not serve an end immanent to itself. It locates this world's powers inside a matrix of fallen powers that transcend the material instantons of their authority. The death and resurrection propose the most revolutionary act because it defeats the material manifestation and disrupts their cosmic end. As such, the life, death, and resurrection of Jesus require those who follow him to relocate themselves within the structures of the world both materially and cosmically. Any reading of Scripture must include this cosmic perspective and move its readers beyond its pages. It is as Psalm 36:9 states, "In your light we see light" (NRSVue). One must see the light shed by the crucified and resurrected Lord that calls us to resist these fallen powers.

What is Scripture, and how does one interpret and follow it? Based on our analysis and images, one can find a way forward. Keeping Augustine at the forefront, one must orient one's reading of Scripture toward God and one's neighbor. Only by keeping these two in view does one come close to the "correct" reading of Scripture. Thus, Scripture does not require the capturing of space *for* God. God is not honored by these empty ceremonies (Amos 5:21–24). Rather, the goal of Scripture requires that the light of God's flourishing shines on our neighbors so that they might live into it. The interpretation is no less lived out and apologetic. Instead, one lives with no expectation that others will follow a particular way. Instead, one lives the concrete love of one's neighbor in an attractive way. It does not seize control of another or a power but celebrates its non-power. Again, not to ask those without to submit to abuse but rather to refuse to use Christianity or the name of Christ to gain power over others.

The crucified Lord crucially informs this way. The one crucified is also resurrected, which lies beyond the immanent frame. Only from that vantage point can one see the cross not as a defeat but something that dialectically reinforms human perception of value. It performs a necessary exorcism of ideological demons and the fallen powers that demonize them. It does this not only through Christ's defeat of the powers but also through the commissioning of those who take up that cross in their standing next to the demonized scapegoats of the world. Worshipping the crucified yet risen Lord (primal narrative) requires changing where one stands. To say that the crucifixion and resurrection interrupt the systems of sin. Seeing the cross as something luminously beautiful means that the cross disrupts our tastes. Rather than coercive power and authority, one finds power and authority in the crucified. Being present to the margins is the presence of the kingdom, not to instrumentalize (technology) that space, but to work and live in a way that disrupts the material instantiation of fallen powers by destabilizing the lure toward fallenness.

Thus, Gilead truly offers a balm because it allows the text to point to the disruptively present yet transcendent Lord who died alongside two criminals executed by the state. The ecclesial power of this confession binds together communities like Gilead, Iowa. Lila describes communities as bodies missing a vital part; without each member present, something essential is lost. Such is a counterculture—one that does not flaunt authority or privilege where the only solution is to deport or execute dissenters; rather, it celebrates how broad and diverse the community becomes.

Such diversity only comes through the reading of the Bible in diverse voices. This is where believers find the surplus of meaning (Ricouer) and subsequent de-demonizing (exorcism). The ecclesia is where we search to detect when our readings do not love our neighbors and, therefore, God. Love must always take material form, as it is where we participate in the cosmic disruption of the fallen powers and are drawn into the transcendent God away from our desire for possession. As Amy Plantinga Pauw writes, exorcism "happens through prophetic words, repentance, efforts at reconciliation, and larger hearted attention to the spiritual gifts and discernment of others. The Spirit's exorcism work is agonizingly difficult and slow because it aims at nothing less than opening heaven and converting earth, bringing all creatures into joyful, eternal fellowship with the triune God."[51] At this moment, when one encounters the surplus of meaning, one experiences freedom in and through the triune fellowship.

At this point, one can find how Jesus before Pilate becomes a compelling image for the liberating interpretation of Romans 13:1–7. For Barth, this is the site of reconciliation and disruption as God the Judge becomes judged by earthly authority. In so doing, he exposes the mimetic desire to scapegoat and assume human pretension in our judgments. Christ is the man of lawlessness, and Pilate the restrainer. The call for order at this moment means the execution of God. It is no small paradox that when God becomes human, humans choose their own "order" over God's kingdom. However, the Judge judged in our place before Pilate reversed the order of

51. Pauw, "Holy Spirit and Scripture," 38.

power. It shows that the powers do not discourage bad behavior, so what do we do with this stumbling block? Returning to the primal narrative, God is the one who raised Jesus from the dead after first raising Israel out of Egypt. Indeed, as Paul finally saw, the realm of life has entered the realm of death and robbed it of its power. Life now will be secured not through the power of Rome or any nation but through the crucified and risen Lord. As such, the way that nations and principalities participate in the material perpetuation of death requires a radical witness. It is only from the perspective of those who are crucified that Romans 13:1–7 makes sense.

Part IV. The Figural Reading of Romans 13:1–7

Romans 13:1–7 is often read as advocating uncritical submission to governing authorities. However, an allegorical reading through the metaphor of marginalized parents teaching their children about systemic power reveals deeper interpretive possibilities. This approach invites readers to see Paul's instructions not merely as abstract theological advice but as practical wisdom emerging from conditions of vulnerability and marginalization. Just as parents in oppressed communities must carefully guide their children through a complex relationship with authority, Paul provides nuanced instructions for a church living under precarious political realities.

Romans 13:1–7, a passage often interpreted as a call for uncritical submission to governing authorities, takes on a profoundly different resonance when viewed through the metaphor of parents in marginalized communities who must teach their children about the dangers posed by systemic power. For these parents, the question of authority is not an abstract theological or philosophical issue—it is a matter of survival. This lived experience provides a lens through which Paul's exhortation can be understood as a nuanced, urgent reflection on the precarious nature of earthly power and its relationship to divine justice.

In marginalized neighborhoods, parents face the harrowing task of explaining to their children how those tasked with maintaining order—such as police officers—can also become agents of harm. For these families, power is not inherently good or evil but a force capable of preserving *and* endangering life. Similarly, Paul's words in Romans 13 reflect a duality in viewing governing authorities. While Paul acknowledges that authorities are "instituted by God" to maintain order and uphold justice

(v. 1–4), he also implicitly warns that their legitimacy hinges on their alignment with God's purposes.

For Paul, the powers are provisional, not absolute. The same God who ordains their existence also stands as their ultimate judge. In the context of a Roman empire known for its oppression of marginalized groups, including the early Christian community, Paul's instructions cannot be read as an unqualified endorsement of state power. Instead, his words must be understood in light of the precarious realities faced by his audience. Like parents teaching their children about systemic power, Paul calls the church to navigate its relationship with authority with wisdom, caution, and an awareness of the risks.

Paul's writings consistently reflect an apocalyptic worldview in which earthly powers are subordinated to the reign of Christ. Romans 13 must be read alongside passages like Ephesians 6:12, where Paul speaks of the struggle "against the rulers, against the authorities, against the cosmic powers over this present darkness." This tension underscores the provisional and contingent nature of earthly authority. For parents of marginalized children, the advice to "submit" to authority often comes with caveats rooted in survival: comply when necessary but always remain vigilant. Similarly, Paul's call to submission reflects a practical concern for the survival of the Christian community under an empire that wielded its power unpredictably and often violently.

The metaphor of marginalized parents also highlights the interpretive tension in Romans 13. Parents instruct their children to navigate systems that can harm them, not out of unquestioning loyalty to those systems but as an act of pragmatic resistance against forces that seek to dehumanize them. In the same way, Paul's instructions to submit to governing authorities may reflect not an endorsement of Rome's authority but a strategy for survival in a hostile context. His directive must be understood as a contingent response to the realities of Roman imperial power, which often demanded compliance to ensure safety, even as it perpetuated injustice.

For parents teaching their children about systemic injustice, the legitimacy of authority depends on its alignment with a higher moral standard. A police officer who acts justly—protecting the vulnerable and upholding fairness—fulfills their role as an agent of order. But an officer who abuses their power becomes an agent of harm, undermining the justice they are tasked to uphold. Paul's words in Romans 13 reflect a similar principle: governing authorities are legitimate only insofar as they serve God's justice. In verse 4, Paul describes the ruler as "God's servant for your good," but this description assumes that the ruler acts by divine justice.

This conditional legitimacy echoes the prophetic tradition, consistently critiquing rulers who fail to uphold justice. When authority becomes an agent of harm rather than good, it forfeits its divine mandate. For parents of marginalized children, the knowledge that power can be corrupt shapes their instruction. They teach their children not to trust uncritically but to approach authority with a discerning awareness of its potential for harm. Similarly, Paul's audience would have understood that their submission was not blind but conditioned by the authority's fidelity to God's purposes.

The metaphor of marginalized parents also exposes the danger of weaponizing Romans 13 to demand uncritical obedience to authority. Just as parents must guard against narratives that place the blame for systemic harm on the children who experience it, interpreters of Romans 13 must resist readings that absolve unjust rulers of accountability. Paul's words have often been used to justify oppressive systems, from slavery to authoritarian regimes, perpetuating harm against the very people the powers are called to protect.

Parents of marginalized children understand that the problem is not merely individual officers but the broader system that enables and perpetuates harm. Likewise, Paul's apocalyptic vision reveals that the ultimate solution to unjust authority lies not in uncritical submission but in the coming reign of Christ, which will expose and overturn systems of oppression. Paul's vision is not passive acquiescence but active hope in the transformative justice of God's kingdom.

For marginalized parents, teaching their children to navigate authority is an act of resistance, a way of preserving dignity and life in the face of systemic injustice. Similarly, Paul's call to submission can be understood as a strategy of resistance, not in the sense of endorsing the status quo but as a way of bearing witness to God's sovereignty over all earthly powers.

When Paul writes that "rulers are not a terror to good conduct, but to bad" (v. 3), he is not describing the reality of Roman governance but articulating the divine ideal against which all rulers are measured. This ideal holds that authority exists to serve justice, protect the vulnerable, and promote the common good. When rulers fail to meet this standard, they reveal their distance from God's purposes, becoming objects of prophetic critique and divine judgment.

Romans 13:1–7, read through the lens of marginalized parents and their teachings about systemic power, reveals a passage deeply attuned to the complexities of authority and its dangers. Paul's call to submit to governing authorities must be understood as a pragmatic response to the realities of power, shaped by his apocalyptic vision of God's ultimate reign. This vision challenges Christians to discern the legitimacy of earthly powers, holding them accountable to the justice of God's kingdom.

For parents teaching their children about the dangers of systemic power, the message is one of caution, discernment, and survival. Similarly, Paul's words in Romans 13 remind Christians that while God institutes authority, it is always provisional, contingent, and accountable to a higher standard. In a world where power often oppresses rather than protects, Romans 13 invites believers to live with an awareness of God's justice, resisting the idolatry of earthly authority and placing their hope in the ultimate reign of Christ.

Paul's perspective becomes clearer when read in conversation with other passages emphasizing the tension between earthly and divine powers. Romans 13 must be read alongside Ephesians 6:12, where Paul explicitly identifies spiritual conflict with oppressive powers. Thus, the authority Paul describes in Romans 13 is neither absolute nor morally neutral but provisional, held accountable to the standard of God's justice. Like parents teaching their children how to navigate harmful systems, Paul instructs believers to adopt pragmatic resistance—not blind compliance—to maintain their integrity in an oppressive society.

This allegory underscores a fundamental interpretive tension. Parents instruct their children to survive within harmful systems without endorsing those systems, just as Paul's call to submission is not an endorsement but a strategic and prophetic acknowledgment of dangerous realities. Governing powers, therefore, derive their legitimacy from their faithfulness to God's purposes of justice and protection. An authority that fails to uphold this standard loses its divine legitimacy, becoming subject to prophetic critique.

Romans 13:1–7, often cited as a call to submission to governing authorities, takes on renewed theological and ethical significance when read figurally through the intersecting images of the lordless powers, exorcism, non-power, and Jesus before Pilate. These images, developed within an apocalyptic and literary theological frame, disrupt readings that justify authoritarianism and invite Christians to discern authority in light of the crucified and risen Christ.

To begin, the image of parents who must teach their children about the dangers posed by police offers a figural key to reading Romans 13. These parents embody a kind of wisdom born of resistance and care. Their lessons—survive and stay alert—are not endorsements of systemic violence but endurance strategies. For them, power is never neutral; it must be navigated for survival. Similarly, Paul's exhortation to submit is not an ideological endorsement of Roman authority but a pragmatic pastoral strategy for a vulnerable community living under imperial threat. As these parents speak not from positions of power but of proximity to harm, Paul speaks from within the shadow of empire, discerning how to live faithfully under unjust rule.

Paul's words lead his readers to the image of exorcism, where they are best understood not as legitimating earthly authority but as revealing deeper cosmic conflict. Beverly Roberts Gaventa's apocalyptic reading of Romans reminds us that a larger struggle between the kingdom of God and the enslaving powers of sin and death frames submission in Romans 13. Authority, then, is not autonomous—it is provisional, always subject to divine judgment. Paul's call to submission becomes a moment of discernment, akin to Jesus's encounter with demonic forces: not obedience for obedience's sake, but the faithful navigation of a world still haunted by forces that must be named and cast out. In short, the approximate action that bridges the text is one of resistance, not submission, to powers destined to be overthrown. To be abundantly clear, Christ's submission is dialectically understood, namely the act of a wholly other God (e.g., a God who expresses power in submission). Thus, those under the powers of oppression and those over policed need not repeat this action, but instead prophetically witness to the demise of the powers and unjust authority. The parent's voice echoes here, too: recognize the danger, but do not lose yourself to it. Survive without surrendering your soul.

Karl Barth's notion of the lordless powers becomes indispensable in this light. These powers—social, political, cultural, even religious—have rejected their place under God's lordship and seek to enthrone themselves in God's stead. When these powers operate without accountability to divine justice, they become demonic, masquerading as order while perpetuating violence. Therefore, Paul's call to submission must be heard within a dialectic: authorities are instituted by God, but they are not God. They can become idols, demanding ultimate allegiance, and thus must be resisted. Barth reminds us that all such powers are already judged in Christ; their defeat is assured, though not fully realized. Minority parents live with the knowledge of these lordless powers, training their children to see through the costume of legitimacy to the deeper truth of whether power serves justice—or simply itself.

Enter the figure of Jesus before Pilate, the Judge judged in our place. This scene in John's Gospel exposes the absurdity and violence of earthly power. Christ, the true Lord, submits not to validate Roman justice but to reveal its corruption. His silence before Pilate, his refusal to wield power to save himself, and his condemnation by religious and political authorities alike unveil the hollowness of human rule. As James Cone critiques, this image must also be located in histories of racial and colonial violence: the trial of Christ echoes the trials of the oppressed, judged and executed by systems that claim divine sanction. Jesus's posture here mirrors that of the marginalized parent: protective, discerning, and deeply aware of the fragility of life under unjust scrutiny. Thus, Jesus before Pilate becomes a figural mirror for Paul's readers, calling them to see their subjugation not as divine fate but as a site of divine solidarity and apocalyptic unveiling.

Finally, Jacques Ellul's theology of non-power and presence offers a vision for how Christians are to live under unjust authorities. However, it must be read critically and dialogically alongside the lived experience of powerlessness. Non-power, for Ellul, is not weakness but the intentional refusal to dominate—the decision to love, serve, and witness without coercion. Non-power means being able and not being willing to do it. However, in the context of systemic injustice, where minority parents do not choose to renounce power but are instead rendered powerless by oppressive systems, the witness of non-power takes on a different hue. Here, James Cone's theology helps push Ellul further: the powerlessness of the oppressed is not a chosen position of moral high ground but a condition imposed by unjust systems. However, marginalized parents enact a form of prophetic resistance in their powerlessness. Their survival strategies, their refusal to respond with violence, and their insistence on dignity and life become a kind of non-power that exposes the moral bankruptcy of state violence. They model a presence that refuses to mirror the coercion they endure, not because they choose powerlessness but because they transform it into resistance.

This rereading of Ellul through Cone invites us to see that non-power can be embodied even without agency when love, memory, and moral clarity interrupt the scripts of domination. It is not merely the refusal to use power but the exposure of its misuse. It reframes Romans 13 not as a passive acquiescence to coercion but as a summons to fidelity that exposes the pretensions of empire. The silent strength of the crucified Christ and the defiant endurance of marginalized parents together form a counter-witness to Christian nationalism's idolatrous fusion of faith and force.

Together, these images converge into a figural reading that unveils Romans 13:1–7 as a text of both warning and witness. It warns against the idolatry of state power and the temptation to equate divine sovereignty with human rule. It bears witness to a crucified Lord whose kingdom comes not through domination but through love. It calls the church to live as a community that discerns, resists, and endures—not in fear but hope. Such a reading challenges any attempt to weaponize Romans 13 in defense of empire. Instead, it invites us to see the definitive judgment of the powers on the cross and, in the resurrection, the promise of a new world in which justice, not fear, will reign.

CONCLUSION

In conclusion, Romans 13:1–7 serves not as a straightforward mandate for unconditional obedience, but as a profound call to discernment, shaped by a Christ-centered, apocalyptic framework. Across history, interpretations of this passage have revealed deep tensions and complexities surrounding authority, justice, and Christian responsibility. From the early church's cautious engagement with imperial power, to Augustine's nuanced critique of authority, and Aquinas's emphasis on justice and the common good, to Barth's and Gaventa's apocalyptic reclamation, Romans 13 continually calls Christians to wrestle with how they embody faithfulness within contested political realities.

Rather than endorsing passive acquiescence or violent rebellion, a figural reading of Romans 13 invites believers to live in active fidelity to the crucified and risen Lord, whose reign relativizes and critiques all earthly powers. To read Romans 13 rightly is thus not to abandon politics but to engage it prophetically, resisting the temptation to idolize any human authority and instead embodying a gospel witness that aligns itself with God's liberating and redemptive work in the world. In short, Romans 13 is neither a blanket endorsement of political submission nor a carte blanche for revolution. It is an invitation to discernment, faithfulness, and courageous witness—an ongoing summons for the church to reflect the justice, mercy, and radical love of Christ's cruciform reign, the true balm in Gilead that makes all people whole.

As a witness to God's living Word, Scripture calls us into a dynamic relationship with God and neighbor. It resists being reduced to a static tool for control or a justification for injustice. By engaging Scripture with humility, imagination, and a commitment to justice, Christians can reclaim its transformative potential, challenging distortions that align faith with exclusion or power. Romans 13, like all Scripture, invites us to participate in God's redemptive mission, advancing justice, mercy, and peace in a broken world.

Conclusion

Resisting the Powers, Awakening the Kingdom

"Working out the terms of moral justification is an unending task."[1]

T. M. Scanlon

INTRODUCTION

Throughout this book, we have grappled deeply with the troubling relationship between Christian nationalism, fundamentalism, and their corrosive interpretations of Scripture—particularly Romans 13:1–7. At the core of this exploration has been a literary, theological imagination, which, unlike the rigid code-based interpretations of fundamentalism and Christian nationalism, approaches Scripture as a revelation of the transcendent God who interrupts and transforms the immanent frame. We have traced these two movements' historical emergence and ideological entanglement, beginning with the Puritans and their theological legacy, extending into modern American political theology. By contrasting the oppressive Republic of Gilead in Margaret Atwood's dystopian vision with Marilynne Robinson's humble community of grace in Gilead, Iowa, we have seen vividly what is at stake: the very heart of how we read Scripture and imagine the role of faith in political life.

In what follows, we conclude this journey by summarizing the major arguments made throughout our exploration. We will reinforce the necessity of resisting fundamentalist distortions of Scripture through a literary theology centered on Christ's transcendent beauty, truth, and goodness.

1. Scanlon, *What We Owe*, 361.

Furthermore, we highlight this theology's practical hermeneutical tools and ethical commitments. Ultimately, we articulate why the struggle against the powers represented by Christian nationalism and fundamentalism is fundamentally an eschatological task—one in which the methods of resistance must mirror the kingdom we proclaim, reflecting God's coming reign of justice, reconciliation, and transformative love. This conclusion synthesizes the theological insights offered thus far. It serves as a call to action, inviting readers to engage Scripture and the world through an eschatological vision of resistance, justice, and radical hospitality.

LOOKING BACK, LOOKING FORWARD

In *Between Two Gileads*, we have examined the deeply intertwined phenomena of Christian nationalism and fundamentalism, particularly as they manifest within American Christianity. These twin movements share a common heritage, deeply rooted in a particular way of reading Scripture that reduces the biblical text to a rigid set of principles and cultural codes, distorting it into a mere tool of domination rather than a revelation of the transcendent, triune God. Throughout our exploration, Romans 13:1–7 has served as a central example, revealing how a fundamentalist reading has historically empowered oppressive regimes, justified violence, and reinforced authoritarian governance.

The two fictional Gileads illustrate starkly different readings and applications of Scripture. Atwood's Gilead embodies the consequences of a fundamentalist interpretation of the Bible: authoritarianism, coercion, and instrumentalization of human lives, especially those at the margins. Robinson's Gilead, conversely, portrays a community whose understanding of Scripture fosters inclusion, wonder, vulnerability, and openness to transcendence.

This book resists reducing biblical texts to mere instruments of power or simplistic propositions by proposing a literary, theological approach to Scripture. Instead, a literary approach cultivates an aesthetic and ethical imagination shaped by the beauty of God's transcendence, revealed most clearly in the crucified and risen Christ. Drawing on theologians and writers such as Karl Barth, Jacques Ellul, Flannery O'Connor, Toni Morrison, and James Cone, we have developed a method that refuses to collapse the biblical witness into a technological society's logic of efficiency and domination. Instead, this approach nurtures a moral discernment deeply attentive to beauty, narrative complexity, and transformative grace.

Ultimately, this book argues that the fight against the destructive forces of Christian nationalism and fundamentalism is an inherently eschatological task. Our methods and practices must reflect the kingdom of God we proclaim, rejecting coercion techniques and embracing a posture of compassionate solidarity, justice, and humility instead. This eschatological vision, exemplified by civil rights leaders and anchored in Pauline apocalyptic theology, enables Christians to embody faithful resistance, always guided by a hope grounded not in domination of the immanent frame but in openness to the God who continually interrupts our histories with liberating, gracious, and transformative power. Thus, *Between Two Gileads* calls Christians to rediscover a vision of Scripture and community life not bound by power and fear but liberated through beauty, wonder, and radical hospitality.

INTERPRETING ROMANS 13:1–7 FOR LIBERATION AND ACCOUNTABILITY

The book provides a rereading of Romans 13:1–7, focusing on its implications for justice and governance. Drawing on early church interpretations, it highlights the passage's affirmation of God's sovereignty over all authorities while emphasizing the conditional nature of human governments' legitimacy. Figures like Augustine, Origen, and Cyprian provide valuable insights into the limits of obedience, asserting that rulers must align with God's justice to fulfill their divinely ordained roles.

This rereading situates Romans 13 within the prophetic and apocalyptic tradition, emphasizing its disruptive and eschatological dimensions. Paul's framing of rulers as "servants of God" points not to their absolute authority but to their accountability to God's cosmic justice. In this context, the text warns against aligning too closely with any human government, as all earthly authorities are provisional and subject to the coming reign of Christ. Paul's apocalyptic vision in Romans invites Christians to live with an awareness of God's ultimate sovereignty, resisting any structures of power that contradict divine justice.

The Eschatological Task: Resisting the Powers with Kingdom Means

To confront the ideological constructs of Christian nationalism and fundamentalism is an eschatological task. In its most profound sense, eschatology shapes our visions of the future and informs how Christians embody their resistance to oppressive systems in the present. This task does not merely aim at dismantling unjust structures as ends in themselves but rather orients itself toward a transcendent hope, a vision of reality radically transformed by the kingdom of God. In other words, the fight against the powers—the dominations, ideologies, and oppressive structures—is fundamentally eschatological. This truth necessitates that the moves we make and the means we employ reflect the kingdom toward which we journey.

This connection emerges clearly from the theological critique developed earlier in this book. The contrast between the two Gileads highlights this eschatological tension. The Republic of Gilead, rooted in fundamentalism and Christian nationalism, seeks domination within the immanent frame through coercive techniques and biblical idolatry, while the town of Gilead, Iowa, embodies a theology informed by transcendent love, humility, and communal vulnerability. Here, Jacques Ellul's powerful critique of "technique" provides insight into why resisting the powers must reflect the nature of the kingdom. Ellul notes that a technological society, which fundamentalist Christian nationalism embraces fully, privileges measurable outcomes, efficiency, and a relentless pursuit of mastery and quantification. In such a society, techniques shape not only tools or instruments but also human beings, transforming them into objects to be manipulated, controlled, and discarded when deemed useless. The politics of Christian nationalism, as represented by Sessions, Sheila, and Marjorie Taylor Greene, exemplify the deployment of Scripture as a technique to create and police a particular vision of nationalistic power, privileging certain bodies and excluding or violently suppressing others.

However, to combat these destructive forces with mere counter-techniques would be to adopt the same logic of the very powers we resist. Ellul argues that the kingdom of God embodies radically different methods, fundamentally at odds with the technique's emphasis on efficiency, domination, and instrumental rationality. The kingdom of God, as revealed in Jesus Christ, disrupts and subverts human techniques precisely because it operates from a logic of sacrificial love, vulnerability, and radical inclusion. Thus, the fight against the powers is never simply pragmatic for Christians. It is rooted in a radical fidelity to the eschatological reality revealed in Jesus Christ, which, in its very nature, refuses to employ oppressive or coercive means.

The apostle Paul's apocalyptic eschatology in Romans provides additional insight into the fundamentally eschatological character of resistance against oppressive authorities. Paul speaks of a reality where all earthly authorities, even those instituted by God, are subject to judgment and relativized by the higher authority of Christ. Romans 13, which Christian nationalists have often co-opted to justify oppressive regimes, must instead be read in light of Paul's larger eschatological vision, which refuses absolute authority to any earthly power. As argued in previous chapters, a literary theology that disrupts fundamentalism must interpret Romans 13 within the eschatological vision provided by the broader Pauline corpus, where the authorities, though necessary, are relativized under Christ's Lordship. They are temporary, fallen, and subject to judgment, and their legitimacy is always provisional, measured against the crucified Christ who stands with the victims rather than the victimizers. Thus, a properly eschatological reading of Romans 13 does not justify authoritarianism but critiques it prophetically from the margins. This way of reading Scripture serves as a radical alternative to the interpretive habits of the Republic of Gilead, which demand absolute submission and use biblical texts as weapons of domination.

Further clarity emerges when one considers the civil rights movement of the mid-twentieth century, which embodied precisely such an eschatological fight against the powers. The pastors and Christian leaders of the civil rights movement in the United States drew heavily upon biblical eschatology as a source of inspiration and guidance. The struggle against segregation, racism, and white supremacy was never simply political for these leaders; rather, it was profoundly theological, shaped by a vision of God's kingdom and an apocalyptic hope for the radical transformation of society. Martin Luther King Jr. and other civil rights pastors understood their work as an expression of eschatological hope, where nonviolence was not merely strategic but reflective of the very nature of God's kingdom. Their means mirrored the kingdom they sought: peaceable, gracious, and oriented to restorative justice rather than domination or retribution.

King's famous "I Have a Dream" speech at the Lincoln Memorial articulates this eschatological vision. The vision of a beloved community was not just aspirational rhetoric; it represented an eschatological alternative to the status quo. King's dream was rooted deeply in the prophetic tradition of Scripture and the radical vision of inclusion in the kingdom of God. For King and others, to participate in the civil rights movement was to embody, in real time, a glimpse of God's coming kingdom—a kingdom that, though not yet fully realized, still guided every act of resistance. King described this clearly when he stated that the arc of the moral universe *bends* toward justice. The struggle was sustained by faith in the ultimate fulfillment of God's kingdom and its promise of liberation, justice, and reconciliation.

This eschatological vision also informed how civil rights leaders engaged in their fight. The commitment to nonviolence, articulated so compellingly by King, was not merely strategic but profoundly theological. To embrace violence would be to capitulate to the powers that oppress and adopt the tools of coercion characteristic of a fallen world. Instead, their nonviolent resistance revealed the deeper truth of the crucified Christ, who overcame the powers through love, suffering, and radical forgiveness. Their means reflected the shape of the kingdom they proclaimed: one marked by humility, vulnerability, and a steadfast refusal to use the methods of domination and violence characteristic of the powers they opposed.

This posture toward the struggle against oppressive powers is precisely what a literary theology articulated in previous chapters demands. Rather than instrumentalizing Scripture or employing a code-based system that excludes and dominates, the fight against the powers must reveal a deeper vision of beauty, truth, and goodness embodied in the crucified Christ. David Bentley Hart captures this eschatological stance beautifully when he critiques the "appallingly bad taste" of readings of Scripture that justify violence or oppression. Hart's insistence on taste underscores the necessity of means consistent with the transcendent reality revealed in Jesus Christ, which breaks open the immanent frame and refuses to let Scripture be used especially as a weapon for power.

Paul's eschatological imagination, Martin Luther King Jr.'s vision of the beloved community, and the prophetic critique of Jacques Ellul collectively underscore why the means of resistance must themselves reflect the eschatological kingdom toward which Christians journey. Only through eschatological faithfulness, which anticipates the ultimate reign of God, can Christians resist fundamentalist Christian nationalism and the idolatry of power. The task ahead is thus twofold: it demands the imagination to see beyond present structures and the discipline to embody kingdom-oriented means. Like Lila in Marilynne Robinson's Gilead, this eschatological task is rooted in presence, openness, and radical hospitality—an embodiment of the gospel that resists, subverts, and ultimately transforms the world.

In sum, the fight against fundamentalist Christian nationalism and all oppressive powers is basically an eschatological task. Our movements, means, and methods must always reflect the kingdom of God as revealed in Jesus Christ. Only in this transcendent vision can the Scriptures function rightly—not as weapons of coercion but as vehicles of grace, justice, and love. This is the path to the life-giving Gilead, to the community of the beloved, and ultimately, to the transcendent kingdom beyond all powers and principalities.

LEAVING GILEAD, ENTERING REST

The journey through *Between Two Gileads* has sought to unveil the profound tension between Christian nationalism and fundamentalist readings of Scripture, exemplified vividly in the symbolic worlds of Margaret Atwood's oppressive Republic of Gilead and Marilynne Robinson's grace-infused town of Gilead, Iowa. These two imaginative landscapes illustrate the stark divergence in how Scripture can shape political theology and communal life through rigid, exclusionary control or openness, humility, and transcendence.

The Republic of Gilead symbolizes the dangers inherent in a fundamentalist hermeneutic—one that insists on strict literalism and transforms religious texts into tools of domination and coercion. Atwood's dystopian vision warns of the consequences when political power marries itself to religious authority without critique or self-awareness. In such a world, Scripture is not a living dialogue between humanity and the divine but a rigid manifesto that reinforces existing power structures. This hermeneutic reduces the Bible to a mere handbook of moral and political codes, and God becomes domesticated and co-opted into endorsing oppressive agendas. Such an approach inevitably leads to violence, exclusion, and a radical distortion of both religious faith and political life.

Conversely, Robinson's Gilead offers a potent and redemptive alternative. Here, Scripture is an expansive narrative inviting humility, reflection, and moral imagination. Rather than providing clear-cut instructions for governance or morality, Robinson's portrayal emphasizes Scripture as a living document that dialogues with readers across contexts, cultures, and personal histories. In Gilead, Iowa, biblical engagement fosters a community characterized by empathy, openness, and an unyielding recognition of human complexity and frailty. Characters like Lila and John Ames embody a profoundly ethical faith precisely because it resists simple categorization or easy answers. Their struggles and redemptive arcs underscore the transformative power of a theology that recognizes divine mystery, transcendence, and an abiding presence that refuses confinement by narrow doctrinal certainty.

These contrasting visions give us critical insights into how the Bible functions within American political theology. The legacy of fundamentalism, with its insistence on biblical literalism and its anti-intellectual rejection of nuanced hermeneutics, has laid fertile ground for Christian nationalism. This ideology seeks a symbiotic relationship with the state, urging the creation of policies reflective of specific conservative Christian interpretations of Scripture, as we have seen historically and contemporaneously through figures such as Jeff Sessions, Marjorie Taylor Greene, and Mike Johnson. The resultant politics is not a mere religious expression but rather an idolization of nationalism, cloaked in religious garb, serving more the pursuit of power and societal control than any genuine spiritual or moral truth.

This idolization distorts not only Scripture but also the very nature of community, faith, and political responsibility. Fundamentalism transforms Christianity into an ideology, a simplistic mechanism of exclusion that prioritizes efficiency, measurable outcomes, and hierarchical authority. It erases the complexity inherent in Scripture and human life, creating an environment ripe for authoritarian impulses. The resulting society, mirrored tragically in Atwood's Republic of Gilead, strips people of dignity and agency, systematically alienating individuals from the transcendent beauty and profound ethical demands that characterize authentic religious experience.

However, Robinson's literary theology offers a counterpoint to this bleak outlook. In her Gilead, readers encounter a community shaped by the recognition of shared humanity, the necessity of grace, and the beauty of imperfection. Here, moral discernment is cultivated through narrative and imagination rather than rigid adherence to fixed rules. Robinson's characters reflect a profound understanding that rightly engaged Scripture directs attention beyond itself toward a transcendent God whose nature is love, compassion, and inclusivity. Through the stories of John Ames, Lila, and the flawed but striving inhabitants of Gilead, Iowa, Robinson articulates a theology capable of disrupting the logic of nationalism and fundamentalism by inviting us toward an ethic rooted deeply in care, empathy, and mutual recognition.

Therefore, the task for contemporary Christian communities and theologians is clear yet demanding. It requires courage to resist the simplistic allure of fundamentalist clarity and nationalist fervor. It demands that readers of Scripture embrace a literary imagination, recognizing the Bible not as a static collection of propositional truths but as a dynamic narrative pointing toward divine transcendence and ethical transformation. Such an approach dismantles the idolization of the Bible, allowing it to breathe, challenge, and invite readers into a profound encounter with God and neighbor alike.

Romans 13:1–7, a text that Christian nationalists have frequently weaponized, provides a crucial test case for this literary theological approach. As we have explored, when placed within the broader narrative of Scripture—particularly the life, death, and resurrection of Jesus—Romans 13 does not uncritically sanction authority but rather demands discernment and responsibility. Authority is accountable to divine justice, and Christians are called not to blind submission but to prophetic witness. The literary theology we advocate challenges readers to engage with Romans 13—and indeed all Scripture—in ways that resist authoritarian misinterpretation, instead cultivating a taste for justice, mercy, and humility.

Such a reading fosters communities resistant to nationalism's violence and fundamentalism's rigidity. Instead, it cultivates a shared life rooted in beauty, wonder, and openness, a life that refuses the closed-off power structures characteristic of oppressive regimes. This approach offers hope—not through dominance or ideological purity but through the slow, patient, transformative power of love enacted daily among neighbors.

Ultimately, the choice presented by the two Gileads is stark. It is a choice between death and life, between idolatrous certainty and humble faithfulness, between oppressive uniformity and vibrant communal diversity. The literary, theological imagination championed in this book beckons Christians and citizens toward a more just, compassionate, and inclusive society. It transcends national boundaries, ideological binaries, and theological simplifications, instead inviting us into the vast, challenging, but infinitely rewarding task of loving God and neighbor in a fractured world.

CONCLUSION: A HIDDEN LIFE, AN UNSEEN KINGDOM

As I conclude the book, I cannot help but remember this quote from George Eliot's elegant work, *Middlemarch*:"for the growing good of the world is partly dependent on unhistoric acts; and that things are not so ill with you and me as they might have been, is half owing to the number who lived faithfully a hidden life, and rest in unvisited tombs."[2] These hauntingly beautiful words summon us into a deeper truth that resonates profoundly with our journey in *Between Two Gileads*. Having traced the dark shadows cast by fundamentalism and Christian nationalism and glimpsed the brighter possibility of a literary theology that refuses domination, we arrive at this quiet revelation: true resistance, true transformation, and true beauty emerge from lives lived beyond the spotlight, far removed from historic heroics. They rise quietly, persistently, faithfully—hidden in acts of love, vulnerability, and unrecognized grace.

This hiddenness defies the logic of a technological society, a logic obsessed with efficiency, measurement, and outcomes. The powers that animate fundamentalism and Christian nationalism thrive on spectacle, craving attention and applause, leveraging Scripture as a means to dominate and coerce. They speak loudly and confidently, seeking to write history in their image, confident in their versions of a triumphant narrative. Yet beneath their noise, within the shadow of these so-called triumphs, lies a more potent and powerful truth: the kingdom of God grows best in obscurity, often far from human acknowledgment or acclaim.

The Republic of Gilead exemplifies precisely the opposite, a dystopian horror born of a twisted desire to control history, to manipulate sacred texts into blunt instruments of power. In such a world, the humanity of countless souls is erased, their stories silenced, their tombs unvisited, marked only by the tragedy of lives reduced to mere tools of an oppressive system. And yet, even there, hope persists in secret gestures—small, unhistoric acts of resistance by Offred and others whose whispers of prayer, whose subtle refusals to be fully conquered, quietly defy the powers that seek absolute control. The spark of liberation endures within those unseen, undocumented moments.

Contrast this with Marilynne Robinson's gentle depiction of Gilead, Iowa—a community whose beauty lies precisely in its hiddenness. Robinson's characters, John Ames and Lila chief among them, embody

2. Eliot, *Middlemarch*, 621.

the quiet dignity of faithful living. Their lives bear witness not through grand gestures or spectacular accomplishments but through humble acts of hospitality, grace, and profound moral courage practiced in obscurity. Their tombs, one imagines, may also remain unvisited by worldly admirers, yet their legacies shape lives in unseen ways, transforming communities quietly, incrementally, yet irrevocably.

Thus, our literary and theological journey points us toward a kingdom whose true measure cannot be captured by instrumental rationality, technological dominance, or nationalistic fervor. It is a kingdom visible only to eyes willing to perceive grace in its most subtle manifestations—a child welcomed, a stranger embraced, the marginalized brought from shadow to communion. The world's powers—fundamentalist certainties and nationalist slogans—seek a visible kingdom that is controlled, measurable, and dominated. However, the kingdom revealed through Scripture rightly read is one of radical hiddenness, like yeast leavening bread unseen, like seeds buried in fertile darkness, rising silently toward the sun.

Paul's apocalyptic vision reminds us forcefully that all earthly powers stand under judgment. They are temporary, provisional, and vulnerable. Ultimately, the power of the crucified and resurrected Christ overcomes precisely because it refuses the tools of domination. There will always be a need for the prophetic, and the apocalyptic cross is the one that begins our vision of the powers against which the prophet speaks. The cross proclaims victory through weakness, triumph through defeat, and revelation through concealment. To live in faithfulness to this eschatological truth is to embody resistance, not through power or violence, but through acts of vulnerable love, quiet sacrifice, and humble fidelity to God's justice.

Herein lies the prophetic spirit of civil rights leaders, whose voices echo softly yet powerfully from the pages of history. Their eschatological vision saw clearly beyond the oppression of their day to the hope of a kingdom not fully realized yet quietly present. King and his contemporaries knew the transformative power of small, unseen acts—marches taken quietly, songs sung gently, prayers offered in darkness, and courage displayed without recognition. Their willingness to embrace the hiddenness of struggle and trust that the God who calls forth justice is present in obscurity gave strength to their movement and beauty to their witness.

As readers now confronted by these two Gileads, the choice before us is profound. It is not merely an intellectual exercise but a call into faithful living—a call not toward the alluring light of public acclaim but the transformative power of humble obscurity. The fight against Christian nationalism and fundamentalism is ultimately won not on grand stages but in countless unhistoric moments of love, in whispered prayers, in unseen kindnesses, in hidden lives that quietly resist the distortions of power. Our hope lies precisely in these quiet revolutions, the kingdom breaking forth unseen, unnoticed, yet unstoppable in its quiet grace.

Like Eliot's hidden souls, we may live and die unknown, our tombs unvisited, our stories unrecorded in the annals of human history. Yet it is precisely such hidden lives, lived faithfully and beautifully in the shadow of the cross, that plant seeds for the world's ultimate renewal. In obscurity, vulnerability, and humility, we defy the powers and open space for God's radical newness, God's gracious intrusion into our broken histories.

And so, leaving behind the seductive certainty of the Republic of Gilead and journeying toward the quiet hospitality of Gilead, Iowa, we step toward home. We step toward that kingdom glimpsed dimly, where the last shall be first, the poor are blessed, and the hidden faithful are finally revealed in radiant glory, for it is these quiet souls, these faithful hidden lives, whose silent witness has always sustained the world. These faithful ones hold the world gently, their prayers and quiet acts of grace sustaining us all, ensuring that things are not nearly as ill as they might have been.

We leave the shadows of oppressive certainty behind and gently step into the sacred uncertainty of love's hidden kingdom. May we, too, live faithfully our hidden lives, quietly sowing seeds of compassion, justice, and grace—awaiting the day when all hidden faithfulness will blossom fully into the dazzling beauty of God's eternal, eschatological light.

Bibliography

Aquinas, Thomas. *Summa Theologica*. Translated by Fathers of the English Dominican Province. Allen, TX: Christian Classics, 1981.

Atwood, Margaret. *The Handmaid's Tale*. Deluxe ed. Boston: Houghton Mifflin Harcourt, 2020.

———. *The Testaments*. New York: Nan A. Talese/Doubleday, 2019.

Augustine. *On Christian Teaching*. Translated by R. P. H. Green. Oxford: Oxford University Press, 1997.

Bachelard, Sarah. *Resurrection and Moral Imagination*. London: Routledge, 2014.

Balmer, Randall. *Bad Faith: Race and the Rise of the Religious Right*. Grand Rapids: Eerdmans, 2021.

———. "Historian's Pickaxe." Andrea Mitchell Center for the Study of Democracy. https://amc.sas.upenn.edu/sites/www.sas.upenn.edu.andrea-mitchell-center/files/Balmer%20-%20Historian's%20Pickaxe.pdf#overlay-context=event/randall-balmer.

Balthasar, Hans Urs von. *The Glory of the Lord: A Theological Aesthetics, Vol. 1: Seeing the Form*. Translated by Erasmo Leiva-Merikakis. San Francisco: Ignatius, 1982.

Bantum, Brian. "Clothed in Flesh." In *Karl Barth and Liberation Theology: Experiments in Reformed Doctrine*, edited by Paul Dafydd Jones and Kaitlyn Dugan, 161–76. London: T&T Clark, 2023.

Barth, Karl. "Christian Ethics." Translated by Matthew A. Frost. Lecture delivered at the Freie Deutsche Hochstift, Frankfurt am Main, June 15, 1946. In *Zwei Vorträge, Theologische Existenz heute* NF 3, 3–10. Munich: Chr. Kaiser Verlag, 1946.

———. *The Christian Life*. Translated by Geoffrey W. Bromiley. London: T&T Clark, 2017.

———. *Church Dogmatics: Study Edition*. Edited by G. W. Bromiley and T. F. Torrance. Translated by Geoffrey W. Bromiley and Thomas F. Torrance. London: T&T Clark, 2010.

———. *The Epistle to the Romans*. Translated by Edwyn C. Hoskyns. 6th ed. Oxford: Oxford University Press, 1933.

Barton, David, and Tim Barton. *The American Story: The Beginnings*. Aledo, TX: WallBuilder, 2020.

Bassett, Paul Merritt. "The Fundamentalist Leavening of the Holiness Movement, 1914–1940: The Church of the Nazarene—A Case Study." *Wesleyan Theological Journal* 13, no. 1 (Spring 1978) 65–91.

Bell, L. Nelson. "A Southern Evangelical on Integration." In *Jerry Falwell and the Rise of the Religious Right*, edited by Matthew Avery Sutton, 51–54. New York: Bedford/St. Martin's, 2012.

Biden, Joseph R., Jr. "Remarks by President Biden on the Terror Attack at Hamid Karzai International Airport." Speech, the White House, August 26, 2021. https://nato.usmission.gov/remarks-by-president-biden-on-the-terror-at-hamid-karzai-international-airport/.

Biggar, Nigel. *Between Kin and Cosmopolis: An Ethic of the Nation*. Cambridge: James Clarke & Co., 2014.

Blakely, Jason. *Lost in Ideology: Interpreting Modern Political Life*. Newcastle upon Tyne: Agenda, 2024.

Bruenig, Elizabeth. "Judgment Days: A Small Town Reckons with God, Trump, and the Meaning of Morality." *Chicago Tribune*, July 21, 2018. https://www.chicagotribune.com/2018/07/21/judgment-days-a-small-town-reckons-with-god-trump-and-the-meaning-of-morality/.

Brueggemann, Walter. *The Bible Makes Sense*. Rev. ed. Cincinnati, OH: Franciscan Media, 2003.

Cone, James H. *The Cross and the Lynching Tree*. Maryknoll, NY: Orbis, 2011.

———. *God of the Oppressed*. Maryknoll, NY: Orbis, 1975.

Cunningham, Conor. *Genealogy of Nihilism: Philosophies of Nothing and the Difference of Theology*. New York: Routledge, 2002.

Driscoll, Mark, and Gerry Breshears. *Doctrine: What Christians Should Believe*. Wheaton, IL: Crossway, 2010.

———. *Vote Like Jesus: Answering 15 Big Questions About God vs. Government*. Scottsdale, AZ: RealFaith, 2024.

Du Bois, W. E. B. "Jesus Christ in Texas." In *Darkwater: Voices from Within the Veil*, 70–77. New York: Harcourt, Brace and Howe, 1920.

Du Mez, Kristin Kobes. *Jesus and John Wayne: How White Evangelicals Corrupted a Faith and Fractured a Nation*. New York: Liveright, 2020.

Eliot, George. *Middlemarch*. Edited by Rosemary Ashton. London: Penguin Classics, 2003.

Elliott, Neil. "Liberating Paul: Pauline 'Evangelization' in the Shadow of Empire." Lecture presented at the International Seminar on Saint Paul, Ariccia, Italy, April 19–29, 2009.

———. *Liberating Paul: The Justice of God and the Politics of the Apostle*. Minneapolis: Fortress, 2005.

Ellul, Jacques. *Hope in Time of Abandonment*. Translated by C. Edward Hopkin. New York: Seabury, 1973.

———. *Living Faith: Belief and Doubt in a Perilous World*. Translated by Peter Heinegg. Eugene, OR: Cascade, 2013.

———. *Presence in the Modern World*. Eugene, OR: Cascade, 2015.

———. *Propaganda: The Formation of Men's Attitudes*. Translated by Konrad Kellen and Jean Lerner. New York: Alfred A. Knopf, 1965.

———. *The Technological Society*. Translated by John Wilkinson. New York: Alfred A. Knopf, 1964.

———. *Theology and Technique: Toward an Ethic of Non-Power*. Translated by Christian Roy, foreword by David W. Gill and Yves Ellul, introduction by Frédéric Rognon. Eugene, OR: Cascade, 2024.

———. *To Will & To Do: An Introduction to Christian Ethics*. Volume One. Translated by Jacob Marques Rollison. Eugene, OR: Cascade, 2020.

———. *To Will & To Do: An Introduction to Christian Ethics*. Volume Two. Translated by Jacob Marques Rollison. Eugene, OR: Cascade, 2021.

Fabrycky, Laura M. *Keys to Bonhoeffer's Haus: Exploring the World and Wisdom of Dietrich Bonhoeffer*. Minneapolis: Fortress, 2020.

Fitzgerald, Frances. *The Evangelicals: The Struggle to Shape America*. New York: Simon & Schuster, 2017.

Frei, Hans. *The Eclipse of Biblical Narrative: A Study in Eighteenth and Nineteenth Century Hermeneutics*. New Haven: Yale University Press, 1974.

Fromm, Erich. *To Have or To Be?* New York: Harper & Row, 1976.

Gadamer, Hans-Georg. *Truth and Method*. 2nd rev. ed. Translated by Joel Weinsheimer and Donald G. Marshall. New York: Bloomsbury Academic, 2004.

Galvin, Daniel. *Party Domination and Base Mobilization: Donald Trump and Republican Party Building in a Polarized Era*. IPR Working Paper WP-20–18. Northwestern University, August 11, 2020. https://www.ipr.northwestern.edu/documents/working-papers/2020/wp-20–18-rev.pdf.

Gaventa, Beverly Roberts. "Reading Romans 13 with Simone Weil: Toward a More Generous Hermeneutic." *Journal of Biblical Literature* 136, no. 1 (2017) 7–22. https://doi.org/10.15699/jbl.1361.2017.1362.

———. *Romans: A Commentary*. New Testament Library. Louisville: Westminster John Knox, 2024.

Girard, René. *I Saw Satan Fall Like Lightning*. Translated by James G. Williams. Maryknoll, NY: Orbis, 2001.

Gorski, Philip S., and Samuel L. Perry. *The Flag and the Cross: White Christian Nationalism and the Threat to American Democracy*. New York: Oxford University Press, 2022.

Gregory of Nyssa. *The Life of Moses*. Translated by Abraham J. Malherbe and Everett Ferguson. San Francisco: HarperCollins, 2006.

Grudem, Wayne. *Politics According to the Bible: A Comprehensive Resource for Understanding Modern Political Issues in Light of Scripture*. Grand Rapids: Zondervan, 2010.

———. *Systematic Theology: An Introduction to Biblical Doctrine*. 2nd ed. Grand Rapids: Zondervan Academic, 2020.

Gutiérrez, Gustavo. *A Theology of Liberation: History, Politics, and Salvation*. Translated and edited by Sister Caridad Inda and John Eagleson. Rev. ed. Maryknoll, NY: Orbis, 1988.

Hall, David D. *The Puritans: A Transatlantic History*. Princeton: Princeton University Press, 2019.

The Handmaid's Tale. Created by Bruce Miller. Hulu, 2017–present.

Hannah-Jones, Nikole, ed. *The 1619 Project: A New Origin Story*. New York: Random House, 2021.

Harris, Harriet A. "Fundamentalist Readings of the Bible." In *The New Cambridge History of the Bible, Volume 4: From 1750 to the Present*, edited by John Riches, 328–46. Cambridge: Cambridge University Press, 2015.

Hart, David Bentley. "A Sense of Style: Beauty and the Christian Moral Life." *Journal of the Society of Christian Ethics* 39, no. 2 (Fall/Winter 2019) 237–50. https://muse.jhu.edu/article/741519.

Hauerwas, Stanley. *The Work of Theology.* Grand Rapids: Eerdmans, 2015.

Hawkins, J. Russell. *The Bible Told Them So: How Southern Evangelicals Fought to Preserve White Supremacy.* New York: Oxford University Press, 2021.

Heyrman, Christine Leigh. *Southern Cross: The Beginnings of the Bible Belt.* Chapel Hill: University of North Carolina Press, 1997.

Hughes, Albert, and Allen Hughes, dirs. *The Book of Eli.* Los Angeles: Warner Bros. Pictures, 2010.

Jeffress, Robert. *How a Christian Should Vote.* Dallas: Pathway to Victory, 2024.

Jenkins, Jack. "Republicans Mostly Mum on Calls to Make GOP the Party of Christian Nationalism." *The Washington Post*, August 19, 2022. https://www.washingtonpost.com/religion/2022/08/19/republicans-mostly-mum-calls-make-gop-party-christian-nationalism/.

Jennings, Willie James. *After Whiteness: An Education in Belonging.* Grand Rapids: Eerdmans, 2020.

Jenson, Robert W. *Systematic Theology, Volume 1: The Triune God.* New York: Oxford University Press, 1997.

Johnson, Mike. "Remarks by Speaker Mike Johnson upon Election." Speech, US House of Representatives, October 25, 2023. https://www.c-span.org/program/us-house-of-representatives/speaker-elect-mike-johnson-floor-speech/634217.

Käsemann, Ernst. *On Being a Disciple of the Crucified Nazarene: Unpublished Lectures and Sermons.* Edited by Rudolf Landau and Wolfgang Kraus. Translated by Roy A. Harrisville. Grand Rapids: Eerdmans, 2010.

Kazin, Michael. *A Godly Hero: The Life of William Jennings Bryan.* New York: Knopf, 2006.

Killian, Mitchell, and Clyde Wilcox. "Do Abortion Attitudes Lead to Party Switching?" *Political Research Quarterly* 61, no. 4 (2008) 561–73. https://www.jstor.org/stable/20299760.

Levendusky, Matthew S. "Why Do Partisan Media Polarize Viewers?" *American Journal of Political Science* 57, no. 3 (2013) 611–23. https://www.jstor.org/stable/23496642.

Lovett, Adam. "The Ethics of Asymmetric Politics." *Politics, Philosophy & Economics* 22, no. 1 (2023) 3–30. https://doi.org/10.1177/1470594X221133445.

Madison, James. *Memorial and Remonstrance Against Religious Assessments, 20 June 1785.* In *Founders Online, National Archives.* https://founders.archives.gov/documents/Madison/01-08-02-0163.

Marsden, George M. *Fundamentalism and American Culture.* New York: Oxford University Press, 1980.

———. *Understanding Fundamentalism and Evangelicalism.* Grand Rapids: Eerdmans, 1991.

Marshall, Wallace. *Puritanism and Natural Theology.* Eugene, OR: Wipf and Stock, 2016.

Martin, William. *With God on Our Side: The Rise of the Religious Right in America.* New York: Broadway, 1996.

Martyn, J. Louis. "Apocalyptic Antinomies in Paul's Letter to the Galatians." In *Theological Issues in the Letters of Paul*, 111–24. Nashville: Abingdon, 1997.

———. *Galatians: A New Translation with Introduction and Commentary.* Anchor Yale Bible 33A. New York: Doubleday, 1997.

———. *Theological Issues in the Letters of Paul.* Nashville: Abingdon, 1997

Mason, Lilliana. "'I Disrespectfully Agree': The Differential Effects of Partisan Sorting on Social and Issue Polarization." *American Journal of Political Science* 59, no. 1 (2015) 128–45. https://doi.org/10.1111/ajps.12089.

Maxwell, Angie, and Todd Shields. *The Long Southern Strategy: How Chasing White Voters in the South Changed American Politics.* New York: Oxford University Press, 2020.

McIntire, Carl. "A Minister Denounces the Civil Rights Act." In *Jerry Falwell and the Rise of the Religious Right*, edited by Matthew Avery Sutton, 54–56. New York: Bedford/St. Martin's, 2012.

McVicar, Michael J. *Christian Reconstruction: R. J. Rushdoony and American Religious Conservatism.* Chapel Hill: University of North Carolina Press, 2015.

Milbank, John. *The Word Made Strange: Theology, Language, Culture.* Oxford: Blackwell, 1997.

Miller, Patrick. "What is Christian Nationalism?" *Christianity Today*, February 3, 2021. https://www.christianitytoday.com/ct/2021/february-web-only/what-is-christian-nationalism.html.

Morrison, Toni. *Beloved.* New York: Alfred A. Knopf, 1987.

———. *The Bluest Eye.* New York: Holt, Rinehart, and Winston, 1970.

———. *Goodness and the Literary Imagination: Harvard Divinity School's 95th Ingersoll Lecture with Essays on Morrison's Moral and Religious Vision.* Edited by David Carrasco, Stephanie Paulsell, and Mara Willard. Charlottesville: University of Virginia Press, 2019.

———. *Nobel Lecture, December 7, 1993.* In *The Nobel Prize.* https://www.nobelprize.org/prizes/literature/1993/morrison/lecture/.

Morse, Christopher. *The Difference Heaven Makes: Rehearing the Gospel as News.* London: T&T Clark, 2010.

Murdoch, Iris. *The Sovereignty of Good.* London: Routledge, 2001.

Noll, Mark A. *The Civil War as a Theological Crisis.* Chapel Hill: University of North Carolina Press, 2006.

———. *The Scandal of the Evangelical Mind.* Grand Rapids: Eerdmans, 1994.

O'Connor, Flannery. "A Good Man Is Hard to Find." In *The Complete Stories*, 117–133. Centennial ed. New York: Picador, 2025.

———. "Revelation." In *The Complete Stories*, 488–509. Centennial ed. New York: Picador, 2025.

Onishi, Bradley. *Preparing for War: The Extremist History of White Christian Nationalism and What Comes Next.* Minneapolis: Broadleaf, 2023.

Origen. *On First Principles.* Translated and edited by John Behr. Oxford: Oxford University Press, 2020.

Pauw, Amy Plantinga. "The Holy Spirit and Scripture." In *The Lord and Giver of Life: Perspectives on Constructive Pneumatology*, edited by David H. Jensen, 25–39. Louisville: Westminster John Knox, 2008.

Pew Research Center. "5 Facts on How Americans View the Bible and Other Religious Texts." April 14, 2017. https://www.pewresearch.org/short-reads/2017/04/14/5-facts-on-how-americans-view-the-bible-and-other-religious-texts/.

Pickstock, Catherine. *After Writing: On the Liturgical Consummation of Philosophy.* Oxford: Blackwell, 1998.

Reno, R. R. *Return of the Strong Gods: Nationalism, Populism, and the Future of the West.* Washington, DC: Regnery Gateway, 2019.

Ricoeur, Paul. *The Conflict of Interpretations: Essays in Hermeneutics.* Edited by Don Ihde. Translated by Willis Domingo et al. Evanston, IL: Northwestern University Press, 1974.

———. *Freud and Philosophy: An Essay on Interpretation.* Translated by Denis Savage. New Haven: Yale University Press, 1970.

———. *From Text to Action: Essays in Hermeneutics II.* Translated by Kathleen Blamey and John B. Thompson. Evanston, IL: Northwestern University Press, 1991.

———. *Interpretation Theory: Discourse and the Surplus of Meaning.* Fort Worth: Texas Christian University Press, 1976.

Robinson, Marilynne. *Gilead.* New York: Farrar, Straus and Giroux, 2004.

———. *Home.* New York: Farrar, Straus and Giroux, 2008.

———. *Jack.* New York: Farrar, Straus and Giroux, 2020.

———. *Lila.* New York: Farrar, Straus and Giroux, 2014.

Root, Andrew. *The Church in an Age of Secular Mysticisms: Why Spiritualities without God Fail to Transform Us.* Grand Rapids: Baker Academic, 2023.

———. *Churches in the Crisis of Decline: A Hopeful, Practical Ecclesiology for a Secular Age.* Grand Rapids: Baker Academic, 2022.

———. *Faith Formation in a Secular Age: Responding to the Church's Obsession with Youthfulness.* Grand Rapids: Baker Academic, 2017.

Rosa, Hartmut. *Democracy Needs Religion.* Translated by Valentine A. Pakis. Cambridge: Polity, 2024.

———. *Social Acceleration: A New Theory of Modernity.* Translated by Jonathan Trejo-Mathys. New York: Columbia University Press, 2013.

Rushdoony, Rousas John. *The Biblical Philosophy of History.* Vallecito, CA: Ross House Books, 1979.

———. Foreword to *Theonomy in Christian Ethics*, by Greg L. Bahnsen, xi–viv. 3rd ed. Nacogdoches, TX: Covenant Media, 2002.

Scanlon, T. M. *What We Owe to Each Other.* Cambridge: Harvard University Press, 1998.

Seidel, Andrew L. *The Founding Myth: Why Christian Nationalism Is Un-American.* New York: Sterling, 2019.

Sessions, Jeff. "Speech to Law Enforcement Officials." Fort Wayne, IN, June 14, 2018.

Smith, James K. A. *How Not to Be Secular: Reading Charles Taylor.* Grand Rapids: Eerdmans, 2014.

Sobrino, Jon. *No Salvation Outside the Poor: Prophetic-Utopian Essays.* Translated by Margaret Wilde. Maryknoll, NY: Orbis, 2008.

Stanley, Harold W., and Richard G. Niemi. "Partisanship and Group Support, 1952–1988." *American Politics Quarterly* 19, no. 2 (1991) 189–210. https://doi.org/10.1177/1532673X9101900203.

Stanley, Jason. *How Propaganda Works.* Princeton: Princeton University Press, 2015.

Tanner, Kathryn. *Theories of Culture: A New Agenda for Theology.* Minneapolis: Fortress, 1997.

Taylor, Charles. *A Secular Age.* Cambridge: Harvard University Press, 2007.

Van Engen, Abram C. *City on a Hill: A History of American Exceptionalism.* New Haven: Yale University Press, 2020.

Van Vleet, Jacob E., and Jacob Marques Rollison. *Jacques Ellul: A Companion to His Major Works.* Eugene, OR: Cascade, 2020.

Webster, John. *Holy Scripture: A Dogmatic Sketch.* Cambridge: Cambridge University Press, 2003.

Wittgenstein, Ludwig. *Philosophical Investigations.* Translated by G. E. M. Anscombe. Oxford: Basil Blackwell, 1958.

The Westminster Confession of Faith and Catechisms: As Adopted by the Orthodox Presbyterian Church. Lawrenceville, GA: The Committee on Christian Education of the Orthodox Presbyterian Church, 2007.

Index

www.ingramcontent.com/pod-product-compliance
Lightning Source LLC
LaVergne TN
LVHW100523110826
845146LV00002B/760